Embodied Enquiry

Embodied Enquiry

Phenomenological Touchstones for Research, Psychotherapy and Spirituality

Les Todres
Department of Psychology, University of Bournemouth, UK

First published in hardback 2007
This paperback edition published 2011 by
PALGRAVE MACMILLAN

Palgrave Macmillan in the UK is an imprint of Macmillan Publishers Limited, registered in England, company number 785998, of Houndmills, Basingstoke, Hampshire RG21 6XS.

Palgrave Macmillan in the US is a division of St Martin's Press LLC, 175 Fifth Avenue, New York, NY 10010.

Palgrave Macmillan is the global academic imprint of the above companies and has companies and representatives throughout the world.

Palgrave® and Macmillan® are registered trademarks in the United States, the United Kingdom, Europe and other countries.

ISBN 978-0- 230- 30230-3   ISBN 978-0-230-59885-0 (eBook)
DOI 10.1057/9780230598850

Logging, pulping and manufacturing

A catalogue record for this book is available from the British Library.

A catalog record for this book is available from the Library of Congress.

10 9 8 7 6 5 4 3 2 1
20 19 18 17 16 15 14 13 12 11

Transferred to Digital Printing in 2013

To Louise

Contents

List of Tables

Foreword

In this innovative exploration of research, psychotherapy, and spirituality, Professor Les Todres helps us to appreciate anew our fundamental embodied connection with the world in which we live. Moreover, he gives us principles and methods for drawing more deeply upon this connection. Following in the tradition of the philosopher and psychologist Eugene Gendlin, Todres makes it plain that concepts such as mind and body and language and experience should be thought of in relational rather than oppositional terms. At one point he writes, 'Sometimes, the bodily depth of what one has lived through is "more than words can say". Yet such experience "looks" for words'. This brief statement goes to the heart of what his book is about. It also speaks profoundly to the depth of our embodied experience.

Let me explain by telling a brief personal story. Around the time I was reading this manuscript, an unusually forceful wind storm hit the coast of Washington state, where I live. It downed large trees that in turn knocked over power lines and left over a million people without electricity. My partner, Kathryn, and I had planned to spend the weekend on Whidbey Island (right off the coast) and to attend an artist's open house. But since there was no electricity on the island we took a ferry to a nearby town on the mainland. However, Kathryn was keen on meeting this artist and seeing her work and so we traveled back to Seattle by way of the island and were pleased to find that electricity had just been restored and that the open house was on. Our persistence was richly rewarded. We were the only ones there and thus we had the good fortune to spend time alone with the artist, who graciously conversed with us at length about her work and her life.

At one point she showed us several of her collages, constructed with pictures taken from various magazines. Each collage focused on an important person in her life. She explained that having put the pictures together, she now had words for the relationship. Intuitively she had known which pictures fitted for each collage, and the assemblage of pictures allowed to her to give voice to what had previously been only an implicit and inarticulate embodied sense of the relationship. This process gave her a greater appreciation of these relationships and of herself as an active participant in them. I was keenly interested in what she showed us, and not only as a psychotherapist. The process of discovery that she described is fundamental to human life and to the search for understanding in which all of us are engaged, however inconsistently or infrequently. Indeed, her reflections brought me to my own as she showed us the view from her backyard.

Her house was situated on an embankment overlooking Puget Sound. The view was spectacular. It was enhanced by the presence of three tall trees rising up from the embankment. They were, one might say, witnesses to the life out there on the body of water – to the movement of the waves, ships passing back and forth, and sunrises and sunsets. For me, there was something compelling about this scene. It was, all at once, serene, overwhelming, and wondrous, and taking in this scene moved me both in body and in spirit. It brought to mind the words of Fr. Stephen Sundborg, the president of the university where I teach, who has said that at its core spirituality as has do with our relationship to mystery. Here again, there was more than words could say. Yet we seek words, sometimes in the form of poetry, as Les Todres suggests, hoping to express something of the transcendent reality that we encounter.

Professor Les Todres is a teacher, scholar, phenomenological researcher, and a psychotherapist. *Embodied Enquiry* is a scholarly book that draws upon the contributions of philosophers, such as Heidegger and Merleau-Ponty, and psychologists and psychiatrists, such as Hillman, Jung, and van den Berg. But it is not, I am happy to say, a publication that is preoccupied with textual analysis as an end in itself. Rather, it is a book that addresses us as embodied beings who seek a deeper appreciation of our existence, as I have suggested in the brief vignette above.

In his discussion of research methodology, Todres' call for an emphasis on qualitative research that 'seeks to show and evoke the presence of a lived experience through words', and his suggestions for how to accomplish such a goal will be welcomed by practitioners and students alike. Similarly, his discussion of the process of psychotherapy and various therapeutic modes of being is simultaneously clarifying and open-ended. That is, while providing a useful and thoughtfully constructed map of the psychotherapy process, Todres never loses sight of how psychotherapy, at its core, involves a relationship between two people. Healing, he suggests, involves the development of a sense of personal truth, self-forgiveness, and hope.

In the last section of his book Todres turns to the arena of spirituality. In my view, he rightly asserts that 'human existence has its essence in its transcendence' and rejects the notion that the transpersonal is a stage in our development rather than a dimension of human life that is always already present. His discussion of spirituality and its relationship to vulnerability deserves careful study and cannot be readily summarized. But as I read the concluding section of his book, it brought to mind the perceptive analysis of Owen Barfield (1981), who suggests that our current sense of estrangement requires reflection on our use of language and a remembering of its metaphorical nature.[1] Such reflection enables us to re-encounter the deepest realm of being where we are all already connected. I believe that Professor Todres takes us in a similar direction, drawing upon Zen writings and the reflections of the later Heidegger as well as his own experience as a psychotherapist. Here the relationship between language and embodied experience continues to be central as Todres looks at the paradoxical relationship between finding oneself and losing oneself, and the necessity of both. At this point I am brought back to my experience of the trees and the water. Contemplating this unforgettable view was an experience of self-forgetfulness and yet it was also a deeply enriching personal experience. I believe that readers of this book will find their own stories that resonate with this evocative study of embodied enquiry and that their personal and professional life journeys will be the richer for it.

Steen Halling
Professor of Psychology, Seattle University

Preface and Acknowledgements

This book essentially wishes to honour the valuable role that the phenomenological tradition has played in disciplining my academic and professional development over many years. As a philosophically oriented psychologist I have been fascinated by a certain coherence and depth within this tradition in spite of its many polemics and differences between the partners within the conversation. My own participation as a philosophically oriented psychologist was to try and take forward some of these ideas into the more applied areas of research methodology, psychotherapy, and spirituality. Recently, when I looked over a 16-year period of publishing articles in academic journals, I realized that there was a story that I wished to tell about this development. A certain latent common theme and sensibility seemed to have been at work and functioned as a touchstone in my thinking and practice. It is this common theme that I wish to articulate in this book by re-presenting a number of my published articles within the context of a thematic unifying narrative. Introductions to various parts of the book, as well as its concluding chapter, articulate the theme of embodied enquiry and how this matters.

I would also like to acknowledge that there is an interesting and valuable groundswell of thought and practice that is leaning towards embodied enquiry in other philosophical orientations, qualitative research approaches, psychotherapeutic approaches, and spiritual practices. For example, the works of Rosemarie Anderson (2001, 2004) in qualitative research and Michael Washburn (2003) in spirituality provide some very interesting directions for more embodied forms of research and spirituality. In the present book, however, I wish to bow to what has emerged for me from phenomenology, and hope that readers and practitioners outside this tradition may be interested in some of the possibilities that have been generated.

I am grateful to my primary mentors in phenomenological psychology: Dreyer Kruger and Amedeo Giorgi. I am also indebted to the work of John Welwood, and thank him for his very helpful conversations about the relationship between spirituality, psychotherapy, and embodiment. The work of Eugene Gendlin has been pivotal in my more recent academic development, and this book attests to the integrating power of his thought in shaping my own version of experiential phenomenology.

I would like to thank Louise Todres, my wife and partner, for being there in many different ways and for her aid in helping me to find better words. And then there is the rich company of my academic friends and existential companions over the years with whom I have shared productive conversations and nourishing projects: Roger Brooke, Immy Holloway, Kate Galvin, Karin Dahlberg, Claire Jankelson, David Jankelson, Greg Madison, Barbara McGavin, Lyn Preston, Frances Rapport, Kip Jones, Steen Halling, Peter Ashworth, Don Polkinghorne, Scott Churchill, Linda Finlay, Peter Willis, Arthur Frank, Rosalind Pearmain and Erik Craig. Sometimes I do not know where I end and they begin: thank you all.

I am grateful to the editorial expertise of Anita Somner, who is courageous in telling me when I write weird; to the help that I have received at Palgrave Macmillan from Dan Bunyard; and to the staff of Macmillan India Ltd.

Publication Acknowledgements

The original sources of the material in this book are as follows:

Chapter 1 is a revised version of 'The qualitative description of human experience: The aesthetic dimension', which originally appeared in *Qualitative Health Research*, 8 (1), 121–127 (1998). Reprinted by permission from Sage Publications.

Chapter 2 is a revised version of 'The meaning of understanding and the open body: Some implications for qualitative research', which originally appeared in *Existential Analysis*, 15 (1), 38–54 (2004).

Chapter 3 is a revised version of 'The bodily complexity of truth-telling in qualitative research: Some implications of Gendlin's philosophy', which originally appeared in the *Humanistic Psychologist*, 23 (3), 283–300 (1999). Reprinted by permission from Lawrence Erlbaum Associates.

Chapter 4 is a revised version of 'Writing phenomenological-psychological description: An illustration attempting to balance texture and structure', which originally appeared in *Auto/Biography*, 3 (1&2), 41–48 (2000). Reprinted by permission from Sage Publications (©British Sociological Association, 2000).

Chapter 5 is a revised version of 'Humanising forces: Phenomenology in science; psychotherapy in technological culture', which originally appeared in two journals: the *Indo-Pacific Journal of Phenomenology*, 3, 1–16 (2002); and *Counselling and Psychotherapy Research*, 3 (3), 196–203 (2003), http://www.tandf.co.uk/journals.

Chapter 6 is a revised version of 'The rhythm of psychotherapeutic attention: A training model', which originally appeared in the *Journal of Phenomenological Psychology*, 21, 32–45 (1990). Reprinted by permission of Koninklijke Brill N.V.

Chapter 7 is a revised version of 'The primacy of phenomenological process and sequence in psychotherapy: A case study' and originally appeared as a book chapter in R van Vuuren (ed.) *Dialogue Beyond Polemics.* Pretoria: Human Science Research Council Publishers, 95–106 (1991).

Chapter 8 is a revised version of 'Globalisation and the complexity of self: The relevance of psychotherapy', which originally appeared in *Existential Analysis*, 13 (1), 98–105 (2002).

Chapter 9 is a revised version of 'Freedom-wound: The embodiment of human openness in Daseinsanalytic Therapy', which originally appeared in D. Martino (ed.) *Daseinsanalysis: The Twenty-Second Annual*

Symposium of the Simon Silverman Phenomenology Center. Pittsburgh, PA: Simon Silverman Phenomenology Center, pp. 111–125 (2005).

Chapter 10 is a revised version of 'Psychological and spiritual freedoms: Reflections inspired by Heidegger', which originally appeared in *Human Studies*, 16, 255–266 (1993). Reprinted by permission of Springer Science and Business Media.

Chapter 11 is a revised version of 'How does liberating self-insight become tacit understanding?' and originally appeared as a book chapter in G. Watson, S. Batchelor & G. Claxton (eds) *The Psychology of Awakening.* London: Rider, 177–186 (1999). Reprinted by permission from the Random House Group.

Chapter 12 is a revised version of 'The wound that connects: A consideration of 'Narcissism' and the creation of soulful space', which originally appeared in *The Indo-Pacific Journal of Phenomenology*, 4 (1), 1–12 (2004), an online journal available from http://www.ipjp.org.

Chapter 13 is a revised version of 'Embracing ambiguity: Transpersonal development and the phenomenological tradition', which originally appeared in *Religion and Health*, 39 (3), 227–237 (2000).

Chapter 14 is a completely new chapter and is partially based on an invited plenary talk that I gave to the 4th Nordic interdisciplinary conference on qualitative methods in the service of health at Växjö Universiteit in Sweden on 18 May 2006.

Introduction: An Embodied Path at Beginning and End

The phenomenological tradition may be seen as a broad but coherent movement that addresses foundational issues in epistemology, ontology, and ethics (Spiegelberg, 1971). Edmund Husserl, considered to be the founder of phenomenology, focused most on epistemological concerns: how knowledge about life and the world can 'come from' a reflection on what appears in consciousness. He wanted to heal a split that had been emerging in Western philosophy between 'inner' and 'outer', mind and body, subject and object. Martin Heidegger focused more on ontological concerns: the kind of being who can understand and know, and what this also tells us about the nature of Being per se, the context within which beings arise. Husserl and Heidegger, although concentrating, respectively, on epistemology and ontology, both understood that these concerns are intimately related, and that they also had ethical implications. Within this tradition, Emmanuel Levinas went further to develop a line of thought that articulated the ethical dimension as essentially intrinsic to epistemology and ontology: how the 'other', that is always beyond summative knowing, tells us more about the kinds of beings that we openly and intersubjectively are, and how this is already an ethical calling. Merleau-Ponty, a scholar steeped in both Husserl and Heidegger also pursued an allied integrative task: how all this, the place where ontology, epistemology, and ethics meet, is primarily located in our bodily being: that embodiment cannot be considered separately from being and knowing. Although there has been much mileage made from the creative differences and even antagonisms that existed between these thinkers, there is beginning to emerge a coherent thematic understanding of some of the continuities and synergistic thrusts of these thinkers (Zahavi, 2003).

One of these coherent developmental strands, beginning with Husserl, is the articulation of the lifeworld and its relation to the lived body. The picture that has emerged is that of a pregnant world of meaning that is 'more than' any constructing or languaging of it, a world of multiple possible meanings. Even though language constitutes the 'house' of Being, and thus provides a place to stand and act from, and change things, there is always a 'more' or a receding horizon to the lifeworld beyond the 'known' perspective. This means that the lifeworld is never 'closed' or 'finished' or 'totalised', and that language and other ways of human meaning-making cannot adequately summarise the lifeworld. So what is it about being human that is 'in touch' with an unsummarised experience of 'what comes', and yet can also interact with and understand, the meaning of 'what comes' for itself in some way? And here is where the role of the lived body becomes crucial as a double realm that both texturally experiences the prereflective 'more' of a world that it is part of, and at the same time, gives perspective and reflection (shared or alone) to this experience. The lived body thus grounds understanding by intimately participating in a world that can show new horizons and meanings. It is this participative and aesthetic dimension that the lived body gives to understanding. As such the lived body also gives to understanding the textures and aliveness of a 'fleshly' world that is relevant to persons. So, embodied understanding is a form of knowing that evokes the possibility of its living, bodilyrelevant textures and meanings. It is different from a disembodied knowing that merely creates plausible, abstract models or explanations, but which cannot easily be brought into the light of one's own lived possibilities. In his philosophy of entry into the implicit, Eugene Gendlin has taken forward the challenge to articulate and work with the complex relationships between the lived body, the lifeworld, and language.

It is here where I have broadly located myself in my work over the last 16 years. As a philosophically oriented psychologist, I have been fascinated by this phenomenon of embodied understanding, both for myself and how to facilitate it for others. In qualitative research, it has moved me to more evocative forms of writing. In relation to psychotherapy I have been very interested in the nature of self-insight as a form of embodied understanding, as well as therapeutic ways of being that may help clients move forward with bodily informed understanding. Philosophically and spiritually, I have engaged myself with how there has been a traditional split between spirituality and bodily life, and this has motivated an interest in what an embodied spirituality may look like.

So I have found that an engagement with such foundational issues grounded in the phenomenological tradition has been very helpful and productive when considering their implications for research methodology, psychotherapy, and spirituality. I now only recognise in retrospect that a certain sensibility and narrative theme has been at work in the way that I have applied myself to these matters. It is this journey that I wish to share with the reader in the hope that the whole may be more than the sum of the parts.

The sensibility and narrative theme centrally refers to how phenomenology grounds human enquiry in a way that marries 'head' and 'heart'. Embodied enquiry is the path by which embodied understanding happens. Sometimes a chapter will focus on embodied understanding as an outcome, such as when considering the dimensions of an embodied spirituality. Sometimes a chapter will focus on embodied enquiry as a path to embodied understanding, such as the use of personal imagery in psychotherapy. The central theme of this book is, however, on the nature of embodied understanding and its implications for the path of embodied enquiry. This theme takes on particular nuances in the three areas of research methodology, spirituality, and psychotherapy:

- In research methodology: how embodied understanding is not just 'cognitive', but involves embodied, aesthetic experience and application.
- In spirituality: how embodied understanding opens up a view of human existence that lies between great freedom and great vulnerability, a view of spirituality that integrates the personal and the transpersonal.
- In psychotherapy: how embodied understanding may occur through the process of psychotherapy where one is able to increasingly experience oneself as 'more than' the ways one has been objectified and defined (freedom), and therefore, more fluidly in accord with the human realm (vulnerability).

These three areas of application, although overlapping, are the foci that organise the three parts of the book: research methodology, psychotherapy, spirituality. Each part comprises a number of chapters that are linked together with the aid of an introduction to each part. The book concludes with a review of the major 'touchstones' that phenomenology provides for each of the three applied areas. It considers how such phenomenologically informed ideas may provide timely and relevant food for thought in our current situation, where the de-personalisation and de-humanisation of self and other is rampant in obscuring the human ground that we share. Could it be that Husserl (1970), in his *The Crisis of the European Sciences and Transcendental Phenomenology: An Introduction to Phenomenological Philosophy*, and Heidegger (1977), in his *Question Concerning Technology and Other Essays*, already saw some of the challenges of a transitional world-view that has not yet learned how to humanise, and ethically encounter, the systems and symptoms of technological progress? Could it be that the touchstones that they provided bring more into focus than ever before the need for a philosophical world-view that pursues the tasks of embodied enquiry?

Part I Research Methodology: Towards Aesthetic and Embodied Practices

This first part on research methodology develops a view of embodied enquiry as an aesthetic pursuit that centrally requires the lived body as the 'place' where intimate understanding of both experience and language happen.

Chapter 1 asks the question: What kinds of qualitative descriptions of human experience produce a feeling of understanding in the reader? The answer to this question may involve not only issues about truth (validity) but also issues about beauty (aesthetics). The themes discussed include the relationship between the structure and texture of an experience, the relationship between the concrete and abstract uses of language, and the relationship between the individual and general levels of description. The chapter draws on the thought of Dilthey, Heidegger, Merleau-Ponty, and Hillman to articulate the need for using language in a way that serves the qualitative dimensions of experience. This tradition would ask for a way of communicating our descriptions that can retain their concrete and embodied occasions; it wishes to return texture to structure and thus involve readers in forms of understanding that cannot be separated from aesthetic participation.

Chapter 2 moves further into the nature of embodied understanding and how such considerations may clarify the purpose and path of phenomenologically oriented qualitative research. It proceeds by developing some foundational thoughts about what is involved in the kind of understanding that is experientially and qualitatively relevant. Such understanding is metaphorised as the play of 'home' and adventure, of the familiar and the unfamiliar. Particular themes from Husserl, Heidegger, and Gadamer are lifted out before gathering them together to settle on the work of Eugene Gendlin. The lived body, characterised as the 'messenger' of the unsaid, provides possibilities for understanding situations that exceed any precise formulation or patterning of it. Such understanding is thus 'alive' in its excess, in that the role of ongoing experience is never exhausted. The chapter concludes with a consideration of how such an emphasis on embodied understanding may reinterpret the tasks of phenomenologically oriented qualitative research. In this view, to facilitate embodied understanding is to make understanding 'habitable' for others in a lively way. The path of embodied enquiry in qualitative research thus seeks to show and evoke the presence of a lived experience through words. It does not arrive at a summative 'essence', but offers instead 'good words' that describe and show, but do not kill, the sense of aliveness that they refer to.

Chapter 3 concentrates more explicitly on Gendlin's philosophy of the body and develops the implications of these ideas for the practice of qualitative research as an embodied methodological practice. It begins by considering an embodied perspective on the 'truth values' of qualitative research. In this view, our bodily participation in life provides a grounded quality to understanding, a shared reference point for an experientially grounded language that can 'work'. This understanding is a bodily informed practice and involves the body's access to 'more than words can say'. As such, the body is intimate to understanding, and such bodily informed sense-making adds a crucial dimension to the ways we have access to truth and present such truth. Implications of this approach for qualitative methodology are discussed, in particular the implications for the informant's task, the interviewer's task, the task of analysis, and the task of the reader.

Chapter 4, the final chapter in this methodological section, pursues one of the practical implications of taking phenomenological methodology towards more aesthetic and embodied forms. It focuses on a certain tension in the way we describe human experience: how to retain the richness and texture of individual experiences when formulating a level of description that applies generally and typically. The terms of this debate refer to the notions of texture and structure as guiding principles. The chapter anticipates the next section on psychotherapy by applying this concern to a phenomenological study of the nature of therapeutic self-insight as an illustration. A practical attempt is made to describe the researched phenomenon in such a way as to achieve an aesthetic balance between texture and structure. It concludes by reflecting on the path of this approach in order to contribute some guidelines about the art of writing when communicating our research discoveries about the qualitative dimensions of human experience.

1
The Qualitative Description of Human Experience: The Aesthetic Dimension

1. Overview

The *Duquesne Studies in Phenomenological Psychology*, Volumes 1 (Giorgi, Fischer & Von Eckartsberg, 1971), 2 (Giorgi, Fischer & Murray, 1975), 3 (Giorgi, Knowles & Smith, 1979), and 4 (Giorgi, Barton & Maes, 1983), was one of the first programmatic approaches to psychological research that attempted to be faithful to the qualitative dimensions of human experience. Interesting and distinctive research topics such as the experience of being criminally victimised (Fischer & Wertz, 1979) and the experience of suspicion and its relationship to delusion as experienced by psychiatric patients (de Koning, 1979) were pursued.

I have been interested in this approach since 1976 after having been inspired by Giorgi's (1970) book *Psychology as a Human Science*. I took this approach in both my master's and PhD research and became increasingly aware of a tension with which I still struggle. The tension refers to how to retain the richness and texture of individual experiences when formulating a level of description that applies generally and typically.

When I read phenomenological descriptions about anxiety or alienation by master writers such as J.P. Sartre and J.H. van den Berg, I am impressed by their insight and ability to produce in me a greater understanding of the phenomenon they are trying to describe. Take Sartre, for example, in his description of trying to give up smoking:

> In giving up smoking I was going to strip the theatre of its interest, the evening meal of its savour, the morning work of its fresh animation. Whatever unexpected happening was going to meet my eye, it seemed to me that it was fundamentally impoverished from the

moment that I could not welcome it while smoking. To-be-capable-of-being-met-by-me-while-smoking: such was the concrete quality which has been spread over everything. (Sartre, 1943, p. 596)

This description is full of aesthetic texture. It does this by staying close to this unique individual, yet at the same time there is a social and perhaps universal significance. It is this texture that can become easily lost in our efforts to generalise and find a broader context-related validity.

In this chapter, I wish to indicate some theoretical justifications for considering texture when writing qualitative descriptions of experience. It is hoped that the incorporation of some of the themes to be discussed will be helpful in explicitly guiding our attempts to deepen the understanding in our readers of what we have researched.

2. What is meant by structure?

The Duquesne tradition in psychological research has provided a disciplined procedure that is designed to ensure that the details of individual experiences intimately contribute to an articulation of a level of generality considered to be psychologically relevant; this has been called the 'general structure'.

The general structure involves a level of description in which context-related themes are expressed such that a variety of readers may further their psychological understanding of a phenomenon in a way that is generally applicable. Such insights do not merely describe various elements or extract various features that correlate positively; rather:

To describe the structure is to describe how the elements of a phenomenon function constitutively; how they interrelate to form the unity of the experience. (Reed, 1987, p. 102)

Such insights are also not necessarily universally applicable but apply within similar contexts. This phase thus involves the movement from individuality to generality. All the diverse cases of individual experiences of a phenomenon are understood to contribute towards a general understanding of its psychological structure. The aim is to establish what is typical of the phenomenon and to express such typicality in an insightful and integrated manner. The danger of this general description is that while it can find terms of reference that essentially fit all cases studied, it may lose a sense of the particular substance of the experience.

This general level of language is often fairly philosophical and abstract. As an example, I will briefly quote from Fischer's (1989) excellent study of anxiety:

> An anxious situation arises when the self-understanding in which one is genuinely invested is rendered problematically uncertain and hence, possibly untrue. (p. 134)

Fischer goes on to insightfully describe some important nuances of anxiety in general, such as being confronted by contradictory meanings, the division between one's self and one's body, and the desire for avoidance. In order to achieve these generalities, the specific texture of individual occasions for this experience is de-emphasised for the sake of being essential. In other words, the general plot of anxiety is expressed at this stage without retaining the concrete examples of how different people lived their anxiety in unique and nuanced ways.

This dilemma about the tension between the abstract and the concrete goes back to Aristotle, who held that no universal is substantial – only particulars are substantial. Within this perspective, the form of something cannot exist (except conceptually) without it 'eventing' in particular (Silverstein, 1988).

Aristotle's challenge

Aristotle's implicit challenge for qualitative research is perhaps to find a level of discourse that reflects both the individual particulars of 'this' experience or situation as it is lived and how such particularity reflects more typical and general themes and categories of human existence. One could err in the extremities of either direction, and this can occur in phenomenological research as well. One could describe the general themes of an experience in such an abstract way that the qualities are devitalised, or one could describe the particular experience in such a way that its general implications for you and me are not articulated.

I would like to argue for a conception of understanding psychological life that flows through the writings of Dilthey, Heidegger, Merleau-Ponty, and Hillman. This tradition would ask for a way of communicating our psychological descriptions that can retain their concrete and embodied occasions; it wishes to return texture to structure, and this involves readers in forms of understanding that cannot be separated from aesthetic participation.

One way of interpreting this task may be to ask the question: What kinds of descriptions produce a feeling of understanding in the reader?

Some directions for beginning to answer this question are indicated with reference to some philosophical points about the nature of understanding.

Dilthey: Understanding is enactment

The philosopher Wilhelm Dilthey reminds us that there is no detached reader of psychological knowledge. He was acutely attuned to how we are embedded in and part of the psychological life we are trying to understand, and so we cannot say that we begin 'objectively' as human scientists from an outside point of view.

In our humanness we are able to evaluate things because we have feelings and purposes, we are able to understand history in a meaningful way because we are historical beings. Dilthey thus called for a *Geisteswissenschaft*, an 'understanding science' which attempts to comprehend the nature of mental life from within rather than from the perspective of an outsider. In this view, a psychology that cannot find a language that discovers the 'I in the Thou' (Dilthey, cited in Rickman, 1976, p. 18) has alienated itself from its subject matter from the beginning.

This process of groping towards a fuller understanding from a less complete understanding is a description of the 'shuttlecock' movement of what has been called the 'hermeneutic circle'. Such a notion clarifies how 'understanding' proceeds by telling us more about what we already understand, experience, and live. In this way, its task is to retain continuity with what is already experientially evident and familiar to us as 'commoner'. Such 'standing-in' what we already understand is clearly full of personal texture. Dilthey uses the term *nacherleben* to designate a form of understanding that roughly translates as to 're-enact'. Within this perspective, to comprehend a human experience, whether one's own or that of another, is to bring it into the light of one's own possibilities – and thus to re-enact it. Dilthey's simple message for us today may be to write in a language that aims to elicit empathy and participation in the reader.

Heidegger: Mood is intimate to understanding

Heidegger worked further to restore texture to understanding. He restores emotional atmosphere or 'heart' to the experience of understanding by indicating how understanding is existentially situated.

In its immediate concreteness, the appearance of things always first tells us about the state of our relationship to them. Before we reflectively abstract our understanding, we 'register' how we are in relation to things in a prereflective and unthematised manner. Such prereflective 'registration' functions as a background quality that is not merely neutral, but colours our perceptions and understandings with emotional texture. This leads one of Heidegger's interpreters to emphasise how mood provides an important ontological context for perception and understanding:

> Disclosure of Dasein is primarily not theoretical but rather mood-like. (Vycinas, 1961, p. 43)

Even in boredom or tranquillity, the world is never colourless but shows a face that emphasises possibilities that are consistent with its mood. Heidegger (1962) has used the term *befindlichkeit* to refer to that form of prereflective understanding that interprets the mood-like disclosure of things. *Befindlichkeit* as a form of understanding is thus always involved when we understand another's experience or when we read the text of a human situation – we relate ourselves to its mood – and can thus understand with our hearts. The message for us may be to use language in a way that communicates the mood of a situation of experience.

Merleau-Ponty: The body takes up language and enlivens it

Merleau-Ponty (1962) is the most explicit about how the human body is intimately present in any act of understanding the structure of an experience:

> Structures are lived rather than known and therefore can never be apprehended passively; but only by living them, assuming them and discovering their immanent significance. (p. 258)

If we come to understand in a bodily participative way, there is a sense in which our bodies know more than we do in an explicit way: Shapiro (1985) expressed it in the following manner:

> I conceive of phenomena as fixed enough in their structures so that through my body I can retain them as a bodily sense and reactivate them or revivify them. (p. 19)

Here the message for us may be to write our descriptions in such a way that they are able to communicate a bodily sense of being-there.

Hillman: Aesthetic understanding is a 'breathing in'

In my view, the post-Jungian psychologist James Hillman is the most radical in arguing for the importance of communicating the aesthetic dimensions of human experience.

According to Hillman, aesthetic awareness involves presence through the senses, and the senses do not stop at the nose, eyes, or skin as if we were non-participant spectators. The senses penetrate the fluids of our bodies, and we go through an experience; we are moved, and a particular form of the world finds a home through our accommodating stance. In this regard, Hillman (1981) elaborates:

> This link between heart and the organs of sense is not simple mechanical sensationalism; it is aesthetic. That is, the activity of perception or sensation in Greek is aesthesis which means at root 'taking in' and 'breathing in' – a gasp, that primary aesthetic response. (p. 31)

Such a perspective would ask whether words can not only show the intelligibility of psychological life but whether they can do so in a way that can be 'breathed in'. Thus, descriptions may not only be valid but beautiful as well. Beauty in this sense does not mean a particular individual response to things where we evaluate things as beautiful or ugly. Rather, with Hillman, the term is used in the way Henry Corbin uses it to indicate the 'howness' of how things appear – how it bodies forth and stands there in a context.

It is in this spirit that Heidegger does not see a separation between truth and beauty when talking of poetic discourse. Poetic language with regard to experience is 'truthful' in that it attempts to retain the prereflective qualities of experiential structures – concrete, embodied, mooded, sensed, interrelated, and always full of the imagination gathered from other times and places. In poetic discourse, one's relatedness to existence is revealed in that it asks the listener to move towards the speaker or the text and to find the body of the occasion, its taste, and mood in his or her own.

With regard to general descriptions, the consideration of poetic discourse may mean writing in such a way that the reader is invited to relate to the description not just logically but also personally. This may be supported in two ways:

- by the writer providing enough individual occasions so that the reader may 'stand before' the concreteness of the experience
- by the writer offering some of her own metaphors and images that reflect her research discoveries. It is believed that this may be helpful as long as it is not presented as the only possible interpretation, and that in the true spirit of the hermeneutic tradition, the writer is explicit about her own interpretive contributions to the text.

In my view, efforts by phenomenologically oriented researchers to return texture to structure include Clark Moustakas's (1994) approach, which achieves a 'textural–structural synthesis', and van Manen's (1990) elucidation of hermeneutic phenomenology.

Full-bodied descriptions of human phenomena such as 'what it means to be tactful as an educator' (van Manen, 1990) or Yoder's textural–structural synthesis of the experience of guilt (cited in Moustakas, 1994) can only be done justice by reading them as unbroken texts, and I would refer readers to the aforementioned books for adequate illustration. It is finally only the reader's participation in engaging with the entire text that can ensure the possibility of an aesthetically rich understanding.

Both Moustakas and van Manen provide suggestions on how to conduct disciplined thematic analyses of our research data. They are both mindful about the issues of validity, trustworthiness, and faithfulness to the phenomena. However, they argue in different ways that, in addition, nothing can replace the researcher's personal digestion of the research experience in producing a description that is both valid and aesthetically communicative. No technique can do this for one, and Sartre forever beckons.

3. Conclusion

This chapter has attempted to offer some philosophical justification for attending to the aesthetic dimensions when communicating our research discoveries. The themes that have preoccupied me may be seen to reflect one dimension of a postmodern struggle: how to find a level of participation that is neither impersonal nor only personal. Within this spirit, the quest for more integration of texture and structure may be one way of defining a qualitative research endeavour that is faithful to a meaningful human world.

2
The Meaning of Understanding and the Open Body: Some Implications for Qualitative Research

I would like to develop some thoughts on the question of 'what it means to understand' as an important guiding principle for qualitative research. I believe that addressing this question can tell us important things about the purpose and aims of qualitative research and that it can also help to refine our methodological sensitivity and procedures. In this pursuit, I am indebted to the broad tradition of phenomenology and, specifically, particular strands of thought that run through Husserl, Heidegger, Gadamer, and Merleau-Ponty. I use these great thinkers inspirationally as a psychologically oriented person with a pragmatic interest in qualitative research. And in this concern to meditate on the theme of what it means to understand, I then move to an emphasis on embodiment as a remedy to a Cartesian tradition that may have overemphasised the 'cognitive' and the abstract dimensions of understanding. Here, the relationship between experience and language becomes a pivotal enquiry. This task is helped centrally by the work of Eugene Gendlin, and I spend time unfolding some of his key thoughts on the matter as well as some possible implications of this for the practice of qualitative research. In this regard, I draw generously on his passion to show how we use much more than our thoughts when we think and how the lived body is full of fertile excess, intimate with crossings and bridges, textures and relationships that are the 'stuff' of understanding.

1. Home

A theme found in Husserl relating to understanding is that of the notion of a 'home-world' which makes understanding relevant. In a book called *Home and Beyond*, Anthony Steinbock (1995) considers the theme of home in Husserl's writings as the place from where understanding begins and the place to which understanding returns.

14

Steinbock interprets Husserl to forge a 'journey' of understanding in which there is a tension between 'home-world' and 'alien-world' – the familiar and the unfamiliar. These two structures define one another, and even the feelings of 'normal' and 'abnormal'. One could even say that where there is only 'home' there is little need to understand. But in this view, neither home-world nor alien-world can be regarded as the 'original sphere' since, in Steinbock's words, they are 'in a continual historical becoming as delimited from one another. This is the sense in which home and alien are co-generative' (1995, p. 179).

Grounding the notion of 'what it means to understand' in the liminal space and experience of 'home' and 'alien', it can become meaningful to talk of understanding as a journey of appropriation and transgression – an interplay of the familiar and the unfamiliar. If it were possible to only have the 'unfamiliar', there would just be wordless shock or even non-recognition. If it were possible to only have the 'familiar' then there would be wordless symbiosis, an eternal womb where understanding is unnecessary.

So, there appears already in Husserl an ontological wound which generates a hunger for understanding – of how to appropriate that which has already transgressed home. Appropriation and transgression may thus be one important aesthetic touchstone for the task of understanding. Steinbock quotes a very illustrative conversation between a Mongol emperor and Marco Polo from a novel by Calvino, which although fiction, highlights 'home' as a crucial aesthetic touchstone:

'There is still one of which you never speak.'
Marco Polo bowed his head.
'Venice', the Khan said.
Marco smiled. 'What else do you believe I have been talking to you about?'
The emperor did not turn a hair. 'And yet I have never heard you mention that name.'
And Polo said: 'Every time I describe a city I am saying something about Venice.'
'When I ask you about other cities, I want to hear about them. And about Venice, when I ask you about Venice.'
'To distinguish the other cities' qualities, I must speak of a first city that remains implicit. For me it is Venice.'
'You should then begin each tale of your travels from the departure, describing Venice as it is, all of it, not omitting anything you remember of it.'
(Calvino in Steinbock, 1995, p. 186)

Implicit in all this is how a home-world is also a we-world – it is inter-subjectively co-constituted. And thus, the shared world of culture and language shows itself as a central feature in the drama of understanding and how this occurs through the productive tension between appropri-ation and transgression. Another word for 'being at home' is to 'dwell'. Bernd Jager (2001) has written that 'only a creature that knows how to dwell can paint, dance, think and write' (p. 134). He is indicating how an experience of dwelling can provide the kind of space and boundaries that are required to humanise our world – to create a space of human habitation in which we can 'appropriate' and make that which is given to us as our own. There are even writers who see an excessive transgres-sion of 'home' as constituting disease and illness: 'Illness is a state of disharmony, dis-equilibrium, dis-ability, and dis-ease which incorpo-rates a loss of the familiar world' (Toombs, 1993, p. 96).

For Husserl, to understand is to imagine, to transgress the concrete event and enter into the horizons of the world, and to find its unities for back home. Here, the meaning of an event is partially constituted by the depth of the world with which one engages – the lifeworld itself speaks and Husserl was most concerned with our mode of access to the eventing of the lifeworld. But we must leave Husserl for now, as we think further about the role of language as bridge-maker in understanding.

2. Adventure

The emphasis on home-making brings out the task of understanding as a cultural quest full of symbolisation and language. Language is the place where alien otherness becomes adventure, so I would like to move here from Husserl's structure of home/alien to a perspective that is more in the spirit of Heidegger; that of home and adventure. In adventure one is both excited and scared to enter the unknown – one is widened and stands in wonder. At its edge is our own finitude – of giving up what we have embodied. One is called by otherness and difference to respond as faithfully as possible – to honour the possibilities that stand out, and to care for the possibilities of phenomena in an attitude of letting-be-ness. The one from home is transformed by this adventure, as such a 'self' is never self-enclosed but always in the openness of relationships. But in adventures of understanding there is not only otherness, as if home is dead. Home is transformed and adventures become meaningful for home. Understanding is bridge-making, and adventure gives the per-spective of distance which refreshes homecoming with people there eager for stories, and dwellings with open windows and doors – a mixing of interpenetrating worlds. The distance-making power of critique gives understanding the possibility of continual renewal – of making the fruits of understanding relevant in a changing world.

Here we come to Gadamer who can tell us a little more about the play of home and adventure and the role of language in understanding. Gadamer acknowledges Schleiermacher and Dilthey for focusing on the question of 'what it means to understand' and how this could form a core guiding principle for the humanities. He also acknowledges Heidegger for seeing 'understanding' as definitive of the kind of being that is human being. For Gadamer, understanding is the linguistic happening of tradition (Gadamer, 1975), but the happening is such that it exceeds tradition. And so, in a way, home is the past and all that it brings in body, community, and meaning. But understanding is also beyond tradition as living event in the way it gathers up the past and lives it forward. In understanding, there is a linguistic reworking of 'home' that arises out of the intersection of this 'carried past' with already adventuring human existence. The aliveness of human living is already exceeding home, so understanding is also an 'exceeding'. The structure, 'adventure' is thus not just elsewhere but is intimately 'in' the ongoing, carried forward 'aliveness' of being human. So for Gadamer, understanding is a linguistic happening in which the play of tradition and ongoing living become interrelated and full of meaning and significance for further living. Understanding is thus not separate from application; it is already telling us what is possible in terms of further living. In this applied sense, understanding is thus a 'living forward'. The way Gadamer expresses this is, that to understand, is to understand differently. Like 'home', tradition has a claim on us, and we are also already claimed by the ongoing living towards the future and new contexts that exceed us. We are thus transformed by this intersection of claims, of the old and the new, and how this intersection comes to us as meaning. To quote Gadamer: 'Understanding is not to be considered so much as an action of subjectivity, but rather as entering into an occurrence of transmission (*Uberlieferungsgeschehen*) in which past and present are being constantly mediated' (Gadamer, 1975, p. 290). Understanding is then properly thought of as neither objective or subjective; it is participatory and cannot be possessed. For Gadamer, the individual is de-throned, and understanding is the happening of Being in the locus of human historical existence (Ferrer, 2002).

So the 'happening' of understanding that is beyond where we were standing is a 'standing under' and is a transformation of who we were.

Both tradition and ourselves are transformed by such a new meaningful event. In being faithful to such happenings Gadamer speaks of a receptive stance of 'opening' and 'allowing', rather than an active methodological stance of subjecting meanings to procedures. The play of home and adventure is primary – home-horizon is expanded, and the home/adventure play is a 'between' that is an ongoing productive conversation with no clear endpoints or paths known in advance. Such play does its work beyond all method and is already a linguistic happening before our conscious participation in it.

What does this play of home and adventure tell us about the nature of the kind of language that is the medium and messenger of such living understanding–happening? There appears to be a certain illusiveness of language in which it 'effaces itself in favour of its subject matter' (Kisiel, 1985, p. 12). Its power is that it is flexible enough to bend itself to the play and intersection of what is between home and adventure, the old and the new, tradition and living forward. It takes on new meanings in different contexts, and works creatively 'in the cracks', not just logically, but metaphorically, poetically, and evocatively. It touches experience and bows down to the excesses of the lifeworld which always exceeds language's precise capture. Yet experience is already languaged and so language reveals its transmitting power. It is there in tradition and in culture before us. But even then it is speculative and always hungry, seeking like a vampire for the alive blood of experiential happenings. Without it, home and adventure would have no storying power, no bridges, no way to move. So languaging is the angel of the between. And understanding is 'refreshed' language and a real happening of pregnant horizons.

3. The 'said' and the 'unsaid'

Here, I need to say a few more words about Heidegger and how, in my view, he was more radical than Gadamer. This is arguable but some commentators have said that Gadamer refers to language as a process of making oneself at home in the world (see Kisiel, 1985). For example, Gadamer has emphasised the importance of holding on to home as follows:

> In order to understand that [the text], he must not seek to disregard himself and his particular hermeneutical situation. He must relate the text to this situation, if he wants to understand at all. (Gadamer, 1975, p. 289)

If so, one may see this as a somewhat domesticising bias in the interplay of home and adventure. My need to say a few words about Heidegger comes from my sense of how he at times, stood in the mystery of Being, the extent to which self was open rather than home-concerned, and the extent to which he grounded the 'said' in the 'unsaid' – of how being-in-the-world always transcended its forms and intrinsically exceeded linguistic capture. So there is insight in understanding that sees through language to the excesses of living and being-in-the-world. The 'said' points to the 'unsaid': 'what is sayable receives its determination from what is not sayable' (Heidegger, 1975, p. 78). There is a mysterious happening in which one is addressed meaningfully by Being, and there is an 'upsurge of the unsaid into the said' (Kissiel, 1985, p. 22). Such penetration from the unsaid emphasises the quality of 'adventure'.

Although obviously interested in the phenomenon of understanding, Heidegger grounds understanding in Being that is beyond understanding – Being that presents itself most intimately in living even before it gives itself to understanding. That Being can show itself and be understood means that it *can* show itself and that such showing itself is a presentation that is linguistic in its broadest sense. For Heidegger, there is a mysterious relation between language and Being, in which the 'unsaid' lives always exceedingly as that which the said is about. Speech in a broad sense is pregnant with this excess.

Human being's participation in the 'unsaid' indicates something of the flavour of the radical openness and continuity of self with the world. Self is 'out there' (being-in-the-world) and disappears into a depth of meaningful happenings that are not separate from its being. It is a knowing by virtue of being, an intimate inhabiting, an 'embodying of the presence of things that is pregnant with meaning' (Ferrer, 2002, p. 122). But being-in-the-world not only disappears into the 'unsaid' of world-happening, intimate with excess, it also appears again in a historical gathering of what this means for living forward with others in situations. So there appears to be a rhythm of self/world understanding, of self-standing in unknowing, and self-appropriating the fruits of such unknowing in some meaningful way. Heidegger is indicating a radical intimacy with being-ongoing, a primary adventure before appropriation. What this emphasis means for the destiny of understanding is that Heidegger is always very respectful of the 'forest' and the 'wild' (metaphorically speaking) and how the 'clearing' in the forest is very tentative and can never be fully domesticated. The enacting self as the shape of understanding is first 'wet through' by the insight of intimate participation and this can come to language in tentative ways.

So I interpret a more radical emphasis in Heidegger than Gadamer, in that understanding is always pointing quite strongly to the flow of the unsaid and its overwhelming adventurous power. Understanding comes into being through 'visiting', even through 'suffering' the unsaid. The insights that come from such adventure transforms us and we are challenged with the question of whether we can come to feel 'at home' with such letting-be-ness of the intimate excesses of what comes. It is in this emphasis of not reducing Being to a domestic home that we come to the notion of embodiment as the messenger of the 'unsaid'. This forges a productive tension between language and the lifeworld, a productive tension to which *the lived body and all its connections are adequate in intersecting the 'said' and the 'unsaid'*. And here we move to embodiment as a focal theme and to the work of Eugene Gendlin as a helpful guide.

4. Experiencing, embodiment and language

I interpret Gendlin as going forward from Husserl on the topic of experiencing as relational, from Gadamer on the topic of understanding as 'carrying forward', and from Heidegger on the topic of the productive tension of the concealed and the revealed. But it is Gendlin's thoughts on how the body is central in all this that may provide us with a coherent framework for understanding the meaning of understanding. Before coming to Gendlin's views let us approach thinking about embodiment first in a holistic and poetic manner. The body is the 'shepherd' of participation; it is in a relationship of belonging to being-in-the-world. It is interwoven with many realms, the perceptual–textural, the languaged, the affective, the immediately responsive, the interpersonal, the temporal, and even the 'unsaid' interweaving of all this together. It is thus not an object, although it can include this, but is rather 'dispersed throughout its lived context' (Merleau-Ponty, 1963, p. 248).

When we think of 'body', we may traditionally think of something solidly there. In the Cartesian sense, there is the body and the world, the body and the mind, inner and outer. But approaching embodying more naïvely, we find a living body that inhabits situations intimately; it interweaves the realms as a matter of being, and is itself often 'lost' out there in the textures, the senses, the flesh, the histories, and the meanings that come from the flowing excesses of the lifeworld. Yet it also carries personal history and prereflective sediments of historical meanings that shape its openness. One could say that embodying is where being and knowing meet, or as Gendlin says: 'The body knows its situation directly' (1997, p. 26), and further: 'A living body knows its environment by being it' (1997, p. 27). The body is an intentional body, primordially relational, and co-arising with its situation that is not just fleshly perceptual but also full of implicit meanings and relational understanding. What are these relational understandings, and how can we talk of bodily relational understandings that are faithful to the way embodiment appears as its interweaving, its non-linearity, its unpackaged presences, and its vague tentative formings? Logical language does not like these cracks, whisperings, and ambiguities where space/time sequences are not simply sequential. For Gendlin, perception is not primary, as perception is already based on a distinction between 'over there' from 'over here' – something important is happening before this spatial distinction in the way that meaning unfolds. As Gendlin describes it: 'Perception is never first and never alone' (1997b, p. 15). Faithful to the depth of bodily relational understandings, we could say that the way we are bodily in situations exceeds any precise formulation or patterning of it. This phenomenon is usefully metaphorised by Gendlin as a 'preseparated multiplicity', and this involves experiencing 'mores'.

Even though these 'mores' can be formulated, languaged, and patterned, (many things can come from 'there') what is referred to in different ways by the languaged formulations is often all together as an interrelated multiplicity, implicitly 'there' in the 'more'. This 'all together' has order, specificity, and vitality and functions intimately and in an ongoing way in the coming to being of meaning. To quote Lieberman (1997): 'It has been [Gendlin's] principal effort to describe, develop, demonstrate that there are lived orders that are orderly in more than formed ways' (p. 253). But like Heidegger's 'unsaid', the 'more' is always what the 'said' is about. The 'more' is the being of the 'said' even though the 'said' can change the 'more'. To make this a little more experiential you may want to sense, for example, the feel of a hot summer's night, just being in that. This whole experience is carried by the body and is 'more' than the heat, 'more' than who you were with, 'more' than other personal times and places that resonate with the hot, summer's night. The experiential sense of all this can be thematised and languaged, and meaningful aspects separated out from this 'preseparated multiplicity'. So the body functions in situations as a background knowing of how the situation is as a whole before perceiving its distinctions. Such lived body sensing of situations, through 'being them' is adequate to the contact with lived meanings that language can be about. Without such an intimate connection before separation, the meanings of language would have no 'about'. Even though language has the power to change the 'about', the lived experience, the 'about' is always grounded in its 'more'. And the body is the intimate medium of the 'more'. The 'more' (situation) present within embodying is not vague and amorphous but 'very exact and precise, more precise than the common phrases and distinctions. But it is not given in convenient cognitive units' (Gendlin, 1997, p. 16).

Gendlin's notion of the 'more' brings together Heidegger's 'unsaid' in a very concrete way to which the body has experiential access and is always already there as part of our everyday lives. The 'more' is:

• Not reflectively already achieved before us; one needs to go into a kind of 'murky' or a kind of 'down there' or 'in there', a 'not quite that but something else'. This involves an aesthetic process of finding the words or differentiating movements, or symbolising something in such a way that does some of this 'more' a degree of justice.
• Very fertile. Many strands or specific meanings can come from it – but it is itself an 'unseparated multiplicity'.
• Very specific even though it is unseparated in direct experiencing. It is specific in that it implies particular directions, actions, and speech. So for example, there may be a sense of something about where I stand in relation to Gadamer. As it finds language, what comes is a particular appreciation of Gadamer's ethics (yes, his 'ethics' is what it is), and this gives me a particular specific direction by which I can position myself in relation to some of Heidegger's thinking. Gadamer's 'ethics' was in the 'more' of my relationship to him, and as this meaning is lifted out of the implicit mesh, it gives me the possibility of a very specific direction for action and speech. In this experiencing/languaging process, Gadamer is much more than a series of completed thoughts in my memory. He is a kind of presence for me with whom I can dialogue. His presence for me is not identical to him but also exceeds any formulated thoughts that I have had about him. His presence is in a sense 'alive' and productive for me, and there is the potential for an ongoing dialogue, where the 'more' comes to me 'through a glass darkly', stirring in its gradually forming shapes as they are bodily felt and recognised, and finding distinctive forms in workable language. 'Yes, his ethics', I say again.

Another way of indicating the body's role in understanding is to put the word 'embodied' together with the word 'experiencing': 'Experiencing is the process of concrete, bodily feeling, which constitutes the basic matter of psychological and personality phenomena' (Gendlin, 1964, p. 111). To express this another way, bodily experiencing is the place where the presence of 'more than orderly patterns' that come to us first gathers.

In relation to bodily experiencing, Gendlin uses the term 'felt sense' to indicate something much more interactional and intentional than subjective inner bodily sensations that only speak of internal events: 'What one feels is not "stuff inside" but the sentience of what is happening in one's living in the outside' (Gendlin, 1997b, p. 41). Referring to some postmodern theorists who overly prioritise language, Lieberman draws on this notion of the interactional open body to which the 'more' comes, to remark that there is a 'texture of life still to be made contact with after deconstruction' (1997, p. 261). This is an important remedy to the notion that signs only point to other signs endlessly, in that the interactional body provides a crucial 'grounding' to language. It is Gendlin's contribution to the relationship between bodily experiencing and language, and the role of this tension for 'what it means to understand', that may be helpfully directional for qualitative research.

Even though language and experience are implicated in one another, they cannot be reduced to one another nor replace one another in the ongoing aliveness that is understanding. Language unfolds distinctions from an embodied sense of the 'more' (experiencing), and these distinctions in turn become part of the specific history of the 'more'. Thus, such explicit unfolding of meanings is not just a meaning-making that leaves the 'more' as it was, as if the process of explication did not carry the 'more' forward into new relationships that reconstitute it as what it itself is. The 'more' is not a box of 'essences' that is unchanged by the process of languaged 'lifting-outs'. Yet, although the 'more' changes in its interaction with language, it still exceeds the way it is packaged, and continues its endless pregnancy. The 'more' of bodily grounded experience is always open beyond cognitive units and is 'always open for further living and action' (Gendlin, 1997, p. 7). So we are talking about a kind of language that is released from the logic of identity, a language that has the power to say more than any circumscribed pattern, one that exceeds its own distinctions. The 'more' of the whole situation is not just a static truth; 'it involves the implying of further situations, events and actions' (Gendlin, 1992, p. 93). So 'language cannot work alone' (Gendlin, 1992, p. 93). It needs the body and the 'more' (a big challenge for computer models of artificial intelligence). And the body cannot work alone either. It needs language to form further from itself until the distinctions are ready to stand out at least for a moment in shared space. It is in this relationship of mixing and separating that language, embodiment, and the 'more' are intimately related, and as such, cannot be fully reduced to one another.

So this 'mesh' of potential lived meanings is in Gendlin's words, 'intricate'; it is not indeterminate even though it is excessive of formed patterns in its aliveness. Meaning-making is thus a bodily inclusive hermeneutic cycle in which one's bodily-sensed-situation-in-relation-to-words 'gives the words a new life' (Gendlin, 1997, p. 8). Such 'life' is beyond any pattern, even though the pattern may have been historically languaged as part of the changing history of the 'intricacy' of the 'more'. And such meanings live freshly: 'Whenever we enter the experiencing of anything that is being talked about, we immediately find an intricacy with vast resources that goes beyond the existing public language' (Gendlin, 1997, p. 37).

5. Back to the question: What it means to understand

The subtle relationship that Gendlin articulates between embodied experience and language may help us to elaborate our question of 'what it means to understand' with a new embodied emphasis. He is attempting to establish a philosophy of understanding that moves forward with the body and language and others, towards meanings that are always at the edge of the play of the old with the new. The qualities of this are both centring and decentring, home and adventure; a vital tension between the familiar and the unfamiliar.

The validity of such understanding can never correspond to the way things are (one cannot get into the same river twice). The validity of such understanding is rather in the way that it 'carries forward' meanings into new productive relationships in the future. Validity in this sense cannot thus be separated from a consideration of use and ethics. In drawing close to experience, words are instructional rather than merely 'descriptive'; they invite us into further experiencing of the 'more' exceeding them and, in languaging the 'more' further, this re-situates the 'more'; and the 'more' itself becomes more intricate. Understanding is a kind of reaching beyond formulated cognitions; it uses 'fuzzy specifics' and the body is intimate to 'fuzzy specifics'. But 'fuzzy specific' as a quality also wants something very precise from language in the way it would like to be 'carried forward'. However, we cannot construct the right words in a very active way: 'Words come to us in much the same way that emotions, appetite, fatigue and other bodily events come; in appropriate ways that cannot be forced or fabricated' (Hatab, 1997, p. 242). It wants just 'these series' of words in explicating the implicit of the 'fuzzy specific'. The 'fuzzy specific' wants a languaged home to rest for a moment before further adventure – a resting in familiar surroundings before all this becomes part of a new 'more' that is full of the new 'unsaid' adventure. Understanding *is* this intersection of bodily adventure and languaged home. Understanding is always asking for 'crossings' and 'intercourse'; it is always richer than it was, and here Gendlin is cautionary about Husserl. Descriptions should not be summative but rather invitational. The danger of summations is that such descriptions could 'replace experience, to make it no longer necessary' (Gendlin, 1997, p. 39). A summation would give experiencing no continuing role in understanding. In an embodied way, understanding is rather a procedure which includes the invitation to experience more. So 'meaning ... is not only a certain *logical* structure (although it can use such fixed statements as well) but also involves a *felt* experiencing' (Gendlin, 1997b, p. 1). And here we come to Gendlin's procedure of 'focusing' as a form of engagement that honours the embodied nature of understanding, its grounding in the 'unsaid', and the power of language to move.

Focusing as embodied enquiry

If we understand with more than thoughts and more than forms, and if conceptual formulations never work alone without reference to an experienced world that disappears into the 'unsaid', then understanding involves a bodily grounded practice in which, *as human beings, we are intimate with the 'unsaid' and intimate with the 'said'*. As human beings, we move in these realms, and in our everyday lives, have already been doing this ever since we can remember. Focusing is a more intentional and disciplined way of doing this. It originated from Gendlin's work with Carl Rogers in which he noted the processes that psychotherapy clients went through when they experienced new understandings that made a difference to the way they felt and lived. He noticed that the 'place' from which their speaking happened was a 'more' and that it first came as a bodily 'felt sense' of their situation. He developed these insights further as both a philosopher and psychotherapist and called the process 'focusing'. It involves a process that can be taught to psychotherapy patients and others, and has also been used in a number of creative pursuits such as poetic writing and doing philosophy. I am not able to give a full exposition of this disciplined process but will lift out some important features that may be relevant to a subsequent discussion on the implications of embodied enquiry for qualitative research:

- I attend to a definitely felt but conceptually vague experiencing. This is done after I bring my awareness into the body and wait for some felt relationships to what I am engaged in to form. There are various aids to this, but a 'felt sense' comes that is recognised as pregnant with some meaning that is not yet articulate, for example, 'something about my unfinished paper that needs attention'.

- I draw on the power of language, gesture, or symbol and begin to be open to 'words' or ways of describing the sense of the 'something'. There is a subtle kind of dipping back and forth between the 'felt sense' and a way of 'languaging' this in a broad sense. For example, the words that come about my unfinished paper are that it needs more 'unfolding' at just 'that' stage, which I can picture.
- I check to see how the phrase or narrative fits with the 'felt sense', how it resonates as an aesthetically satisfying experience. How do those words or phrases work? In my example, the phrase 'more unfolding' is not quite what it is; the phrase 'it needs more air' fits better.
- The phrase may become part of a new experiencing that is productive of further explicit meanings. In my example, the words that fitted better were: 'it needs more air'. My body resonated with this and took it up in a way that implicitly interacted with a whole lot of other meanings which fitted. This new experiencing generated new phrases and words which told me more about the precise manner of my paper 'needing more air': 'yes, that place is too condensed where I said that – it is not just too condensed but it also needs more air in the sense of allowing my readers to bring their own interpretations to it – I have been too specific in defining things at that place'.
- This back and forth between the 'more' of experiencing and the differentiations of language continue as a productive process of more refined understanding. And this is welcome and received as almost a relief of tension in my body. The meanings feel more digested and I would feel in a better position to dialogue these meanings with others and bring them into the shared world of intersubjective understanding.
- This would then set up a new process in which others would become part of the depth of the 'more'.

Two important things could be highlighted about this process:

- Referring to the 'more' usually appears to need some silence, a kind of 'waiting' and a willingness to feel the meanings of what may need attention or what wants to be said.
- The 'manner of experiencing' seems important: a certain 'immediacy' of what is living about all this now, its presence, its fresh detail. This 'manner of experiencing' can be helped by another's presence, and both Gendlin and Carl Rogers have spent much time trying to articulate the characteristics of another's presence that is facilitative in this kind of way.

So now we are ready to come to the implications of embodied enquiry for qualitative research.

6. Embodied understanding and phenomenologically oriented qualitative research

Max van Manen provides a succinct and helpful starting point for a consideration of phenomenology as applied to qualitative research: 'It is best to think of the basic method of phenomenology as the taking up of a certain attitude and practicing a certain attentive awareness to the things of the world as we live them rather than as we conceptualize or theorize them' (Van Manen, 2000, p. 460). This requires us to use accounts of experiences that may be gathered in different ways (interviews, written descriptions, even fictional narratives). So far, this is consistent with Gendlin who would 'seek to articulate experience as actually had rather than laying some invented theoretical scheme on experience' (Gendlin, 1973, p. 317).

The phenomenologically oriented researcher engages with accounts of experiences in a way that can articulate important understandings from these experiences and that may be relevant to others and take intersubjective understanding further. The ongoing controversy is whether we can call these literary articulations and understandings 'essences' in the sense that Husserl originally meant them. He was interested in the possibility of the almost mathematical quest of finding what is most invariant across examples of phenomena so that if those invariants changed, the phenomenon could no longer be what it is. This is a certain kind of philosophical and imaginative thinking which is designed to produce understandings about what is most general about experienced phenomena. However, the previous consideration about understanding requiring ongoing experiencing would suggest that what is 'most general' about experienced phenomena can never be the final thing said about that phenomenon. So, for example, we could say that anger has a potentially 'explosive' quality and that we can recognise this quality in many examples of anger. As soon as we see and say 'explosiveness' about anger, we have already begun to engage in how this word 'explosiveness' takes us in an experiential direction that opens up certain further meanings and closes others off.

So a new nuance on the meaning of anger is evoked, and we understand so-called essences only in terms of how the received generality opens up further specific aspects of the experience. There is always a 'more' in living and we cannot say this all at once and finally.

The phenomenon 'anger' can be understood in richer ways but each new word or phrase is not an 'essence' but rather a 'gathering'. It is a gathering that is instructional, as if to say: when the 'explosiveness' of anger is named, see how 'anger' in the contexts you are interested in is better understood and leads to even further productive understandings and meaningful connections. The word, 'explosiveness' is thus a 'lived platform' and bridge rather than an 'essence'. It is an intersubjective bridge as well as a bridge between the experienced phenomenon (anger) and its 'more' – the as yet unsaid about anger. Gendlin deals with a possible worry about the fluidity and endless progression of this journey as follows:

> The method may seem as if it launches us on an endless progression, but even here there are methodic ways of knowing when a desirable stopping point is reached; again the stopping point is not a final statement *of* (Gendlin's emphasis) an experience, but rather a way of structuring words or situations so that some living, some action, or some intellectual task may be carried out. With respect to the final nature of experience, there is no stopping point to statement, because the nature of experiencing vis-à-vis further structuring is precisely that it can be further structured and in several different ways. (Gendlin, 1973, p. 305)

What this means for qualitative research is that it repositions our task as one that is an ongoing 'conversation' that seeks to share 'good words' and phrases that are evocative and 'carry understanding' further. It is a community journey. Such embodied understanding is also a further invitation to experiencing in that it seeks to show and evoke the presence of a lived experience through words. Fresh sense-making occurs as a bodily experienced recognition, and the one who understands further provides a temporary home for what is understood. She crosses this 'other', this phenomenon, this adventure, with her own possibilities. In such embodied understandings, the language 'works' in ways that are open to that which is beyond formal boundaries, the unsaid life of the phenomenon. The qualitative researcher within this spirit is a mediator and facilitator who carries forward understandings distilled from informants' accounts into a shared world. The task is to share understanding in a habitable way. So, to facilitate embodied understanding is to make understanding 'habitable' for others. This kind of qualitative research serves a communal, cultural quest that straddles 'home' and 'adventure'. In order for qualitative research to pursue embodied understanding, it requires procedures that show phenomena in both experientially evocative as well as structurally coherent ways. Such home-making is finally a narrative offering which can be poetic in its evocative power but is not just poetry; it includes the kind of details and examples that show phenomena in a systematic and even logical manner. The 'words' from 'embodied understanding' participate in a paradoxical quality:

* On one hand, they forge a fruitful distance from the specific embodied occasion by allowing some generalities that are transferable across these occasions.
* On the other hand, they remain responsively connected to the aliveness of the specific experiential occasions, inviting the bodily 'more' of participation.

Such an emphasis would reframe the idea of 'essence' to be that of an 'authentic productive linguistic gathering'. This term takes into account how the outcome of phenomenologically oriented enquiry is grounded in textured bodily experience that it takes its validity from 'good' words that work in a productive (and perhaps ethical) way, and that the status of the 'linguistic gathering' refers to 'real' happenings that are neither absolute nor relative but 'always on the way', in play with 'home' and 'adventure'. Such an 'authentic productive linguistic gathering' keeps experiencing alive in ongoing embodied understanding.

I believe that all this puts a particular emphasis on the goal of phenomenologically oriented qualitative research, and that this has important implications for the path and practice of such research; how we formulate our research enquiry, how we interview and dialogue with research respondents, how we analyse and explicate the experiences of others, and how we write up and offer for reading the products of our understanding. In these specific pursuits, the practice of focusing that has developed out of Gendlin's philosophy may become a very helpful innovation for phenomenologically oriented research. Incorporating this practice of focusing may result in outcomes that are different and deeper than other qualitative research approaches. This is because it 'opens up the whole vast implicit experiential level' (Gendlin, 2003, personal communication).

3
The Bodily Complexity of Truth-Telling in Qualitative Research

When we talk to one another about the ways in which we have personally built meaningful knowledge that has both theoretical and practical implications, it often comes down to the experience of 'sense-making' and how this 'sense-making' can be carried into the 'give and take' of shared life. Such 'sense-making' appears to be an ongoing and progressive, though not linear, practice. I would like to suggest that a consideration of 'sense-making' as a process in qualitative research may be a fruitful line of enquiry when pursuing the nature of truth in qualitative research. In differentiating between a logical and responsive order, Gendlin emphasises an aesthetic dimension to the practice of 'sense-making', and this may need to be given greater attention when considering the 'quality of qualitative research' (cf. Seale, 1999).

1. Overview of argument

A number of different writers have contributed to epistemological debates in qualitative research and have discussed the 'truth values' of qualitative research that have deepened the natural scientific notion of validity. Terms such as trustworthiness, credibility, dependability, confirmability, and others have been put forward to indicate a certain multidimensionality in the ways we legitimate qualitative enquiry (see, for example, Denzin & Lincoln, 1994). Drawing on the work of Eugene Gendlin, I want to suggest that such notions may need to address not only the public or shared dimension, but the personal and experiential dimension as well. In this view, the 'authenticity' of a qualitative description or interpretation is also valued in terms of its ability to deepen personal insight in listeners and readers. In Chapter 1, I have referred to this as the 'aesthetic' dimension of qualitative description.

However, the implications of Gendlin's thought would take this further: In this view, 'sense-making' is not just a personal cognitive process but requires the participation of the 'lived body' as an authenticating or validating procedure. Such lived body participation is always 'more than words can say', and the experience of 'sense-making' involves an engagement with a kind of language that is bodily and sensorily involved. Such a process is not arbitrary, but involves what Gendlin calls a 'felt sense' (Gendlin, 1997a; Gendlin, 1981). A 'felt sense' refers to a way of knowing that is not just 'logical' but 'responsive', that is, awake to the bodily evocative dimensions that makes words personally relevant and workable. Taking this one step further, one may wonder about the extent to which such embodied understanding can be communicated or shared. The chapter thus considers the notion of 'interembodiment' as a possible component of 'intersubjective validity' and one which can accommodate both unique personal references as well as shared dimensions.

In developing these themes, the chapter progresses as follows: first, a consideration of the nature of knowledge within a postmodern debate; second, a consideration of one particular emphasis in Gendlin's philosophy: the relation between language and the lived body; and third, a consideration of some practical implications for qualitative research. These practical implications are identified as: the informant's task, the interviewer's task, the task of analysis, and the reader's task.

2. The question of knowledge

Before focusing on Gendlin's thought in greater detail, it may be helpful to situate him within a particular range of epistemological and hermeneutic concerns relevant to qualitative enquiry. Postmodern movements in philosophy and epistemology have been concerned with getting away from the notion that knowledge is there as an absolute ideal with absolute unassailable and unchanging content. A more existential claim is being made that knowledge is *for* experience and action – for making sense of all that we are in relationship with and how we act in such contexts. The difference from modernism is that there is no non-positional understanding – the observer is always part of the story of the observed. Within this perspective, 'knowledge for whom' can never be left out of the equation on what knowledge is – the question of relevance reaches philosophical status.

However, where does this leave us? Does this mean that understanding is arbitrary and that anything goes in the multiple ways that we interpret experience, situations, and contexts? In his book, *Beyond Objectivism and Relativism*, Richard Bernstein (1988) draws on the work of Gadamer, Habermas, and Arendt, and forges an epistemological position that is open but not arbitrary. Within this view, when we move to inhabit or share a particular engaged perspective (practice), shared understanding proceeds and works. Such shared understanding is not merely 'constructed' as if we were 'making' the world as an exercise of group omnipotence. In remembering knowledge as a relational practice rather than as something inside that is imposed on the world (subjectivism) or as something outside about the inalienable way that things are (objectivism), Bernstein attempts to heal the Cartesian legacy and finds worlds in progress that are real but intimately responsive. Such relational reality (rather than relative reality) is a movement that is both beyond and within us – the snake swallows its tail, and we belong to tradition, history, and language just as they belong to us as an unfinished story.

3. Embodied meaning in the work of Eugene Gendlin

In his philosophical work, Gendlin is pleased about certain aspects of postmodernism and worried about others. He is pleased with the insight that 'no matter how we proceed, there are always other ways' (Gendlin, 1997b, p. 5). However, he is concerned with the question of 'what sort of saying and thinking is possible after the insight that every standpoint centers' (Gendlin, 1997b, p. 5). Like Bernstein, he wishes to show that the rejection of objectivism can lead to more intricate forms of understanding rather than arbitrariness. He takes this further, however, in that his analysis of the lived body provides the intimacy required for knowledge as a meaningful practice.

Gendlin has pursued a calling in both philosophy and psychotherapy. He has worked with Carl Rogers in developing the foundations of client-centred therapy and was the originator of the therapeutic approach called 'focusing'. As a member of the Philosophy Department at the University of Chicago, he pursued his philosophical interests and is well known for his 1963 book (new edition: Gendlin, 1997a) entitled *Experiencing and the Creation of Meaning*. A number of philosophers and scholars in the humanities and social studies have discussed his philosophical ideas with reference to the timely question: 'What comes after postmodernism?' (Levin, 1997a). His main philosophical influences have been the broad tradition of phenomenology, notably Husserl, Merleau-Ponty, and Heidegger. He has also acknowledged, among others, the writings of Wittgenstein and Polanyi.

Within the space of this chapter, I cannot do justice to the breadth of his concerns and some of his distinctive arguments. I thus cannot dwell on the important ways he differs from Gadamer, Merleau-Ponty, and others who are swimming in a similar ocean. I can merely indicate one particular strand of his thought which involves the tension between language and the lived body. It is this tension that may have important implications for the practice of the kind of qualitative research that draws on the experience of others.

The primacy of the lived body

Gendlin's thought about the primacy of the body begins in a philosophical tradition which understands intimate participation in life as the ground that makes knowing possible:

> We can build on the work of Wittgenstein and Heidegger: We do not first interpret things; we live and act in them. We inhale and cry and feed. We are always already within interactions (situations, practice, action, performance ...). (Gendlin, 1997c, p. 405)

This has implications for the role the 'lived body' plays as a source of meaningful understanding. Gendlin indicates a phase of knowing that is prior to symbolisation. Here, the intimate inhabiting that the lived body experiences in its interaction with its world is the primary source of knowing that makes language meaningful and possible. We often take this level of knowing for granted. Although such knowing lends itself to language, it is prereflective. There is understanding 'in it' but it is not yet separated into the discrete forms of 'this' and 'that' within which language works. Such an intimate, responsive knowing is felt as a whole and serves as a meaningful reference for words. This has implications for language and the way we say things: 'Logic works only with what has been separated. But a situation is a preseparated multiplicity and carrying it forward opens up new possibilities that were not separately there before' (Gendlin, 1991, p. 92).

This thrust recovers what has been a minority voice in postmodern dialogue: the involvement of the body. There has been an overemphasis on language – understandably so as language is always already implicated in what things mean – and cultural context is a profound stakeholder in language. However, Gendlin wants to remind us of how the body is intimately implicated in what things mean in that we live meanings through bodily participation in the world. One implication of this is that language and bodily experience cannot simply be reduced to one another – both require one another as partners in a conversation, and both phases (embodying and languaging) constitute both limits and freedoms in this conversation – hopefully, a productive tension. Sometimes, the bodily depth of what one has lived through is 'more than words can say'. Yet such experience 'looks for' words. Sometimes, the language of what things mean changes bodily experience, and the words disappear; in and out of language. Embodying language; languaging the body: each has its day in an ongoing process.

In recovering the bodily emphasis, Gendlin says: 'Speaking is a special case of bodily interaction' (Gendlin, 1997b, p. 28). In highlighting the primacy of the body and its close relationship to language, Gendlin forges a continuity in which knowing is both an embodied and languaged process. These components of knowing cannot be reduced to one another and are both required in the rhythm of closeness and distance that is required for meaningful knowing to occur. 'Closeness' refers to bodily-participative-knowing, while 'distance' refers to the language-formulating process. Knowledge is thus not just reasoned but recognised, and this involves an aesthetic dimension in which the intimacy of bodily responsiveness is implicated. And here we turn to Gendlin's notion of the responsive order.

The responsive order

In privileging a logical order, Descartes has written that when justifying claims to knowledge, there should be no appeal other than the appeal to reason – a reason which is universal, not limited by historical contingencies, and shared by all rational beings. However, in moving towards a responsive order that is 'more than words can say', David Michael Levin, a commentator on Gendlin's philosophy, indicates how knowledge can neither be separated from interpretation nor enclosed in a static way:

> In response to any interpretation, the body of experience talks back with more intricacy than was contained in the interpretation. (Levin, 1997b, p. 55)

This responsiveness means that it is not just the logical meaning about whether things make sense that is important (that is, the contents of what people say), but rather the lived process by which languaging and embodying interact (Gendlin has used the metaphor 'cross and dip' – see Gendlin, 1985). This responsive process is more than checking against a logical conception of whether an interpretation hangs together and 'makes sense'. Rather, such 'sense-making' requires this more complex tension between languaging and embodying – so that logical rules and computers cannot validate interpretations: only beings who participate bodily and move in and out of language and situations can. Within the responsive order, both the separation of languaging and the nonseparated 'more' of bodily-contextual-intimacy are utilised as sources of ongoing authentic understanding. This 'more' in which the body intimately reveals a world is never completely in view – it is not an object that is presented in front of us – it is always dispersed – we are 'in it'.

This form of understanding and authentication in which both languaging and embodying occur is thus a procedure in which its 'doing' produces more intricate possibilities for 'knowing' – the final word is never said but each step 'makes sense' not just in terms of logical consistency but as a bodily responsiveness that can confirm the lived relevance of meanings. As such, more intricate meanings can become languaged in this process, and in turn, open up more 'things' to be seen. This is a circular or spiralling process, but in a responsive sense that is aesthetic and not just according to the intersubjective logic of good argument. Bodily mediated intricacy is greater than conceptualisation. We 'always already' use the 'more' that our bodies open up to us when we speak, and can speak from this 'more' in different ways – logically and more-than-logically – both contribute to the more intricate understanding.

Gendlin's notion of the more intricate understanding that is given by the responsive order is not arbitrary. Although open to different sayings, there is a specificity about it. The body and situations talk back in unanticipated ways. We are not simply free to 'construct' new realities or ways of saying things without how we find ourselves in body, time, interpersonal context, and place. These notions are closer to the phenomenologies of Husserl and Heidegger than to the postmodern thought of Derrida and Rorty. So, to lift out this emphasis in Gendlin's thought, we could summarise as follows: (1) bodily interaction functions in language; (2) the rejection of representational truth must lead us to a more intricate understanding, rather than arbitrariness; (3) the notion of a 'responsive order' honours 'flow' and embodied understanding, and provides a healthy counter-point to a 'logical order' that provides abstract principles; (4) this 'flow' has 'reality', in that phenomena talk back in surprising ways and not merely in accordance with our horizons.

Let us now take all this forward more explicitly into the area of qualitative research. If it is not language on its own that can describe, interpret, carry forward the meaning of things, actions, and situations but language in relation to the bodily sensing of all this, what are the implications for our practice of qualitative research? Some initial questions arise that may provide direction. Although these questions are not new, they will help to focus the subsequent discussion:

- What are the ways of interviewing which include procedures whereby both the respondent and the interviewer do not just talk, but pay more attention to the bodily sense of meanings that are 'more than words can say'?
- What are the ways of analysing qualitative data that pay more explicit attention, not just to the logical organisation of themes, but to the more responsive, aesthetic experience of encountering the data that are given with embodiment?
- What are the ways of including our reader as 'journey-person', so that the style of our writing can speak to both the logical and responsive orders?

In addressing these questions, four phases of 'showing' a qualitative phenomenon will be considered: the informant's task, the interviewer's task, the task of the analysis, and the task of the reader.

4. The informant's task: Language which presences

Let us imagine that I was interviewing Mandy about her experience of homelessness. When we are speaking together I can see that at times she struggles to find the right words to convey the complexity of her situation. She is 'in' a situation that is a 'preseparated multiplicity'. There are meanings of this situation that she is in touch with that 'are more than words can say'. Yet her sense of her situation is not vague but very specific. It is intricate and carries an intimacy and immediacy that is greater than any conceptualisation. Her struggle to find words is an authentic expression of how any words that she can find are not a mere representation or simple reflection of her situation. But she wants the words to be 'faithful' in some way to what she is in touch with. Such 'faithfulness' means that the situation with which she is intimate is the crucial standard for her when attempting to communicate what it is about. This bodily mediated intimacy is what she refers to when 'trying on' words or phrases. Some words or phrases fit better than others and she appears to have an aesthetic ability of knowing when one phrase is closer or 'works better' than another. She is engaged in a kind of process in

which there is a creative tension between language and her more intimate bodily felt sense of her situation. One could say that bodily interaction functions in language. She is engaged in including the kind of
intimacy required for qualitative knowledge. Her 'lived body' is the way
she mediates her sense of participation in situations – it is that which is
sensorially intimate enough to 'be in touch with' and 'be faithful to' the
intricacy of experiential situations in their 'preseparated multiplicity'.
For her, such a process of 'lived body' referencing is an authenticating
procedure for the words she uses to communicate her experience.
Although language is not a simple representation of her experience, it
does have a relationship with her experience that 'works'. And it needs
to 'work', first for her and then hopefully, for me and you.

Given this analysis, the first component of a 'truth value' that
acknowledges the responsive order would be a consideration of how our
methodological inquiries allow language to 'work' for Mandy. This
would require much more than simple agreements in understanding
between the interviewer and interviewee. It would require Mandy, as a
co-researcher at this phase, to engage in a process in which she became
not only the informant of *what* she was saying but also the practitioner
of *how* she was finding words that 'worked'.

In his experiential method of 'focusing', Gendlin (1996) provides
some guidelines relevant to psychotherapy that may nevertheless be
valuable for qualitative research at this stage. It involves a way of
attending to the words one says to see if they are not just logical but
responsive. Such responsiveness is an experience in which language is
most alive in awakening the sense of presence of what it is referring to.
The 'validity' of such an 'aliveness' rests on the extent to which it opens
up further ways of talking that 'comes from' this sense of aliveness of
the phenomenon. When such 'focusing' is productively occurring, the
informant is able to report that it is happening in a way that feels satisfying, that is, that what the words are showing is 'coming from' her
'contact' with the experience. Alternatively, she is also able to report
both generally and specifically when the words do not 'work'.

There are many challenges and questions about the informant's task
suggested here. There is much more we need to understand about finding
words that 'work' and its implications for methodological strategy and
research informants. However, all I would like to argue at this point is
that by highlighting important issues about the process by which
an informant brings phenomena to language, Gendlin provides one
component of a 'truth value' that may need more acknowledgement in
qualitative research. The 'truth value' at this level could be referred to

as a faithfulness to the bodily felt sense that opens or touches the holistic presence of the phenomenon as it is experienced. If it is left out as a consideration, then one could argue that the opportunity for a rigorous connection to the fullness of the phenomenon-as-experienced has been lost.

5. The interviewer's task: Facilitating the informant's task and interembodied listening

In interviewing Mandy about her experience of homelessness I am aware that the 'what' of the words that she is expressing are often provisional and secondary to the process in which the contours of her experience are taking communicative shape. The words are not final packaged products that form 'objective' data (simply extracted from within her) and do not carry understanding in themselves. Rather, it is the way they 'work' that interests me more at this stage. I am interested in their 'working' at two levels: firstly, how they work for Mandy and secondly, how they work between us, interactively. In attending to the first concern, my task as interviewer is to act in such a way that my presence does not excessively obscure her faithfulness to the lived bodily process in which words stay connected with the 'felt sense' of what they are referring to (preseparated multiplicity/situation). My words and questions need to serve this process. The process could easily become excessively diverted by the social circumstance of myself as a 'demanding other'. If so, Mandy may sacrifice the primacy of her faithfulness to her 'felt sense' and adapt her responses to my concerns. As we are social beings, my presence is obviously co-constitutive of the way Mandy is focused, and such faithfulness to 'felt experience' can never exclude the gaze of the other, whether represented by me or some internal part of herself. Understanding this tension, my task is partially one which champions the 'how' of what is said and I may indicate in different ways my interest in her valuing this process of 'faithful presencing'.

On the other hand, I am also interested in how the words work between us, interactively. I am representing the world of the 'other' but an 'other' who wishes to join with her in finding a way to 'show' in language what is situationally embedded in the complexity of her situation. In representing a larger public world, I am there as a listener who is also focused on understanding as an embodied experience. Just as words are a bodily lived experience for Mandy, so are they for me.

Because of the possibility of some degree of interembodied experience, I often find that when words work for Mandy, they begin to work for me, not only in deepening my understanding, but also in awakening something of the lived 'sense' of her situation. This is usually a gradual process and a momentum often builds in which the experience of 'sense-making' in me happens. My task in this regard is to be open to the process in me by which the words do not just make logical sense but which open up the possibility of seeing something together. Such 'seeing together' cannot include the uniqueness of our personal references and histories, but does include a credible sense in which I understand in an embodied way. Embodied understanding does not mean that I have or have had the same experience as Mandy, but it means that the words show me something 'more' that involves a bodily sense of being present to a whole situation. In such an interembodied process both of us have 'mores' and see through language in order that these 'mores' can have some common dimensions. I can check out to some degree the extent of our interembodied understanding by sharing some implications of my embodied understanding with Mandy that were not necessarily explicit in her expressions. Such confirmation happens although it remains a large task to consider the extent to which this can happen and what should be considered sufficient concordance at this level.

Another dimension of such interembodied understanding is that it seems to further facilitate Mandy's ongoing ability to bring her 'sense' to language. The quality of the conversation within this spirit is one of 'flow' rather than conclusiveness, and Mandy may talk further 'from' her 'felt sense' in ways that are surprising to both of us. Such freshness of meanings can again be experienced as 'making sense' by her and by me in the ways already discussed. The nature of the responsive order is such that there are potentially always new meanings to be expressed from a situation and that the very process of 'sense-making' allows these new meanings to appear. The truth value of these new meanings within this paradigm is about their qualitative ability to 'work' further in 'sense-making'. This is a conception of truth as progressive flow rather than as a dichotomous 'true or false'. In other words, to reinvoke Bernstein, when we move to inhabit or share a particular engaged perspective (practice), shared understanding proceeds and works. And to reinvoke Gendlin, the lived body provides the intimacy needed for knowledge as a meaningful practice. Languaging and embodying is thus a procedure in which it's 'doing' produces more intricate possibilities for knowing.

6. The task of the analysis: Showing qualities with words that work

Whatever questions or modes of analysis I may bring to Mandy's as well as other informants' testimonies about the experience of homelessness, a consideration of the responsive order would ask me to consider the kind of understanding that I have achieved as an important source of my analysis and writing. Both the phenomenological and hermeneutic research traditions have emphasised the importance of beginning one's analysis by 'getting a sense of the whole' when reading an interview transcript or other meaningful text (see, for example, Giorgi, 1985a; Packer & Addison, 1989). Such a sense of the whole ensures that the details are not just merely accurate but rather, meaningful within their context. Gendlin's thought is more explicit about where this 'sense of the whole' comes from. Words have worked, not just for Mandy but also for me in showing me to some degree the 'more' to which her words refer. As a human being it is given to me to understand or be present to this 'more' through words. However, it is not merely these words that are my understanding but how they have opened up the presence of something, and the source of this understanding is more intimate than the logic of language – it involves a participative dimension. So as indicated earlier, within the responsive order, both the separation of language and the nonseparated 'more' of bodily-contextual-intimacy are utilised as sources of ongoing authentic understanding. In my analysis and writing then, I am coming from a place of tension in which what Mandy has shown is carried forward by me into a more public arena. There are both freedoms and constraints in this. My interembodied responsiveness to the 'more' that Mandy has shown constitutes an understanding that has a certain presence, shape, or 'whole' which is the 'grounding' of the 'what' of any analysis. This 'what' provides a disciplined constraint to the journeys of language. Language can be used to enhance meaning by coming from different contexts and questions, and thus has a certain freedom in opening new insights and meanings. However, the embodied understanding of what has been shown is always there as a source of accountability for whether the words are working.

In functioning as a bridge between Mandy's experience and the world of shared understanding, my analysis and writing engages in a process of focusing in which I am responsively present to both Mandy's experience and a greater chorus of voices from others, colleagues, and an existing body of knowledge about the topic area. Such a process provides an ongoing intuitive reference whose tension only leaves me when the words have sufficiently worked for the sake of Mandy, my own understanding, and a care for the audience or reader. The resolution of this sense of tension is a minimum authenticating source. Both Mandy and my readers would be meaningful participants in judging the extent to which my resolution of tension also does it for them.

7. The task of the reader: Responsive hospitality

When readers engage with the research report about the experience of homelessness, they are active in different ways at different times with differing emphases. Sometimes they may read with specific conceptual questions in mind and at other times may engage imaginatively with the implications of homelessness as an experience. In Gendlin's terminology, they are, as understanding beings, involved in both the logical and responsive orders. In this view it is possible that a growing sense of understanding can involve both 'head' and 'heart'. In such engagement the reader has access not just to principles, explanations, and conclusions about the topic of homelessness but is intuitively empowered through the words to engage with the phenomenon in a more direct and personal way. It can be argued that such responsive engagement is a crucial part of the process of understanding in that, as human beings we participate in understanding in personal ways that are more complex than the outcomes and conclusions of theoretical explanation. If words can 'show' then readers can actively take up what is 'shown' in an aesthetic encounter in which the 'presence' of the phenomenon is there in a textured way. The artistic dimensions of what is 'shown' can then not be excluded from its 'truth'.

There is still the question of adequacy of understanding (both in terms of the writing and the reading) but a view of reality as relational will not imagine that such adequacy can be unequivocally objectified. Rather, criteria for 'adequate understanding' as something that 'works' for different purposes may still need to be articulated.

So within the responsive order, the readers may engage with the 'shown presence' of the phenomenon themselves and this is in dialogue not only with the writer, the research respondents, and the reader's personal references but includes an interembodied dimension in which both unique and common experiences are accessed. Such responsive hospitality to the 'shown phenomenon' often results in a situation in which the phenomenon 'talks back' in new ways. That is, although Mandy has served as one 'window' to showing or 'opening' the experience of homelessness, and the writer has taken it further into the shared world of wider and more general contexts, the reader brings her own bodily sensed references to bear. And more intricate meanings may be seen that were unanticipated by both Mandy and the writer. Again, the nature of art comes to mind. Thus the reader's responsive hospitality becomes a new 'home' for truth as an ongoing and plural phenomenon as she engages in the lived process by which languaging and embodying interact.

8. Summary and conclusion

In summary, I would like to put forward five points which progressively outlines the extent to which Gendlin's thought may build on others in the hermeneutic tradition in order to advance the boundaries of what it means to 'faithfully show' qualitative phenomena:

- A number of authors have indicated how in qualitative research, 'truth values' are a plural phenomenon and that we 'make authentic sense' in more than one way (see, for example, Sparkes, 1995; Kvale 1996).
- Drawing on the hermeneutic tradition, such 'sense-making', which is an intersubjective enterprise, requires standards that are still under debate (for example, trustworthiness, authenticity, faithfulness). This is a practice and involves the question of what languaged understandings we move towards together.
- Drawing on Gendlin, such authentic 'sense-making' does not just involve logical, intersubjective agreement but involves the 'responsive order' in which the lived body makes authentic sense of language and connects such language to an embodied world of meanings.
- This is not just about agreements in cognitive judgment. It is more aesthetic and demanding and would ask: what ways of bodily-responsive-knowing can we move towards together?
- Such a notion challenges us to find methodological procedures that produce 'words that work'. The section on the four tasks attempted to illustrate how Gendlin's thought on 'words that work' may stretch our notions of truth to include both an inner and outer dimension – knowing by being and knowing by sharing.

In conclusion, I would like to commend Gendlin's philosophical writings as representing a postmodern approach which keeps a healthy tension between language and the lived embodied world without either making them into separate 'things' or simply reducing one to the other. With reference to qualitative research, an inclusion of his notion of the 'responsive order' may contribute an added aesthetic dimension to the way in which we can faithfully bring the textures of the lifeworld to language.

4
Writing Phenomenological–Psychological Descriptions: An Illustration Attempting to Balance Texture and Structure

Reflexive knowledge (Hertz, 1997; Myerhoff & Ruby, 1982) provides insight into the workings of the social and experiential worlds as well as into how that knowledge came into existence. This concern is a theme in reflexive feminist ethnography (Reinharz, 1997), in hermeneutic phenomenology (Van Manen, 1990), and in auto/biographical studies (Sparkes, 1995). Within this perspective there is no 'voiceless' writing (Charmaz & Mitchell, 1997), and there is an increasing concern in qualitative research to pursue the epistemological, ethical, and methodological implications of such reflexivity. Such a challenge includes a concern to care for our informants' voices, to care for the human phenomena that are being expressed, to care for how our own voice as writer reveals, conceals, and co-creates, and to care for our readers as part of the ongoing conversation. All of these things are co-constitutive of human understanding and there are interesting attempts to write up our insights from qualitative enquiry that respects such complexity. It is within this spirit that Day Sclater (1998b) draws on the work of Donald Winnicott to show how informants' stories can be seen as 'transitional phenomena' which are part of an ongoing conversation between private and public worlds, between interviewer and interviewee, and between the discovery and co-creation of meanings and subjectivities.

One emphasis in this broad development is a debate about the kinds of writing that engages both 'head' and 'heart'. Feminist contributions to psychology (Gilligan, 1982) and sociology (Oakley, 2000) have noted how scientific enquiry has been dominated by a patriarchal emphasis which 'knows about' the 'externals' of things and happenings in an excessively distant manner and which decontextualises our participation in our world, obscuring the more intimate dimensions of our capacities 'to know' as aesthetic, interembodied beings.

Within this spirit Charmaz & Mitchell (1997) have written about the necessity to pursue more evocative forms of writing. Feminist writers such as Stanley & Wise (1983) insist that emotion is vital to systematic knowledge about the social world and that a feminist epistemology creatively draws on women's everyday experiences as an aesthetically potent way to enhance enquiry and deepen understanding.

The literary traditions have also contributed useful perspectives and practices. For example, Booth (1987) in his book *The Rhetoric of Fiction* provides helpful directions for more self-aware forms of writing which can deepen their aesthetic appeal and engage the 'hearts' of readers in an invitational rather than authoritarian manner. In pursuing the implications of the power of narrative expression for the human and social sciences, Richardson (1990), Bruner (1990), and Polkinghorne (1988) have all indicated how narrative construction is crucial to understanding human experience in a temporally meaningful way: it attends to the qualitative, aesthetic dimensions of experience, honours context, diversity and fluidity (Robertson, 1999), is close to our intuitive sensibilities, and can help others find themselves in the experiences described.

This ground swell from different traditions to recover the 'heart' of experience has a long history in the phenomenological movement (Spiegelberg, 1971). The present chapter wishes to draw on this broad tradition that began with Edmund Husserl and which took a more hermeneutic and existential turn with his student, Martin Heidegger (Todres & Wheeler, 2001). The continuities and discontinuities between these two thinkers reflect a creative tension that is still alive in contemporary hermeneutic phenomenology.

One way of expressing this tension is to refer to the 'pros' and 'cons' of academic writing versus more poetic forms of writing. Husserl, in championing academic forms of writing, was interested in the most general categories of knowing, which can communicate experiences at their most shared or common levels. Heidegger, especially in his later years, was more interested in poetic forms of writing that invoke more empathic forms of knowing.

In the present chapter, I attempt to keep open what I believe to be a complementary tension between academic and more narrative/poetic forms of writing. I believe that this concern to hold or harmonise the academic with the poetic is consistent with a view of human existence in which self and other are intimately connected. Day Sclater (1998a) expresses this sensibility as follows: 'Embedded in our uniqueness are common threads which connect us all, common matrices within which our experiences, our lives and our selves make sense to us and others' (p. 67).

It is within this context of expressing both the shared and the unique that I would like to pursue the notions of *structure* and *texture* (Moustakas, 1994) as useful conceptual touchstones when pursuing writing within the phenomenological research tradition. Other qualitative researchers have also expressed an interest in more poetic forms of re-presentation in their writing (Willis, 2002). For example, Robertson (1999), in researching with bulimics, includes different phases of her understanding at different times which reflect an autobiographical dimension, a more academic reflection, a poem, and a reflective discussion which pursues some of the implications of these different phases and modes of understanding.

Different moments of 'head' and 'heart' and all the places in between are all part of the ongoing conversation that *is* understanding.

I would now like to move towards the phenomenological tradition and pursue these concerns in three phases:

- A brief conceptual account of the value of attending to the balance of texture and structure when writing our qualitative descriptions of experience.
- An attempt to utilise these concerns with reference to a practical example: a phenomenological enquiry into the experience of therapeutic self-insight.
- Some reflections about my personal experience of such writing in order to contribute to the debate about the art of presenting our research discoveries in a meaningful and helpful manner.

1. Structure and texture: A conceptual consideration

What does it mean to facilitate the understanding of human experience in our readers? It was argued in Chapter 1 that there is some philosophical justification for attending to both the structural as well as textural dimensions when communicating our understandings of human experience. Let us first consider the notion of 'texture' and its relevance to facilitating the understanding of human experience.

Dilthey (1979) was one of the first theorists to consider how 'understanding' is more than 'explanation'. In this conception, we as human beings actively participate in understanding in personal ways that are more complex than the outcomes and conclusions of theoretical explanation.

It has been argued that communicating understanding is not just about truth, that is, that something is revealed, but about beauty as well

(Hillman, 1981). This involves an aesthetic dimension in which what is revealed has the possibility of being personally appropriated; that is, that it can be empathically understood as something that is within the realm of human participative experience.

Such aesthetic requirement, when communicating the richness or 'thickness' of experience has been referred to as 'texture'. The value of communicating such a dimension is that it gives readers access not just to principles, explanations, and conclusions, but grants the possibility of intuitive empowerment, that is, access to a range of implications about the phenomenon that serves as a rich personal reference when acting in relation to the phenomenon. Within such a concern, understanding of the phenomenon is alive in the sense that it is potentially present not just as theory or principles but as an intuitive essence or 'felt sense' (Gendlin, 1997). The phenomenological movement (Spiegelberg, 1971) has attempted to develop an approach to knowledge and existence in which the presence of phenomena can never be simply reduced to the ways we represent phenomena. Any perceived phenomenon is, in a sense, alive and can be related to holistically and intuitively. This relationship includes a qualitative, aesthetic dimension and is always 'more' than any particular words can determine, co-create, or say.

This aesthetic dimension, the texture, is a closeness to phenomena that however, in itself, is incomplete in attempting to achieve any balanced understanding. One also needs a degree of distance in which questions are asked and answered of the phenomenon. Thus it is not enough to know what a phenomenon such as 'therapeutic self-insight' feels like, but it is also important to thematise its inner logic, inner relationships, and some of the interdependent boundaries with other experiences and contexts. This 'distancing', in which themes are expressed, has been referred to as 'structure' and is based on the analytic question of how much the constituents of the phenomenon can be varied before it becomes something else.

In communicating our research discoveries, the challenge is to find some degree of balance or harmony between communicating the 'texture' and 'structure' of human phenomena. One can err in either extreme: in attending excessively to the structural dimensions, one can over-generalise and become too distant and abstract, thus losing texture and intuitive presence; or in attending excessively to the textural dimensions, one can become overly poetic where the intuitive presence of the phenomenon is palpable but where its meaning is left implicit, without reflection, far from answering relevant questions for a community of interested people.

The possibility of erring on the side of 'texture' or 'structure' raises a question about whether it is possible to be sensitive to both these dimensions when communicating the results of phenomenological–psychological research.

Towards application: A personal attempt

I would like to turn to my own doctoral studies of therapeutic self-insight which I completed many years ago (Todres, 1990). I recently re-read the dissertation and noticed a certain schism in the way that I had presented my research discoveries. On the one hand there was an interesting structural description of therapeutic self-insight which answered some relevant questions about how it occurs, its interpersonal context, what is freeing about it, and how different theories of self-insight have missed its central essence and over-emphasised side-issues.

On the other hand, I produced a long poem at the end that attempted to communicate more of my digested experience of the texture of the experience of therapeutic self-insight.

I wondered whether it would be possible to harmonise 'texture' and 'structure' within one movement without splitting them excessively into different concerns. So I tried again. This is an ongoing attempt and I offer my latest version in this chapter. It begins personally by explicating some of my own horizons in order to situate the study. I then present the essential insights of the study to attempt a facilitation of a movement of understanding which interweaves the 'textural' and 'structural' dimensions. This is done by including a 'story' level, a level that draws out the nature of psychotherapy as a context, and a level that attempts to articulate the essence of therapeutic self-insight as a phenomenon. The final section of the chapter documents my personal reflections on how I approached this endeavour.

2. A phenomenological enquiry into the kind of therapeutic self-insight that carries a greater sense of freedom

For a long time I have been fascinated by how understanding oneself more, one's motives, thoughts, feelings, and position can lead to a greater sense of felt freedom. Socrates talked about this, Freud talked about this, and I, friends, family, and clients all have had this experience at one time or another: that certain kinds of self-insight appear to carry a greater sense of freedom.

The rationale of a particular cultural practice in the twentieth century, psychotherapy, is based on this possibility: an interpersonal situation which is specifically set up to help people feel freer and act more coherently in their personal lives through self-insight.

So as a practising psychotherapist, I was interested in self-insight, felt freedom, and the practice of psychotherapy. Although different theories had certain explanations of what self-insight is, very few were able to let go of their particular theoretical framework (for example, 'reorganising psychic energy' or 'cognitive restructuring') and describe what was occurring in a more naive and context-rich way.

Being familiar with phenomenology and existentialism I was interested in the question: what is the nature of the kind of psychotherapeutic self-insight that leads to a greater sense of freedom? Put another way, what does it mean to have this kind of therapeutic self-insight? 'Having' means an experience one lives through that needs to be described. 'Meaning' means that the experience is related to one's life in some intelligible way.

My concern in attempting to elucidate these questions is connected to another concern: to help myself and other health practitioners to practise psychotherapy in a more thoughtful and helpful manner so that our clients benefit. I was thus interested in this discovery-oriented research in order to help myself and other practitioners to learn for the sake of acting (Van Manen, 1990).

In writing my description of therapeutic self-insight I was thus preoccupied with this question of 'learning for acting' and its implications for how my discoveries would be presented. I was not sure in advance what this mode of presentation was, but considered the following initial signposts:

- It would be more than a definition or series of statements about therapeutic self-insight.
- It would tell us something that connects with universal human qualities so that the reader can relate personally to the themes.
- It would tell a story which readers could imagine in a personal way.
- It would attempt to contribute to new understanding about therapeutic self-insight.
- It would not attempt to exhaust the topic but would attempt to allow it to be seen more clearly: like shining a light which increases the reader's sense of contact with this phenomenon without fully possessing it.

These orientations disciplined my enquiry and helped to make its scope and value more explicit.

Having explicated my orientation to the study, I will now refer to the phenomenological research design that was informed by the *Duquesne Studies in Phenomenological Psychology*, Volumes 1 to 4 (Giorgi, Fischer & Von Eckartsberg, 1971; Giorgi, Fischer & Murray, 1975; Giorgi, Knowles & Smith, 1979; Giorgi, Barton & Maes, 1983).

In conducting the original research, I had conversed with a number of people who had been in psychotherapy. I attempted to explicate their experiences utilising phases of procedural discipline pioneered by Giorgi (1985b). I further attempted to reflect both the essence of the experience for each participant, as well as something about the nature of the experience in a general way. For the purposes of this paper I will not dwell further on the details of this methodological approach that is well documented (*interalia* in Giorgi, 1985a; Wertz, 1985; Anstoos, 1987). Rather, the results of the study will be presented in a different way, one that attempts to balance texture and structure. As such, the 'reflective story' draws on the composite picture that emerged from my informants. It does this, however, by using the personal pronoun 'I' to indicate the client in the first-person sense as someone who typifies the general experience within a living and situated context. The challenge is how to be general while retaining the 'thickness' and texture of the phenomenon as an experience.

A story of therapeutic self-insight: A composite description with possibilities

I, as client, am in the presence of a person, a psychotherapist, who is not simply like a friend or a family member. As a therapist she is rather an ambiguous presence, not someone who I know much about, but someone with whom I feel comfortable. We are there to discuss my life, not hers. We have met for some time at a regular interval for a set period. This gives the sessions a structural shape – a space in which we have a certain life together – a life of exploration – that has something of the quality of play. I mostly am free to set the content and direction of our conversations. She helps me to relate to what I have been saying and helps me to reflect on my life, my actions, feelings, thoughts, and relationships.

So there is a general context of interpersonal learning where my life is the focus and I feel increasingly free to say things as honestly as I can.

In experimenting with what I can say, I usually find myself beginning with describing what is on my mind. 'The children have been fighting'; 'I don't have enough time to do things'; 'I feel frustrated, angry, unfulfilled, a nameless worry that I cannot yet say'.

So these are very specific descriptions that progressively tell a story that link my situation, feelings, thoughts, actions, and relationships together. As I talk and progressively tell the story that have my preoccupations as a starting point, I sometimes feel the emotional tone of what I am saying in the sessions: depressed, sad, giggly, dead, longing. Sometimes I feel depersonalised as if another person was telling the story.

The very specific details of what I am saying unfold and start making sense as a narrative with emotional qualities; and here is where I begin learning something in the process of talking.

I learn how some of the emotions that I was feeling tell me things about myself that I had not previously put into words in exactly that way. For example, in talking about my depression I start talking about the extent to which I have resigned myself to a hopeless future. Or, in talking about some of my actions during the week I learn how they tell me things about myself that I had not put into words: for example, how turning down an invitation hid a fear of rejection that I have only now realised was the motivation behind the refusal.

So through the narrative unfolding, I feel more, think further, and learn more about my feelings, thoughts, actions, and motives, and in this process begin to see more holistic patterns or themes that run through the different parts of my experience; how actions connect to feelings connect to thoughts connect to relationships and situations. Together, my therapist and I develop a shared language which has a narrative and synthetic quality, a quality which feels in touch with the details of my life and is thus credible, but at the same time, articulates some general themes which enable me to understand a pattern in how I am living.

In the narrative, some central themes begin to emerge and are captured by language, such as 'I often expect to lose someone' or 'I am careful to avoid criticism'. Other central themes that may have become clearer over time are beliefs such as 'I better look out for myself or no-one else will' or 'If someone doesn't save me at the last moment, they will be sorry'. Such ways of understanding the patterns by which I have been living are built on a number of details of action, thoughts, feelings, and relationships that have been talked about. It is this connecting pattern of action, thoughts, feelings, and actions that gives the theme in each case a sense of felt credibility. With another therapist we might have articulated the themes in slightly different ways or with a different emphasis.

The themes make sense of various historical details, emotional qualities, and characteristic interpersonal interactions in my life.
And these general themes do not stop here. I find that they have a
power to organise other details of my life that I had not anticipated
to talk about until the themes made them relevant and significant:
memories, dreams, habits; all details which are recalled in the light of
the theme.

So general themes or narrative structures are like lights within which
further details are illuminated, not in a haphazard free-associative
kind of way, but in an organised way. It is like a game of leapfrog
between general themes and specific details – and such interaction
gives the work a sense of felt credibility, a narrative unfolding, a
dialectical process which is mutually supportive. Such progression
develops a felt quality that there is a 'work' that is going on. There is
a certain momentum and energy to this work of self-understanding
that feels increasingly intrinsically motivating, almost as if the wish
for self-understanding comes from some deep place within the human
spirit. I am somewhat energised by this spirit of self-discovery and
later come to understand this energy as a deep longing for some kind
of freedom as yet not fully understood.

At some point in this dialectic of detail and theme, part and whole,
client and therapist, I begin to become aware of the parts of the story
where a level of personal agency and responsibility is more possible
than previously. Many unfortunate things have happened to me. In
many respects I am a victim to time, circumstance, nature, others, and
the complexities of the human heart. I have talked about my anger,
sadness, depression, fights, avoidance. I can see what has happened to
me more clearly than in the past. 'My mother was less than perfect'.
'I didn't deserve to be hurt'.

As I increasingly face the themes and details of my life, I develop a
particular kind of relationship to my own experience, one in which I am
both observer and participant, commentator and actor. The therapist
supports this activity by generally being an interested and caring
bystander, one who wishes to understand me as a human being who
deserves some degree of understanding and care. This helps me to
regard my own experience as worthy of some degree of respect, whether
it is good or bad, hurt or happy.

So such a growing permission to be both observer and participant to
my experience increasingly constitutes a kind of self-forgiveness for
having the experiences I have. This does not necessarily condone any of
my behaviour, but it makes me feel that my behaviour and experience

are part of a human story, and this makes me feel more human and less of an object or thing that is defined in a very narrow way.

This whole experience of relating to myself in this way constitutes a generic emotional atmosphere that is very conducive to learning about myself and how my inner and outer worlds connect. Such emotional atmosphere is conducive because I increasingly feel that the truth as it emerges about me and my life is understood in a fair, non-simplistic, and caring way. Such truth-telling seems to require this kind of emotional freedom for it to be authentic and productive. I experience myself more clearly as both victim and agent, and this constitutes a growing self-insight into the complexity of myself and my human story: 'I am not only hurt but expect to be hurt, so hurt others out of self-protection and fear', 'I am familiar with an insecurity I need to hide but am disappointed when others only treat me as strong': both victim and agent of the human condition. Complexity.

How does such self-insight into my complexity carry with it a greater sense of freedom?

In psychotherapy I had particular self-insights about themes, which I had not fully understood, for example, how I was repeating an expectation of disappointment that was no longer needed. Such specific self-insights freed me by giving me confidence that the future could be different from the past, and that I could consciously change something that was restricting me. So, there is an increased sense of personal agency.

However, the experience of a greater sense of freedom went deeper than just these specific self-insights that revealed places of increased personal agency.

Rather, self-insight into my complexity per se gave me a background feeling of increased flexibility and confidence.

Why is this?

I realise that I now see the world as a more complex place than before and I experience myself as more competent to deal with such complexity. I somehow feel initiated into a secret of seasons; that I and the world can be many things, and I have moved closer to giving up ready-made answers or simple solutions that are attempted in all situations. I find myself sometimes responding in less ready-made ways and I sometimes feel more reconciled to such open-endedness. Now that I am engaging a bit more with the unknown, life itself seems to have the capacity to be my 'therapy'. I experiment in life and get feedback from life, and so learn what I can trust and where I can have confidence.

So the broad thrust of therapeutic self-insight has been to initiate me further into my complexity. And such a process has given me some confidence and permission to retain bits of the old and embrace bits of the new. This gives me a feeling of freedom that is not too scary. End.

The narrative unfolding of this typical experience may be further summarised and understood in terms of two foci:

- The context and process of therapeutic self-insight.
- Some essential themes of the experience of the kind of therapeutic self-insight that carries a greater sense of freedom.

The context and process of therapeutic self-insight

Psychotherapy is an interpersonal context, which increasingly enables the client to be and talk truthfully. It is a human environment that provides psychological safety and permission to explore the details and themes of the client's life. In this process the general themes and details of her life cohere and make sense in a credible way. The client comes to see how thoughts, feelings, actions, and relationships intelligibly cohere into a complex story in which she is both victim and agent. The experience of self-enquiry increasingly takes on the feeling-quality of a 'work' that has intrinsic motivation. With the help of the therapist, the client develops a relationship to her own experience in which she is both observer and participant.

In this context, therapeutic self-insights occur which are both specific and general. The more specific self-insights constitute experiences of greater personal agency in specific life situations that one had not seen before. This is a specific perception of how things are different or could be different from the way things were before. However, there is a deeper, more generic self-insight that occurs which constitutes an experience of a more complex personal identity than one had previously realised.

The essence of the kind of therapeutic self-insight that carries a greater sense of freedom

Therapeutic self-insight gives freedom by revealing one's human personal identity as a complex story that is not like a 'thing' and so is more open to the 'new' than one had previously thought. Increased entitlement to, and competence for, such a more open personal identity constitutes a greater sense of freedom and is initiated by psychotherapy, and becomes tested in the fire of life. Thus, the kind of therapeutic self-insight that carries a greater sense of freedom reveals that 'I' am more than any definition of 'me' and this 'more' opens oneself to the possibility of some degree of self-renewal and world-renewal.

3. Reflections on my writing

In writing I was guided by two general concerns:

- What could I say about the phenomenon that would enable readers to enter the phenomenon imaginatively themselves?
- What could I say about the phenomenon that would answer questions which are relevant in this time and place to an imagined audience, and which can further facilitate insight in particular communities of readers? There are some decisions here about whom one is writing for, for example, user groups, sociologists, or psychologists, and it is helpful to make this explicit.

In writing, I implicitly referred to my present understanding of broad human themes: human development, existential dimensions of life, and my personal and cultural life history. Such a background matrix had obviously been informed by reading and interaction, specifically in the existential–phenomenological and psychological traditions. So I was personally and interpretively always there and hoped that the way I was there could care for mutual understanding. I thus attempted to make some of my interests and concerns explicit in the hope that it could find a shared interest so that it is not just *I* who proceeds, but *we* who proceed.

I was less concerned than I used to be to attempt to completely capture and pin everything down in words. I was more tolerant of giving some imaginative space to readers to enter and validate the phenomenon for themselves. This seems to require a balance between providing enough committed boundaries about the description, yet leaving some gaps or indications which need to be filled in by the depth of the reader's imagination and/or interest in engaging with where the description leads. This involves an aesthetic balance between language as poetic pointing and language as analytically precise.

I also attempted to pay attention to an aesthetic intuition about the balance between whole and part. This seemed to require a broadly musical sense of the rhythm of rich, varied details and thematic generalities. At times such rhythm would result in moments of feeling that the description was 'coming together' and I would find words that named this 'coming together', for example, 'complexity', 'agency', 'narrative'.

Further, I attempted to pay attention to an aesthetic balance between closeness to and distance from the phenomenon. This seemed to require a willingness to become intimate with the qualities of the phenomenon and to suffer these qualities as well as a willingness to separate and to let go of these qualities in order to reflect on them. The aesthetic balance appeared to require that engagement and reflection support one another – that engagement informs reflection and that reflection clarifies engagement. In clarifying engagement, I took risks in going into some of the possible implications of the phenomenon. In returning to engagement, I stood humbled by the 'just-so-ness' and specificity of the way the phenomenon was present and appeared in body, mood, time, space, and between us.

Was this writing successful?

I believe that this question is both necessary and problematic. It raises questions about intersubjective validity and how any interpretation is always partial and 'on the way'.

Like much phenomenologically oriented enquiry, a different writer may have facilitated more and deeper insights for the reader. However, it is even more complex than this. It also involves a 'meeting' between writer and reader (cf. Gadamer, 1997, pp. 367–9 for a discussion on the art of conversation).

Given the inevitable ambiguity about whether the writing was successful, it may become more important to specify the purposes for which different kinds of presentations are helpful (that is, knowledge 'for whom' and knowledge 'for what'). For example, one may argue that the form of presentation offered in this paper could:

- Help beginning psychotherapists refine their practice in some way.
- Help theorists in the area of self-insight to clarify relevant debates.
- Provide lay people and prospective psychotherapy users with a greater understanding of conversational psychotherapy and the value of therapeutic self-insight.

A consideration of such purposes would indicate that a plurality of styles of presentation would be helpful, depending on the context and the reader. The particular style adopted in this paper reflects a concern that would wish to appeal to the possibility of a way of knowing that is grounded in both 'head' and 'heart'.

In communicating 'texture' and 'structure' an existential–phenomenological approach does not claim to characterise 'absolute essences', but rather indicates possible themes that help our understanding move together in that vital space between commonality and diversity.

4. Closing thoughts

The description of therapeutic self-insight attempted to pay attention to the balancing of 'texture' and 'structure' in the written presentation of research discoveries.

It paid attention to *structure* by articulating essential themes in order to communicate the boundaries of the phenomenon, that is, what it essentially appears to be. In communicating such structure, the presentation may further our knowledge about therapeutic self-insight. The implications of the description could be developed further in relation to other theories and research endeavours. It could thus be used to support, criticise, or develop a wider body of knowledge and debate *about* therapeutic self-insight (for example, the relationship between self-insight and memory). Such knowledge is primarily conceptual in its grasp.

Within this conceptual spirit, the understanding of therapeutic self-insight that is generated in this paper tends to support a view of psychotherapy that emphasises the power of self-narrative in recreating our 'selves' (Spence, 1982; Hillman, 1983; Hunt, 1998b). The different ways in which this can happen is an ongoing and rich area for enquiry in which the traditional boundaries and purposes of psychotherapy are being both expanded and questioned (Hillman & Ventura, 1993; Hunt, 1998a).

On the other hand, the description paid attention to *texture* by articulating the phenomenon as a narrative movement that was embodied by a person in a concrete situation. This allowed the reader the possibility of going through the experience in a more *enacted* way. The value of such textural considerations is that it is more directly concerned with practical knowledge, that is, knowledge for action. In this context, the reader may be able to come to understand the phenomenon in a more intuitive way, and such intuitive awakening may serve as an implicitly informed reference for acting. It may connect more directly with personal references, and thus does not only ground conceptual understanding, but may provide further personal insights not explicitly provided by the writer's description.

As indicated in the introduction to this chapter, I wished to keep open a complementary tension between academic and more poetic forms of writing. This involved the enactment of a rhythmical gesture in which

I, as researcher and writer, moved between moments of closeness and distance in my engagement with the phenomenon of therapeutic self-insight. In exercising 'closeness' I attempted to enter my informants' experiences and bring the 'heart' of these textures to language. In exercising 'distance' I entered a more academic moment and attempted to tease out some of the meanings in a more thematic way. Such thematising does not wish to locate my informants in any fixed way. Rather, the textured story is presented as a composite with possibilities. Following the inspiration of Winnicott (1953/1971), such a device employs both 'play' and 'reality' in the service of insight and communication and could be called 'transitional biography'.

In conclusion, the concern to balance 'texture' and 'structure' in our qualitative enquiries into human experience may be one way of serving more holistic and resonant forms of knowing which are neither too fixed nor too disembodied. This is where we live.

Part II Psychotherapy: Embodying Complex Identity

This part of the book considers a number of interrelated themes that are relevant to the 'what' and 'how' of psychotherapy: the nature of psychotherapeutic self-insight, how this is facilitated by the therapist from a phenomenological point of view, and some cultural reflections on the nature of psychotherapy relative to the emerging phenomenon of globalisation. The section culminates in a review of how Heidegger's ontology and Gendlin's philosophy may provide a foundational framework for psychotherapy as an embodied practice.

Chapter 5 examines how the findings of a phenomenological study of self-insight in psychotherapy reflects a movement by clients to recover their sense of human identity in ways that always transcend any form of objectification. Their human complexity is somewhat restored as they move back towards the concrete details of their lives where the human order has its life. The chapter also nods back to the previous methodological section by demonstrating how a phenomenological research study results in valuable insights about the nature of self-insight in psychotherapy. In so doing, it reviews how a phenomenological approach provides alternative criteria for human science by championing the value of the human individual as a starting point in human science. This concern results in a practical approach that includes a return to concrete experiences, the balance between unique variations and the ground that we share, and the movement from the particular to the general.

Chapter 6 moves into the 'how' of psychotherapy. Drawing on phenomenological insights, it considers four foci of attention that inform psychotherapists' interaction with clients: attentive, focusing, interactive, and invitational. These forms of attention are characterised as 'ways of being with' and, although they can also be described in behavioural terms (what the therapist does), their essence most crucially lies in the way in which the therapist's attention is focused in any moment, whether primarily on the world of the client, the interaction between them, the implicit meanings of the client's verbalisations, or the possibility of a meaningful future that 'calls'. Although the four ways of 'being with' can be discretely experienced and enacted by the therapist, it is also indicated how these emphases interweave and overlap. In acknowledging this, the chapter title refers to the 'rhythm' of psychotherapeutic attention. The main concern is to use these formulations of psychotherapeutic ways of being with in order to serve the training of psychotherapy students.

Chapter 7 focuses on one of the touchstones from phenomenology for psychotherapeutic practice: how self-knowledge is a phenomenon that is not just cognitive, but requires a rhythmical process between embodied immersion in one's experience and grounded reflections on that experience. It is this rhythm of closeness and distance between immersion and reflection that is often neglected in psychotherapeutic theory and research. With reference to a case study as illustration, this chapter elaborates on four central dimensions of phenomenological process and sequence in psychotherapy: the important facilitative power of 'not knowing', the indirect path to insight, the 'embodied alchemy' between therapist and client, and the experience of a growing complexity of personal identity rather than the finding of 'answers'. The case study illustrates how the client is living through the psychotherapy session as a whole movement, like a piece of music, thus making it artificial to isolate particular therapeutic moments as significant in themselves.

Chapter 8 takes phenomenological enquiry into the broader cultural arena by considering how the nature of the self is changing through globalisation. In such a context, the task of psychotherapy also changes to address the challenges of embodying a more complex personal identity. In acknowledging such complexity and diversity, it raises the question about what it is that is fundamentally human, that is, what it is that transcends cultural differences. As such, one may begin to consider a form of human support and facilitation that is presently referred to as 'psychotherapy', but which does not necessarily need to survive in its present forms. Psychotherapy, as one way of embodying complex identity is then required to become more sensitive to both cultural variation as well as foundational existential issues.

Chapter 9 is a reflection on how the thoughts of Martin Heidegger and Medard Boss have been pivotal in influencing my understanding and practice of psychotherapy. The chapter is based on a talk I gave to the Simon Silverman Phenomenology Centre at Duquesne University. It anticipates the next section on spirituality by offering a view of the human realm that is both psychological and spiritual. It is, however, placed at the end of this section as it shows how Heidegger's ontology gives concrete direction to psychotherapy through the Daseinsanalytic approach of Medard Boss. It draws on the Zollikon Seminars (Heidegger, 2001) which document Heidegger's talks to Boss's psychiatry students. By using two metaphoric images of the human condition: 'belonging to freedom' and 'belonging to wound', the scene is set for the psychotherapeutic task of embodying such dimensions in everyday life. The chapter closes with a consideration of how Gendlin's philosophy of the body provides further innovative directions for psychotherapeutic practice within such a world-view.

5
Humanising Forces: Phenomenology in Science; Psychotherapy in Technological Culture

This chapter would like to show how a phenomenological approach to qualitative research can be a humanising force in the context of science, and how psychotherapy can be a humanising force in the context of technological culture. These two themes have a common concern, that is, to find alternatives to views and practices that depersonalise the human order.

Much has been written about the human implications of living in a world of proliferating technology, from Heidegger (1977) in the phenomenological tradition to Roszak (1992) and others in the field of ecopsychology. The pressure to become more specialised and efficient has become a powerful value and quest. Both contemporary culture and science enables a view of human identity that focuses on our 'parts' and the compartmentalisation of our lives into specialised 'bits'. This is a kind of abstraction which psychology has also, at times, taken in its concern to mimic the natural sciences. As such, it may unconsciously collude with a cultural trend to view humans as objects like other objects and so, fit 'normatively' into the emerging world of specialised and efficient systems.

This chapter describes a study that empowers an alternative view of both science and persons. As such I will pursue two levels of argument:

- How a phenomenological research method tries to remember an essentially human order in its view of persons, one that includes the qualities of a unique individual as well as the qualities of shared human existence.
- How the results of a study into psychotherapy reveal psychotherapy as a humanising force that enables clients to remember a sense of identity which transcends objectification, compartmentalisation, and specialisation.

Both these concerns address the overall task of the chapter to consider the role that they play in helping science and people remember the human scale of things, and thus how they function as humanising forces in different ways.

I will begin with the first level of my argument about methodology and how it is able to reveal an adequate view of persons.

1. Phenomenological methodology as a humanising force

I was interested in studying the nature of self-insight in psychotherapy: what is it about this kind of self-insight that makes a difference to the way clients feel and live? I will come back to this question later. At this point, however, I wish to articulate some of the methodological concerns I had in approaching such a task. I was familiar with a body of literature in the humanistic, existential, and phenomenological traditions that presented a coherent critique of simply adopting natural science as *the* paradigm for human science research (see, for example, Giorgi, 1970). Within this tradition, I was particularly concerned with the critique that a natural–scientific world-view and methodological approach carried with it the danger of defining human beings in reductionistic and utilitarian ways, and that obscured the essence of the uniquely human dimensions of human identity. As such, I found in phenomenologically oriented methodologies the following three remedies:

- A language which cares for the human order.
- The importance of individual concrete experiences as a starting point for enquiry.
- 'Research results' as possibilities with actual variations; that is, expressing 'results' in ways that are not deterministic in nature.

I would like to briefly elaborate on each of these concerns.

A language which cares for the human order

As indicated in Chapter 4, phenomenologically informed methodology demonstrates a concern to care for our informants' voices, to care for the human phenomena that are being expressed, to care for how our own voices as writers and researchers reveal, conceal, and co-create, and to care for our readers as part of the ongoing conversation of understanding.

If one is faithful to the human order and cares in these ways, one finds words to show our informants' experiences that do not just reflect its 'bare bones' (structure), but also its 'flesh and heart' (textures). As previously argued, one could then say that we are not only concerned with 'truth' but also with 'aesthetics'.

In my study of therapeutic self-insight this involved an attempt to present findings in a way that tried to retain the richness and texture of individual experiences while at the same time offering a level of description that applies more generally and typically.

Achieving such an aesthetic balance between presenting the individual level and the more general levels is something that I would argue is necessary in being faithful to a human order, where a language of finding the 'I in the thou' (Buber, 1970) is central. Such a language helps to retain the participative and shared qualities of human phenomena and reveals humans not as outsiders, strangers, mechanisms, clusters of behaviours, and chemicals, but as intentional beings that are not reducible to variables or causes and effects.

Individual experience as a starting point for enquiry

In spite of all the philosophical moves that have tried to deconstruct subjectivity, I still find myself with Husserl's self-evident intuition that individual experience as it appears is our first access to understanding anything.

So this asks us for a methodological approach which moves from the particular to the general, and justifies the use of descriptions of experiences as a crucial starting point for psychological enquiry (Giorgi, 1986).

When asking psychotherapy clients to describe experiences of self-insight, they were naturally and intuitively able to refer to a whole world of meaningful experience. They expressed these experiences as a story in progress, and yet this story also revealed certain structures beyond their active construction.

The point of this theme for this chapter is that such a methodology which grounds itself in the concrete experiences of informants is more likely not to lose sight of the fact that human living is an unfolding narrative in which *meaning* rather than *measurement* is the appropriate currency of understanding.

'Results' as possibilities with actual variations: Expressing 'research results' in a way that is not deterministic in nature

In writing a description of therapeutic self-insight, I was interested in expressing the results of the study in a way that was thematic rather than final. Thus, themes and structures have more the quality of possibilities around which unique variations can occur. Expressing general themes as possibilities do not wish to deny the unique variations of the experience nor the freedom to respond differently. Rather, the themes are ways of organising meanings that have a shared and communicative value, and are faithful to examples of their unique occasions, but which give them a potentially transferable meaning for others.

Such a way of expressing the results of the study tries to reflect the particular in the general; the dance of the unique and the shared. It allows a degree of open-endedness and freedom in the way we express the ongoing nature of human beings. In relation to the theme of this chapter, this is a remedy to a view of the person that is conclusively determined and enclosed in a thing-like manner.

Having made these three points about a methodology that tries to avoid depersonalising, technological, and objectifying ways of thinking about human beings, I will now turn to how the results of my study on psychotherapy may do something similar for how clients come to experience and reflect on themselves.

2. Psychotherapy as a humanising force

One of Freud's enduring insights is about how, as human beings, we can compartmentalise ourselves in ways that are both helpful and problematic. For example, he saw how, in defining ourselves too narrowly, we can become preoccupied and stuck in a way that restricts our capacities for intimacy and work. Such 'stuckness' takes up energy and what we have repressed fights back, and expresses itself in various ways. On the other hand, he saw certain kinds of compartmentalisation at different stages of development as being necessary and healthy. Although couched within a problematic meta-theoretical jargon, his writings on sublimation and repression (Freud, 1914) articulate their constructive role in achieving an organised self that can flexibly de-emphasise certain desires in order to resolve inner conflict and achieve workable forms of functioning.

Whatever jargon he used, the developing self that he was describing, was one that was much more complex than that simply given by the world of nature or the world of society. It is this experience of 'more than' that I found, in my own research on psychotherapy clients, to be pivotal in understanding the kind of therapeutic self-insight that leads to a greater sense of freedom.

The results of my study led me to believe that the clients' experience and understanding of themselves of being 'more than' any fixed definition given by 'nature' or 'nurture' is an important liberating factor in psychotherapy. Such an experience and understanding may be crucial in generically restoring psychotherapy clients to a sense of themselves that remembers a freedom at the centre of human identity that transcends all the ways that they are defined into specialised categories and judgements.

In order to elaborate and unpack some of the implications of this, I would like to spend a bit of time describing the process and results of my study.

3. A phenomenological study of the kind of therapeutic self-insight that carries a greater sense of freedom

Process and goal of study

Ten people (six men and four women) who had been in psychotherapy for a minimum of four months were asked to describe a situation in psychotherapy in which they saw or understood something which carried with it a greater sense of freedom. In order to protect anonymity, all identifying features of the participants have been changed.

I was interested in a particular kind of therapeutic self-insight that they had experienced, one that carried with it a greater sense of freedom. All could recognise such an experience. A pilot study had already revealed that there were certain kinds of therapeutic self-insights that did not carry a greater sense of freedom. For the purposes of this study, I was not primarily interested in these.

Because of time constraints, I will not go into the detailed methodological steps that I took in gathering and analysing the descriptions in a phenomenological way. Suffice to say that I was mainly informed by Giorgi's (1985a, 1987) recommendations, modifications of this suggested by Wertz (1985) and Anstoos (1987), as well as some stylistic concerns that I emphasised in the first section of this chapter. The goal of such procedures is to arrive at an insightful expression of the invariant structure of the phenomenon: the kind of therapeutic self-insight that leads to a greater sense of freedom. The concern with formulating an invariant structure involves a question about what makes it what it is. And this involves a description of its essential constituents and how these constituents form a meaningful whole. The articulation of such a structure is based on an analysis of particular and concrete experiences that were lived through.

Results of the study

The study resulted in the following analysis of themes and their meaning:

Enabling factors of the therapeutic situation and the person of the therapist

The first thing that the analysis revealed was about the enabling situation of psychotherapy.

A structured freedom

Both the therapist and the situation provide a kind of human space that has an ambiguous quality. This ambiguity expresses how there are certain dimensions of the situation that provide clear structures and other dimensions that emphasise a lack of structure. The ambiguity of such a situation articulates a certain 'shape' to psychotherapy, one that is expressed in the phrase: a structured freedom.

On the one hand a sense of structure is constituted by experiences of continuity of time, place, and person, a growing sense of familiarity with the focus on the client's life, a growing sense of comfort and safety to explore within this context. Such a safe structure is a shape that does not emerge complete, all at once, but one which is realised and tested for over time.

Sometimes an informant would speak more about how the person of the therapist provided the sense of a safe structure and shape. Other informants would speak more of how the situation of therapy, the room, and the timing were important in facilitating this sense of safe structure. But in all this, a certain experience of familiarity and continuity were important – a settling down, a gathering together, an interpersonal 'home-coming'.

On the other hand, there was a certain freedom, a lack of structure in the happenings within the session and the interpersonal space of client and therapist.

This freedom essentially involved an unknown dimension: neither client nor therapist knew much in advance about the direction that the specific content of the conversation would take. No matter how theoretically sophisticated the therapist or how much the client rehearsed in advance what would be talked about, both came to accept that surprising directions were always possible. For some clients this was scary, for others, this was exciting, and usually clients had both these experiences at different times in response to the open freedom of the potential content of the sessions.

The paradoxical nature of the tension between structure and freedom as the 'shape' of the psychotherapy situation appeared to provide an

important enabling balance to the client, as if to give the following productively ambiguous message:

> There is something familiar and safe here which appeals to a need
> that we may have for security. Yet, at the same time, there is some-
> thing challenging or invitational about the freedom within this that
> appeals to a need we may have for adventure and discovery. It is
> sometimes scary and sometimes exciting to play with this.

The ambiguity of this structure means that whatever learning takes
place, the client has participated in such learning in an emotionally
meaningful way. It is not a sanitised or theoretically abstract learning
environment. Rather, the tension that has been described is emotionally
engaged, a tension that is 'moving' and 'involving'.

The second thing that the analysis revealed was about the quality and
nature of the therapeutic self-insight that occurs.

The quality and nature of this kind of therapeutic self-insight

We now move on to the nature of the kind of therapeutic self-insight
that carries a greater sense of freedom. What is the nature of this phenomenon that has been enabled by the structured freedom given by the
situation and person of the therapist? There are a number of dimensions
and sub-components of this phenomenon:

i.   *It is not the self-insight on its own that has power: rather it is its 'before'
     and 'after', the entire narrative that is understood and experienced that
     has freeing power.*

Firstly, although there were often particular self-insights that were
important, their credibility was only meaningful because of the personal
narrative that had been forged as their context. Here are some examples
of specific self-insights that occurred:

- I have been living as if I always expect to be rejected.
- There were some important and valid reasons why I needed to hide
  and protect myself, which often no longer apply.
- Although trying to be like my sister has been restrictive for me, it has
  given me a sense of security.
- If I am more assertive towards women, I am afraid that I will lose the
  relationship.

These were important moments of self-insight but they were only given
freeing power by the narrative that came both before and after these

moments. It appears that it is the whole quality of the meaningful personal narrative that is crucial to the value of the therapeutic self-insight. This becomes clearer as we consider the qualities of the narratives that came 'before' and 'after'.

ii.   *A meaningful personal narrative is a linguistic and emotional work of understanding patterns and linkages over time: particular self-insights imply the work of 'patterning' that has preceded it, and the implied directions that can come after it.*

Over time, descriptions of personal behaviours, feelings, and interactions are seen in a way that forms a pattern. For example, for Mary, the theme of wanting to be a 'good girl' first became vividly articulated in terms of the therapist–client relationship. She became aware that she was trying very hard to 'produce the goods' in therapy in order to please her therapist. She then became aware of this theme occurring in other interpersonal situations as well. She also began to remember situations that took place earlier in her life, particularly with her mother, where this was an important concern. This personal narrative of pattern-making/discovery is a linguistic and emotional work that links parts into wholes. It both feels and sees this relationship. As such the client is both a participant as well as an observer, and develops a rhythm of closeness and distance to her own experience in which seeing patterns give distance, whereas the experiencing of details, give closeness and emotional authenticity. The insightful quality of this pattern discovery/creation is in its 'sense-making' and such 'sense-making' is emotionally healing in a number of ways. This becomes clearer as we consider the emotional implications of such a 'sense-making' narrative activity.

iii.   *There is an emotional healing to 'sense-making'*

There were three interrelated ways in which the narrative linguistic work was emotionally healing:

The felt credibility of 'sense-making' and our need for personal truth

The 'sense-making' process of the personal narrative in which part and whole, or particular events and their themes, come together, produces a sense of felt credibility and personal truth. This is not just a freely imaginative process – it is much more rigorous than that if the sense of felt credibility is going to occur. Personal 'sense-making' needs the 'evidence' of details almost as if there is an inner demand for rigour and truth-seeking. It is as if there are certain intuitive standards and questions in the process for the client: 'Is this theme supported by the details of my life? Does this way of saying things, say it better than an alternative phrase or word?' There appears to be an aesthetic quality that satisfies a client emotionally when words fit experiences. For example, when a therapist used the phrase 'You seem to be saying that you want to develop further in this way', the client paused and said: 'Not so much *develop* but rather *moving on*'.

This is a kind of 'sense-making' that is credible to the client. The client herself is the only one who can emotionally validate a theme or an interpretation, as it is only she that has a complex enough access to the textures of her lived experience. The healing quality of such credible 'sense-making' involves the emotional relief that happens when words are felt to serve the uniqueness of personal experience. Such 'goodness of fit' is a pleasing reassurance that the private world can enter the shared space of language, and bridge the 'inner' and the 'outer' in a credible way. Such 'sense-making' also embodies the relief that one's life is not just made up of fragmented bits and pieces, but has some sense of temporal order and continuity. And here we move to two related qualities of therapeutic self-insight that brings the past, present, and future into a workable relationship.

Self-forgiveness
In the personal narratives that were forged, there was usually an understanding in which repetitive patterns were seen as understandable within a human story.

Thus early on in Bill's therapy he saw himself in a judgemental way as 'pathetic' and 'weak' about his lack of assertiveness. As the narrative evolved, he found credible details about his present and past interactions in which his lack of assertion took on a more complex meaning. He saw how he was afraid of being more powerful in a number of present interactions and also remembered how, as a boy, he wanted to show his little sister that he was not scary like their abusive father – he remembers how much he wanted to protect her. His protective wishes towards others could be seen not just as a weakness but also as a strength and even an admirable quality. So the emerging narrative recovers a more complex, human story and this can constitute a sense of self-forgiveness about being the way one is. This does not necessarily condone one's behaviour, but at least makes one less worthy of simple rejection. The healing factor of such self-forgiveness or self-accepting–understanding is that it empowers the kind of self-care that is needed to 'unhook' one from premature, conclusive self-definitions and judgements. And here we come to hope.

Hope

This dimension involves a component of self-insight in which:

- A present restrictive, repetitive pattern that has been articulated, is seen as *not inevitable*.
- Also, the client sees more about where *personal agency* is possible and where it is not. As such, the client sees a different path forward from a mere repetition of the pattern and this constitutes an experience of *hope*.

Here is an illustration of these components taken from the study:

> Jane came into therapy because she felt that her anger could destroy people she cared about. In therapy, a narrative emerged in which she came to realise that a pervasive angry attitude towards her ex-husband obscured a 'huge grief' about what had happened to her and her children. As the narrative progressed, a de-centring of her anger as a central determinant of her existence occurred and was expressed by her in the following way: 'Behind the walls is not an overwhelming anger that is going to make me kill someone.' This was a great relief and a 'hope' that she needed. The sense of increased personal agency came with a dream that made her realise that significant relationships do not have to end painfully or threateningly. This helped her to feel that she could tolerate her youngest child leaving home. Subsequently their relationship improved. The healing factor of such increased personal agency is that it recovers the sense in which one is not merely a victim of circumstance and that the future does not have to be determined by the past.

All in all, the quality and nature of this kind of therapeutic self-insight describes a 'sense-making' personal narrative, with moments of liberating self-insight that are credible, and that 'unfreezes' personal time so that one can move into the future in a more active and hopeful way. Going one step beyond this, however, all this is able to tell us something more essential about the kind of freedom that occurs.

iv. The sense of freedom that occurs is essentially an experience of 'being more than ...'

Here, the question that is addressed is: What is the essential nature of the kind of *freedom* that occurs in a self-insightful narrative process?

Here we move to a more philosophical level of phenomenological analysis, one that was approached in the transcendental phenomenological tradition. Here I am interested in the phenomenology of freedom. Such a question focuses on the implicit preconditions that underlie the kinds of freedoms expressed by the informants. Within this task, the essential meaning that I intuited from the whole structure of the experience was that the phenomenology of this kind of freedom is revealed by articulating the phenomenology of experiencing personal identity as 'being more than'. What is *in* this experience of *being more than*?

- Being more than what I had previously thought and felt.
- Being more than what I had said up till now.
- Being more than any premature judgement of myself – good or bad.
- Being more than any 'thing' or self-enclosed entity that reacts to forces and causes.

To elaborate on some of these themes: there was always a 'more' to the narrative. Any particular conclusions, no matter how valid at the time are too 'thing-like' in themselves and always have a 'before' and 'after'. The 'more' has its life in the specificity of the lifeworld (Gendlin, 1997c) that is always larger than the 'known' (Merleau-Ponty, 1962). Premature self-judgements and self-definitions also stop the flow of time-as-possibility and the call of 'the new'. In the experience of 'being more than ...' a self as agent is recovered in which there is a potentially transcendental quality beyond a self that is reduced to the sum total of its past experiences. On the other hand, such freedom is not an absolute freedom. The results of the study revealed how the terms of the freedom arose out of a consideration of personal limits and repetitions. The open space of the freedom only makes sense in relation to these limits and restrictions.

At the end of this analysis, I am prompted to say that therapeutic self-insight is not the fundamental point of psychotherapy: it is more a means to an end, and points to an experience of 'more'. It is this experience of 'of being more than' or of 'being as possibility' that is the essential power of psychotherapy.

4. Concluding thoughts

To return to the theme of this chapter: How did the existential–phenomenological method avoid depersonalising forces that may arise within a natural–scientific world-view?

In this regard, I concentrated on demonstrating three implications of my methodological approach:

- That it tries to find a language that cares for the human order. This is a language that is full of human participation and that allows us as human beings to intuitively share in the phenomena described; a language that finds the 'I in the thou'; a language of experience on its own terms.
- That it champions the value of the human individual as a starting point in human science. This includes a return to concrete experiences, the balance between articulating unique variations of experience with the ground that we share. The approach moves from the particular to the general, attempting to honour both levels of understanding and their complementarity (the hermeneutic circle).
- That it remembers the freedom of the unique human occasion by expressing essences and themes, not as final and conclusive law-like absolutes, but rather as possibilities around which unique variations and actualities can occur. Truth in this perspective is thus an ongoing conversation which is not arbitrary but which is never finished and depends on questions and context. And the conversation is 'melodic' in the sense that it has shape, themes, and variations.

How does psychotherapy help people avoid depersonalising forces that may arise from the way that technological culture defines us?

- The psychotherapy situation enables a form of learning and exploration that embraces head and heart is playful, and does not know in advance how things will happen. It is a work of un-specialisation.
- The nature of discovering/creating an emotionally meaningful narrative is such that it reveals the future as possibility. It is a work of de-role-ing and involves an emerging sense of the complexity of personal identity that is 'more than' any definition can capture. Science and technology has up till recently felt most comfortable with definitions and their uses.
- In learning about the restrictions and limitations of repetitive patterns of living and meaning, psychotherapy clients move beyond such self-enclosure. The intentional open essence of consciousness or being-in-the world is remembered, and as such, finds a transcendental dimension of being human that can never fully be objectified or turned into a 'thing'.
- In 'sense-making', self-forgiveness, and hope, the client moves back towards being grounded in the concrete details of her/his life.

The flow and ongoing story of such concrete details are always 'more than' any simple abstraction or self-definition. Human complexity is somewhat restored, and this empowers the intuition of one's bodily grounded situation as a valid way of knowing. Such personal knowing is a crucial remedy to a form of knowing that tries to regard the self from an external, outside, and measured point of view.

All this may be an alternative to the pressure to become more specialised and efficient, and the pressure to study one another in technologically useful ways.

And as we stretch between earth and sky, there may be a sigh of relief as we remember something of being at home – its view and its feeling.

6
The Rhythm of Psychotherapeutic Attention: A Training Model

In training students for the practice of individual adult psychotherapy, I have found myself challenged to look naively at some of the ways that a psychotherapist may be present during his moment-to-moment contact with his/her client.

This chapter will describe four phases or emphases of the psychotherapeutic stance which together form a rhythm or continuum of interaction. Although these modes of being overlap and may implicitly carry elements of each other, I have found that the categories are discrete enough that inexperienced therapists may consistently recognise the movement from one emphasis to another, both in themselves and by watching videotapes of colleagues. In this way, the model has served as a meaningful scheme in the context of group supervision for considering both personal style and client needs.

Although the four emphases of interaction may be behaviourally recognised, their teaching value rests most crucially on the fact that students can differentiate each modality, by noticing their own focus of attention in the psychotherapy session. Once they are able to recognise the 'inner feel' or quality of these gestures, they have a valuable range of experiential referents on which to begin discussing psychotherapeutic process.

The essence of each of the four modalities will thus be described in terms of the act and place of attention. In this way students learn to differentiate 'where one's attention is' and this can lead to a range of appropriate questions. For example: Is the therapist's attention absorbed in the client? Is the therapist preoccupied with the quality of the interaction between therapist and client? Is the therapist's attention bound up in an external perspective that is seeking repetitive patterns or themes? Is focus on the interaction called for while the therapist's inclination is to be excessively absorbed in the client's phenomenological world? These and other questions of therapeutic attention tend to become naturally generated when the shared vocabulary has been learned. Students have found that the categories are natural enough to be experientially differentiated, and, through discussion and watching themselves on videotape, they are able to obtain some insight into their own attentional styles. Although this is experienced as self-consciously inhibiting to begin with, students soon learn to integrate these dimensions into a more natural rhythm.

Although indebted to the broad tradition of depth psychology, this model of teaching psychotherapy fits most comfortably within the existential–phenomenological tradition with regard to its view of persons (Boss, 1963) and its understanding of psychotherapeutic change (Gendlin, 1964; Mahrer, 1983). Some of the assumptions of this perspective will become more explicit as the chapter progresses.

The four emphases of attention will now be described. Each category is expressed as a mode of 'being-with' the client in order to indicate the intersubjective foundation on which psychotherapy rests. For the sake of convenience and brevity the four modalities are designated as follows (see Table 6.1):

- Attentive being-with.
- Focusing being-with.
- Interactive being-with.
- Invitational being-with.

1. Attentive being-with

In this mode of being, the therapist allows his/her attention to be absorbed into the phenomenological world of the other. This stance has been well documented in the literature of phenomenological philosophy and psychology (Ellenberger, 1958; Mahrer, 1978). The concern here is to suspend one's own preoccupations and concerns as much as possible in an attitude of letting-be-ness. One's attentional space is very close to or 'contains' the attentional space of the other. The therapist's ability to experientially participate in and imagine the foreground and background of the patient's world carries with it understandings far greater than just the explicit themes of the patient's verbalisations. A coherent world of the other opens up which provides an intelligible context within which specific verbalisations demonstrate significance. In such a phase, the therapist is not concerned with 'explaining' the communicated phenomena

Table 6.1:   Therapeutic modes of being

	Attentive	Focusing	Interactive	Invitational
Place of therapist's attention	Other's world as revealed. Attention – absorbed	Other's world as concealed Themes, gaps, 'shadows' – less absorbed	In the immediacy of the 'between'	Sense of direction DESIRE/ FUTURE
Discourse that this opens up	Unique, specific, coherent world	General, common structures: ambiguities	How each is present to the other. Dilemma of self and other	World of playful imagination, 'authentic' strivings
What therapist does	Let us be, follows, DESCRIBES	Focuses LANGUAGE ACTIVE contribution	Gives permission to make this a valid and safe area to explore	Represents 'callings', participates in story-telling
Theoretical affinities	Rogers, Van Den Berg, Mahrer	Gendlin, Murray	Buber	Boss, Jung, Milton Erikson
Healing power	Sense of continuity – 'self'	Differentiation and integration	Value of human contact	Hope – spirit of invitation
Inter-personal description of the situation	'Holding', nurturing, 'mirroring'	Collaborative	Awareness of inter-personal boundaries	Invitational – 'why not?'
Capacity that therapist exercises	'Dwelling' – 'survive'	Experiential use of language to link	Freedom for distance and closeness	Aesthetic sense of story
Qualitative feel of this mode of being for therapist	Unpreoccupied; self-forgetting in listening	Need for coherence, sense of ambiguity	Become self-conscious or aware of inter personal dimension	Sense of anticipation 'being stirred'

with reference to any theory or generalisation. Rather, he/she behaves in a way that facilitates the *description* of the patient's experiential situation. Such an activity by the psychotherapist includes, but is more than, Carl Rogers' (1951) earlier descriptions of the reflection of feelings.

The emphasis in a phenomenological perspective lies in the description of perceived relationships of self and world. Such an approach is interested in the elucidation of a personal 'topography'. The descriptive act is thus focused on how different qualities of the world, fellow beings, personal time and space, and one's body appear in a coherent and thematic relationship to one another. In this way, rather than emphasising the 'inner' feelings of sadness, the therapist will be just as interested in the kind of world 'out there' that the sadness reveals (Van den Berg, 1972). For example, for a middle-aged woman, the sadness is particularly found in a park that reminds her of a lost mother who took her there after school. She sees the ducks in the old pond. They appear to be out of place, as if they belonged in the bygone era of her youth. The more she looks at the ducks, the more it seems that the new high-rise buildings around the park are where she should try to be. They are not soothing and carefree like the park she remembers and now cannot recover; but they seem to have more life, and more of a future, and that is what she feels she needs. A man glances at her as he passes and she suddenly realises with shame that she has been sitting on the grass in a 'child-like' manner. As she immediately resumes the shape of her 'grown-up' body, her back becomes taut, and she regains a power that enables her to nod politely at the passing stranger. She sighs as she rises, taking comfort as she fills her immediate future with tasks that call from her everyday life.

In attending to, and facilitating, such a description, the psychotherapist becomes absorbed in a personal world that has 'come from' somewhere and is attempting to 'go' somewhere. It is a world that is very specific in revealing restricted and accessible directions. In this description, there is 'much more' than she says. As psychotherapists, our imaginative absorption in this world can plausibly move into wider and wider backgrounds. As the description unfolds, a coherent logic begins to appear in which the background and the moving foreground of further explicit verbalisations connect. More and more, therapist and client get a feeling of how it all hangs together, like a good story or a poem. This is one of the healing powers of psychotherapeutic interaction and contains a number of related facets.

This everyday poetic language of how one is meaningfully located provides the feeling that psychological life is understandable, in the sense that one's thoughts, feelings, and actions are not isolated fragments appearing without sense. This experience constitutes the recovery of a greater context from which to see; a context that corresponds to the experience of a deeper or more continuous self. To this extent the client feels less helpless regarding the relentlessness of what previously appeared to be isolated experiences and meanings.

As an interpersonal experience the client feels contained and understood by the therapist. This phase may reinvoke in the client an experience that corresponds to a nurturant mother; a continuous presence who mirrors or validates the growing organisation of a child's experience. Such an interpersonal experience effectively reduces the kind of anxiety that comes from the threat of self-fragmentation and a chaotic world.

In feeling more connected with one's self and with another who validates this self, the experience of isolation is reduced and greater intimacy, both with oneself and another, is enhanced.

In the therapist, attentive being-with is not just a technique, but also an act of attention that implies a certain emotional capacity. In order to sustain such attention and facilitate experiential description, the therapist must be able to 'hold' the client's experience without detracting from it or turning it into something else. In attending to more of 'what it's like to be you', the therapist is able to face what is revealed in terms of its emotional significance; and if the therapist has difficulty being-there-with the client in that space, a meta-message will be communicated which discourages permissive exploration of that area. In attentive being-with, the therapist lends courage to the client. Some of the implicit attitudes that are communicated in this stance are: 'Being there in your situation can be faced; avoiding your situation is not necessarily the only possible stance; "dwelling" with "more" of where you are may be more multidimensional than the way you are presently conceiving of it or reacting to it.'

Through the reception of these meta-messages, clients often find that deeper description of their experiential world constitutes a 'dwelling' that is fertile ground for new possibilities of perceiving and living. In this sense, attentive being-with is a 'dwelling' which is an invitation to depth; and this invitation to depth is a movement which is both scary and hopeful.

In attentive being-with, although the therapist is willing to experientially participate in the client's world, he does not necessarily react in the same way as the client to this world, as if he has come to the same conclusion about the meaning of it all. This would constitute a 'closing of accounts' with the multidimensionality of things, the very prematurity from which the client is often suffering. It is important that the client feel that the therapist can 'survive' the emotional impact of the client's felt situation. Indeed, such an ability to experientially participate, but survive, improves the therapist's ability to 'let-be' what is emerging without too much overstatement or under-statement.

The qualitative feel of such a mode of being is one of absorption in the other's world. As therapist, one has forgotten oneself and is willingly helping to describe and live in the expanding horizons of that description.

2. Focusing being-with

In the previous mode of being, the therapist's attention followed the client and respectfully assisted in the description of the client's experiential situation. In this way, progressively more facets of the client's world came into conscious focus.

Through this process the therapist, by sharing the experience of what is being revealed, becomes aware of themes, gaps, or fuzzy areas in the emerging personal topography. The attentive concern of the therapist may increasingly be struck by what appears to be implicit to what is being revealed. In such a process the therapist's attention becomes more focused than his/her previous mode of 'following' and 'letting be'. In attentive being-with, the therapist attends to what is emerging; in focusing being-with the therapist attends to his/her own ongoing sense of understanding in the presence of the other's world.

Such a focus of concern derives from a motive in the therapist towards greater coherence. The desire is to assist the client in encountering ways of imagining, talking, and feeling that can 'find a place for' the multi-plicities and ambiguities of his/her experiential life. The focus is thus more active and searching than the more open-ended descriptions sought through the attentive mode. The therapist is internally active in his/her attempt to understand more of how the client's experience and action occurs. In this mode of being-with, the therapist's attention is less absorbed in the client. An internal imaginative dialogue occurs between the specific and unique issues of this particular client and the more general and collective themes of human existence that appear to be relevant. The therapist brings both an intuitive capacity and a body of understanding together in such a way as to highlight a particular focus to the ongoing discourse. Focusing being-with is a contribution by the therapist in attempting to provide a direction for exploration that can integrate what is happening with what has gone before.

In practical terms we are talking here about the artistic use of language with its powers of differentiation and integration (Murray, 1974). The artistic use of interpretations and metaphors does not refer, as much to its aesthetics or truth, as to whether it is experientially meaningful to the client in integrating his experience. Such a notion of the experiential use of language is elaborated by Gendlin (1978), in his description of a holistic and implicit felt sense of 'how we are in relation to our world'. It is this holistic, pre-verbal sense of ourselves-in-relation that enables us to have or not have a sense of recognition as to whether an interpretation or verbal description fits or not.

The focusing that is facilitated in this modality is thus grounded by the client, and essentially speaks to the experiential concerns that are emerging. In facilitating such an act of focus, it is not the technique that is primary, but a sensitivity by the therapist that the evolving language gives the client's experience a 'place to go'. In this way, the focus, whether historical or metaphorical, has life in the sense of unfolding more of the person beyond his/her premature self-conceptualisations.

The facilitation of focus in psychotherapy provides some perspective on what one was previously embedded in. We live in contexts that exceed what we articulate. It would be an exhausting destiny if we felt that we had to make conscious much of what is unconscious. In moments that are relatively free of conflict we let the background simply be the background. However, sometimes we seek distance from our embedded context. In psychotherapy the client experiences this in various ways, but essentially has a global felt sense that he/she is carrying something, feels confused, or has a number of different symptoms that speak of something unspoken.

The therapist, through offering a way of languaging what was experientially bound up with everything else, facilitates an experience of differentiation in which the client breathes a small sigh of relief. The sigh of relief has to do with the sense of mastery that comes with the distance of perspective. Such a distance from what one was embedded in is also a closeness to a social world of meaning where what one has carried gets back into dialogue with the shared world of meanings.

Such naming becomes a temporary vantage point from which to see more of one's lived context and therefore increases the sense of connection between the lived and the known. Such a sense of connection between these two aspects of our existence is another way that a sense of self becomes enhanced. The differentiation of languaging what 'one is in' is thus not just a differentiation from mother and father, or one's childhood, but an act of differentiation from and re-relating to a matrix that is more immediately surrounding us in its embedding power. There is an 'embedding' that is stultifying and an 'embedding' that is supportive, and the power of naming is a magic whose labour is welcome.

As an interpersonal stance, this mode of being-with is collaborative in that it involves the negotiation of meaning (Hobson, 1985). The therapist is exercising a poetic sensibility in which language shows its fluidity by means of links, metaphors, expressions of difference, and so on. He/she is particularly sensitive to whether the naming process opens up experiential directions more than it closes them off. Colloquially this has been referred to as the deepening of rapport.

The qualitative feel of such a mode of being for the therapist is of attention to the background of what is expressed. As a therapist, one becomes alerted to an image, theme, or feeling that appears to make sense of what is being expressed, but goes beyond it. In such a venture, language is sought which gives focus, and names what is in the shadows.

3. Interactive being-with

In this mode of being, the therapist's attention becomes focused on the space between therapist and client. The therapist becomes aware of the quality of the relationship in the here and now, in the consulting room. This may occur either actively or passively; that is, either the therapist may actively wonder how the themes that the client has spoken of are being played out between them, or the therapist finds himself or herself passively responding or feeling something about the quality of the relationship that, to begin with, he/she may not be able to quite articulate.

In both these situations, the immediacy of what is happening becomes an issue. In such an interpersonal focus, therapist and client are part of each other's world, and this constitutes both a dilemma and a hope. The dilemma refers to the therapist's growing awareness that he/she is not free from involvement as part of the client's interpersonal world. Often the therapist feels freer in an attentive or focusing mode to be emotionally available to the client, since he/she is not self-conscious about his/her own mode of presence. The hope refers to the therapist's growing awareness that the interactive focus in the consulting room is a potent arena for therapeutic enquiry, and that the ambiguity of interpersonal life is one important arena in which the therapeutic drama unfolds.

When an interactive focus becomes a concern, the therapist who is aware to some degree of the historical roots of interpersonal perception often feels a need for a heightened sense of alertness. This heightened sense of alertness arises out of the demand to be both part of what is happening and yet also to be apart. One has to be able to distance oneself from the process in order to comment, if necessary (either silently to oneself or to the client), on what is happening in the process between therapist and client. Such an interactive focus involves a meta-perspective in which the therapist's attention is guided to look at the way that both therapist and client are present to each other. Whereas the attentive mode requires a capacity to be close to the world of the client, the awareness of interactive process requires a momentary distance from the interpersonal involvement. In this phase, the therapist's attention is thus, in a sense, in the third person mode, where the attentional space surrounds both therapist and client as a phenomenon.

What different psychotherapeutic traditions do with the interactive focus of attention is a matter of ongoing debate and reflects different understandings of interpersonal process. The approach taken here is grounded in Martin Buber's philosophy of encounter (Friedman, 1985; Brice, 1984) with a particular emphasis on the experience of 'newness' (Shainberg, 1980). The therapeutic principle in this mode of being involves opening up the interactive focus in such a way that restrictive interpersonal patterns become less necessary as well as allowing for the possibility that new ones can be experienced. This principle is already facilitated by the two previous modes of being-with the client, but develop into a specific focus that is explicitly or implicitly communicated as follows: 'This is a place where the immediacy of what is happening between us can sometimes be addressed, survived, and even serve to deepen our faith in the value of human contact.'

This message appreciates some of the ambiguities and ambivalences in differentiating self and other. The therapist is attuned to the Buberian question: Is it possible for us to meet, without excessively reducing me to you or you to me, and without us becoming isolated from each other? Is it irrevocably either merger or separation? To a psychotherapist, the focus is on the difficulties of embodying such an offer. If the offer were a demand, it would become persecutory. The therapist in this modality thus takes seriously the phenomenological world of the client, where each level of recoil from encounter is only released when its concerns are cared for.

The interactive focus thus carries the therapeutic process forward best when it is formulated in terms that give the client permission to explore feelings about the present interpersonal situation without the fearful implications that such an acknowledgement would have in other everyday contexts. When this form of interaction is therapeutic, the client learns that he is neither 'swallowed up' by the other nor destructive of the other; and this may lead to greater courage regarding the freedoms and limits of interpersonal interaction. In this way the interactive focus serves in the client a growing experiential ability to contain and manage the ambiguity of being the 'one and the many' (Scott, 1978) that we are in different interpersonal situations. The healing power of interactive being-with has thus to do with experiences regarding the value of human contact.

The therapist, in responding to an interactive focus of awareness, is developing the ability to use himself or herself in the therapy situation so as to be humanly present, without loss of access to a meta-perspective that can formulate comments about what is occurring between therapist and client. The challenge of this form of attention is to extend one's flexibility for both interpersonal closeness and distance, not excessively needing or getting stuck in either mode. This obviously has implications for the therapist's own development regarding intimacy and separation issues. Supervision thus often focuses on the therapist's own hopes and fears about encountering the client.

The qualitative feel of the interactive mode of being for the therapist is of attention to the sense of immediate interpersonal process of self and other. It is a form of awareness that reveals *how* I as therapist am present and how client as other is present in the dialogue. It is a rhythmical attention in that it involves the intersubjective, mirror-like perspective of 'I in you and you in me'. As therapist, one often becomes alerted to this sense or presence by a growing self-awareness of who one is in the other's eyes. One may feel idealised or even violated and may be tempted to react to what one is being turned into by this spell of perception. The challenge of this mode of awareness is to be able to develop a rhythm; that is, of being close enough to the immediacy of the situation to experience what is happening, yet also to be able to distance oneself from such immediacy in order to become interested in the quality of interaction as a phenomenon. It is this latter ability that gives the therapist a much-needed degree of freedom, a freedom that allows him or her to focus on the quality of the interaction with some degree of empathy. This ability is often difficult to maintain, and supervision in this area focuses on the therapist's experience of confusion. The therapist brings the experience of confusion to the supervisor, and together they attempt the work of distancing, that is, working towards an understanding of who the therapist is in the client's eyes and who the client is in the therapist's eyes. Such consideration empowers the therapist to enter again the stream of ambiguity of the therapeutic situation in a helpful way.

When the therapist is able to maintain this balance of closeness and distance to some degree, the client will be provided with a context in which the dilemmas of relating to another as 'other' can be negotiated. This is a land of many colours, of rage and hope, and the therapist is asked to be resilient, often to wait and to grant the gifts of both aloneness and sharing.

4. Invitational being-with

The rhythm of the previous modes of being sometimes ripens and gives birth to an invitational focus that comes out of the foundations already laid. In this mode of being, the therapist's attention becomes focused in a particular way. Here the therapist is listening more distinctly to a sense of *direction* that is revealing itself as possible. It is not a direction that comes from the therapist-in-himself/herself, as if he/she could simply invite the client into a different world. Nor is it a direction that comes from the client-in-himself/herself, as if he/she could wilfully decide where to go. The direction demands more respect than that and has a degree of necessity as to its authentic possibilities. The phenomenon of a person's story, its restrictions and possibilities, has a life far bigger than the therapist or client's will. It is multidimensionally grounded, and the future possibilities have to answer to such situatedness. Even beginning again demands an ending, and the nature of the beginning is not unrelated to the ending. In this process, the therapist's attention is drawn to a sense of becoming; that is, a sense of how the experiential themes are always already an attempt to be on the way to something. This involves an appreciation of how different futures clamour to be present, and in order to be authentic, these possibilities require a shape that can gather up the past themes and carry them forward.

This aesthetic sense of story, of listening to the presence of future, can be found in the alchemical poetry of Jung (1972), in the tales of Milton Erickson (Rosen, 1982), and in the 'anticipatory care' of Medard Boss (1963). It can also be seen in the 'reframing' of systemic family therapists (White, 1983). This mode of awareness occurs most often in older psychotherapists who have lived and heard many stories and who have begun to find a story big enough to gather together many possibilities – mortals and gods, sky and earth.

In invitational being-with, the therapist is attending to the experiential themes of the client with an ear grounded in this aesthetic of becoming. It is the ear of Eros. The therapist is listening to the themes and attempting to recognise the nature of the authentic strivings already dimly expressed. Whatever degree of isolation or sense of stuckness the client is expressing, the therapist is already attending to the isolation from *what* and the stuckness of *what*. He listens to the *call* that the client cannot take up or sees the *condition* from which the client feels abandoned. He 'remembers' what is looked for and tries to find a voice that can say it in a way that has a future.

Such a mode of attention is supported by a number of theoretical perspectives and is lucidly expressed in the Daseinsanalytic view of pathology and health. In this view, psychopathology is a truncated attempt to achieve healthy existential possibilities. Thus Medard Boss could recognise, in the case of a sadistic pervert, the extremely frustrated desire to be one with a lover, where the client could only angrily express the wish to devour and own (1983, pp. 186–208). Carl Jung could hear the call to a more receptive way of being where another might only experience depression in the realisation of his futile attempts to be heroic (1972, pp. 168–9).

Attention in this mode is thus listening for the healthy potential that is implicit. This is a healing vision and thus, in a sense, a message from the gods. At its outer edge it is the stuff that dreams and prophecies are made of. There is a great danger to this, for, one hopes, such a vision should not just heal the therapist. In moving into this mode of being as a therapeutic activity, the crucial question becomes: How is it possible to represent such callings in a way that a client can authentically integrate and take up as his own?

Although some theorists take refuge in the assertion that the hidden potential comes from the client-in-himself/herself when the way is cleared, or that the archetypes are pre-existently formed, waiting to be heard, the existential–phenomenological perspective sees it in a less determined way. In this perspective, the potential is implicit not in a predetermined form, but as questions which seek answers that still need to be born. In metaphorical language, it is a spirit looking for a shape whose existence is not yet guaranteed.

Such a perspective of human potential requires the co-constructive activity of both therapist and client for its actualisation (Barton, 1974). The therapist in this mode of being is thus responsible for participating in story-telling in a way that has both freedom and limits. The flights of imaginative possibilities require a form that binds the central experiential issues that the client has expressed. In Hillman's (1977) words, it is 'soul-making' in the sense that it gathers up some core issues and provides a wider, plausible context within which these issues can have life. The imaginative realm is not yet actual but gives space for actualities to be born. It thus needs to be respected as a playful but valid realm for authentic becoming. In this spirit, the therapist encourages imaginative explorations that are grounded in central themes, and may even offer from time to time an imaginative scenario where the client 'tastes' the dilemmas and hopes of living out certain scenarios.

Such imaginative activity is most fruitful when its themes are guided by an appreciation of the call or existential question that has emerged in the details of the client's life. The invitation is most loud when it comes from a sense of the 'incomplete' that is felt in its emergence. In this sense it comes from the client but he/she is not alone in its answering. Food reaches its clearest form in the space of hunger, and the dialectics of mutuality require an appreciation of the seasons of emotional fertility – a time for expression and a time for reception.

The essential emphasis in the invitational mode of being is thus on providing the context within which the client's phenomenological situation can be given a direction. Such a direction is most likely to be authentic when it constitutes an inclusive space in which the present configuration of felt meanings is implicitly or explicitly taken up in a new light. In this meeting there is something old and something new. The former component provides authenticity, the latter, hope. The healing power of this mode of being has to do with hope and the life of adventure. Whereas the more 'maternal' attentive being-with provides a home, the more 'paternal' invitational being-with tempts one with the hidden treasures of as yet unknown lands. Such different powers have given rise to different therapeutic schools and sometimes embody a natural form of self-selection as to the kind of therapists they attract. Different clients also respond differentially to these different healing powers – an interesting line of enquiry that cannot be pursued here.

The qualitative feel of the invitational mode of being for the therapist is of attention to 'where the desire is'. Therapists often express this modality in terms such as 'the growing edge' or 'where things need to go'. A sense of such vitality from the therapist's point of view is not necessarily pleasant for the client as he moves into the unknown. The therapist, however, does have an anticipatory sense of how such invitational experiences open up a wider world with a larger range of authentic possibilities.

In the therapist, the capacity for the invitational mode of being involves both an appreciation of how past, present, and future are always in dialogue, as well as a healing imaginative capability that is not unrelated to the givens of clinical material. The latter capability can be informed by theory, the knowledge of psychodynamics, myths and stories of transformation, and the knowledge of how symptoms carry the seeds of meaningful directions. However, it is most authentically grounded in the therapist's own struggles for human reconciliation. When the therapist brings an invitational emphasis to the encounter in a meaningful way, the client is provided with a context where a less linear vision of time is offered. That is, the client may progressively grow into unanticipated experiences that require a changing body and a changing mind. Such experiences may sometimes constitute a growing faith about 'being on the way' without being obsessed about outcome. Thus invitations do not hold guarantees but at least add the spirit of responding to a call, and it is such a spirit that makes all the difference as it reveals Hermes, the messenger of the gods.

5. Concluding thoughts

The danger of too much systematisation of psychotherapeutic attention is that it may be understood prescriptively as if it can be turned into a technique. Peter Lomas (1981, p. 138) asserts that any learned technique in psychotherapy 'not only cannot substitute for a more elemental capacity to heal but may actually inhibit this capacity'. In this perspective, the individual's capacity to help is more of a human than a technical enterprise. It is with this insight that Lomas can say that 'in judging the competence of a therapist we should therefore not depart radically from the way in which we judge any body's capacity to help' (1981, p. 138).

In attempting to give emphasis to some dimensions of psychotherapeutic attention, I am offering one way of languaging our everyday capacities for human interaction. Such capacities are carried forward in a perhaps more disciplined way into the unique structures of the psychotherapeutic space. Such an exercise of abstracting and articulating four modes of being-with the client constitutes an act of self-consciousness and is artificial to the extent that such self-consciousness obscures the overlapping and interpenetrating rhythm of psychotherapeutic attention.

Despite this it is suggested that such self-reflection can serve to provide an experiential language for the beginning psychotherapist that connects his/her own experience to the nature of the situation. In this model of training, the psychotherapist learns in a way that is similar to a client's learning in psychotherapy: that is, through self-awareness. In a group of trainees, a common language is found to be experientially relevant, and differences and similarities about personal styles and client needs are considered. Once each member of the training group can recognise and relate to his/her own experience of the four emphases of attention, further questioning does not follow a preconceived system, but rather is generated by the unique concerns of each training group. This model of training in psychotherapy is thus most successful when it is person-centred.

Although very little of what has been said will be surprising to practicing psychotherapists, a difficulty in teaching psychotherapy remains; that is, where does one begin? This chapter chronicles one such tale of beginning.

7
The Primacy of Phenomenological Process and Sequence in Psychotherapy: A Case Study

There is an increasing emphasis in psychotherapeutic literature on the *ways* in which insights and interpretations occur rather than on the *content* of these insights and interpretations (cf. Mindell, 1985; Kruger, 1988; Teyber, 1988). Thus, for example, in the psychoanalytic tradition (cf. Langs, 1982), sensitivity to the 'context' of the interpretation is considered of crucial importance, that is, how the insight relates to the current meaningful experience of the client in relation to the therapist. Similarly, in cognitive therapy (cf. Edwards, 1989), a person's experiencing of imagery meaningfully contextualises the client's insights about his/her 'outmoded beliefs'.

As it is grounded in a philosophical heritage that centres on how we come to know ourselves and the world, the phenomenological tradition is eminently qualified to offer some interesting perspectives regarding the primacy of process issues in psychotherapy.

To this end, an example of a psychotherapy session is presented in order to illustrate the movement of phenomenological process and sequence in psychotherapy. Such a sense of phenomenological process refers to an aesthetic quality, which guides the therapist's interventions. It is a vision in which priority is given to the way the session happens as a whole. Thus, like music, it becomes artificial to isolate particular therapeutic moments or insights that can be understood as if separate from the total experience of the session. Although certain meaningful themes may be highlighted at various points during the session, such *content* derives its therapeutic power not from itself, but from *living* through the session.

In the past, insight-oriented approaches have overemphasised what becomes *known* between client and therapist. This can obscure a description of the rhythm and interplay of the lived and the known.

The emphasis on psychotherapy as *process* reflects how the situation becomes both lived and known.

Precedents for this emphasis occur in psychoanalytic literature where terms such as 'corrective emotional experience' and Winnicott's term 'holding environment' have become more prominent.

This chapter tries to communicate the quality of phenomenological process through the literary description of a psychotherapy session. It hopes to show that the valuing of such a holistic quality gets away from emphasising specific therapeutic factors in themselves as being primary. Thus, feeling-in-itself, insightful cognition-in-itself, encounter-in-itself, and other abstracted therapeutic factors are de-emphasised and balanced by their interrelated flow, sequence, and context.

In Part 1 of the chapter, I describe the therapeutic session in such a way that it attempts to capture the 'taste' and flow of the session.

I wish to show how a number of different images, thoughts, feelings, and interactions occur in sequence in a co-constituted situation. I do not attempt to make such a sequence appear particularly logical. The way that I have described the session has been confirmed by the client as essentially consistent with his experience as well. In Part 2 of the chapter, I reflect on this quality and propose four explicit themes that go to make up an appreciation of phenomenological movement in psychotherapy. I am aware that the session poses more questions than I have been able to answer in the reflective phase. This is consistent with the hermeneutic endeavour, where other readers may have different questions and concerns.

1. Part 1: A description of a psychotherapy session

Person

Len lived some important dimensions of his existence within obsessive–compulsive constraints. He was cautious and vigilant, condemned to care. He took a lot of responsibility for interpersonal situations, measuring his responses with integrity and thoughtfulness. Other people usually found him a sincere friend. Yet, in many ways, Len was a reluctant hero. He felt anguish at the compartmentalisation of his life, where things always asked to be put in their proper places. He felt resentment about this and was tired of being the one who was vigilant. Yet Len was afraid that if he withdrew his vigilant care from the world around him, he would become horribly schizoid or narcissistic. At times, depression, tiredness, or sickness made him withdraw, but this constituted for him a failure of interpersonal life. He was deeply engaged with the question of how he could be less effortful in intimate situations and he was fearful that such naturalness would not be enough to sustain the self and other.

The psychotherapy session I will describe is one where Len remembered the joy of 'being in his own world', something he had sometimes defended against as a betrayal of relational possibilities. In this session, I did not focus on the everyday, interpersonal context of 'being in his own world' as I had done on some previous occasions. For example, I did not interpret that there was no one to hold him when he wanders off, far away, all on his own (a perspective informed by Winnicott). Nor did I interpret any fear of 'destroying' others by 'leaving them' as a Kleinian perspective may have encouraged. Rather, an image of 'going far away' possessed us both and we became fascinated. We thus listened to the *reluctance* of the hero more, and took the reluctance further. We withdrew and went far away, to see what was there. 'Far away' was back in time and into dream and had a quality that brought life.

Near and Far

The session began in a way that was 'near' to his immediate, everyday concerns. Len had recently said goodbye to a close friend who had left town. Once again he was reminded of his loneliness. He talked stoically, and then longingly, and stoically again. The mood of stoicism was an old strength in which he reminds himself, like a limiting father, that his interpersonal expectations are excessive. A nobility to such 'bracing of himself' also comes through: contemplating adjustment to more aloneness in his life opens up an image of greater self-sufficiency with much less anxiety. Yet this image is immediately juxtaposed by memories of intimacy in a past-valued relationship and he speaks in the mood of longing. Although this relationship was fraught with conflict and anguish, what is most remembered at this time were moments of intense togetherness in which he cared devotedly for the vulnerability of the other and where the other filled up his vision. Yet the relationship ended in an unsatisfactory manner. Len spoke again with insightful stoicism. By this time it felt like there was a thick atmosphere in the consulting room. Needing and not needing. Needing and not needing. Not only this but the intensity of it.

We explored both of these images further. There was joy and pain in both positions. In the aloneness of 'not needing', he experienced the relief of being 'natural', not burdened by obligation and the necessity to be a healer. But the wound of loneliness called out into empty space. In the phase of intimate interdependence, he experienced the quenching of loneliness, not preoccupied with the 'outsider's' long wait. But the anxiety of sustaining intimacy would strangle the 'natural' man, who felt he could breathe more easily on his own. I do not know whether the exclusivity and power of these two images accurately reflected the details of Len's life, but at the time we were both struck by the felt validity of these themes.

There was not only pain and joy in both positions, but another pain as well; the anguish of lack where Len seemed to be condemned to oscillate between the two positions, the absence of a space where both self and other could be.

Both Len and I dwelt with the mood of despair. The intimate relationship he had talked of earlier came into focus again. It literally confirmed his sense that he was condemned to oscillate, that moving towards someone meant moving away from his 'natural' self. A consideration of the previous relationship that he had referred to, demonstrated by means of a number of details how he was vigilant in intimacy. We were struck dumb by the nearness of the concrete situation. An implicit meaning pattern appeared to call from the silence: 'In life, having your own world is an abandonment of the other; moving away is not allowed if you want others there.' For some reason I said: 'Moving away is not allowed if you want others there.' Between the situation saying it and myself saying it, something important had already occurred. In the midst of the oppression of Len's literal past relationship, I became child-like, seeking refuge in the playful world of metaphor. Len did not know this at the time, and it only gradually dawned upon me that this was the case.

I became more literal and less literal, and said: 'This image of going towards someone or away from someone is very different from the world of the dream where you could conceivably go towards someone by going away from them.' I did not say whether I meant this literally or metaphorically. Both possibilities can occur in dreams.

This world of the dream began to catch our imagination. He took this up (I did not know where we were going) and he remembered incidents when, as a child, he went through phases of being intensely 'magical'. He remembered himself closing his eyes and wishing for a bicycle, even imagining the corner of the room where the bicycle would appear. He remembered how disappointed he was when he opened his eyes and how this constituted part of his disillusionment with prayer and the world of religion. I noted that 'magic' must have really been 'in the air' for him before his disillusionment. He said 'yes', and remembered the 'sacred' attitude he felt when watching his father making things out of wood. In many ways Len was ashamed of the kind of fathering he had received, but now he revealed for the first time that he saw something admirable in the way his father approached wood with respect. He remembered visiting the garage on his own where his father kept odds and ends from which he would make things. I started feeling that Len had gone far away from his attitude of realistic stoicism. In describing the garage, he said that it almost had a temple-like quality to it. The important thing about it was that it was a very private place. Hardly anybody went into it apart from him and his father, and then seldom together. Certainly no friends. Here we found a place where he had found a form of privacy that was not only free of anxiety, but which did not remind him of loneliness. He went on to describe the garage as being a place that seemed pregnant with possibility. He felt both at home there and a little excited. We were silent with this for quite a while.

Then it felt like I woke up and he woke up. This experience of 'waking up' made me think that the memory had been like a dream. For some reason I became interested in exploring the experience with an interpersonal perspective in mind. He noted that his experience 'in the garage' did not feel like a denial or rejection of others. It did not feel like he was spoiling the potential for interpersonal relationships by being withdrawn and what he had sometimes called 'schizoid'. Rather, it was just another way of being, not competing with an interpersonal way of being. He even felt that going to that place could enrich his interpersonal way of being but in a secret, private kind of way. I do not know how Len's struggle, to find permission from himself and others to be himself with others, will go. However, I do believe that this session constituted one initiation into the possibility that his private world could enrich interpersonal existence.

2. Part 2: A reflection on how the psychotherapy session was informed by a sense of phenomenological process and sequence

A sense of phenomenological process values the faith of 'not knowing' as being fundamentally conducive to the free emergence of the client's ways of being

Both client and therapist allow themselves to be compelled by the unfolding depth of experience as it is progressively described. In this phase, we get 'swept along' in the experience and become present to a movement that feels larger than us. This sense of 'being compelled' was described in Part 1 as 'an image of going far away possessed us both and we became fascinated'.

Within a phenomenological perspective, we thus allow things to become present in the ways they want to show themselves. In this process we do not necessarily prefer phenomena that are based on consensus reality or concrete events, or make judgements about their logic from a 'reasonable' point of view (cf. Boss, 1985). Thus, if an image of 'going far away' presents itself, we do not immediately try to link it to the continuous life events of the 'subject'. In this process, the subject is not primary; nor necessarily, is our relationship of therapist and client. The phenomenon at that moment is primary and we subject ourselves to the manner in which it wishes to speak. As therapist, I am not in relation to the client as one who is receiving information from another, an ear to a mouth. Rather, our subject–object separation recedes into the background. We are then both turned towards the presencing of the phenomenon whether it is an image, feeling, or other object of concern. In becoming 'fascinated' we are called beyond ourselves to movements and 'beings' that are trying to happen.

I am reminded here of Ricoeur's distinction between the hermeneutics of faith and the hermeneutics of suspicion. To over-simplify, in a hermeneutics of suspicion, one listens to a phenomenon with an interest in what it is deceptively hiding. Thus, for example, within a Freudian framework, one is suspicious that an umbrella may more significantly stand for a penis. In the hermeneutics of faith, the rich appearance of a phenomenon conveys rather than hides its meaning. Thus an umbrella is usually more involved in the power to protect than the power to penetrate.

In valuing the 'faith of not knowing', one is suspending, as much as possible, one's preconceived notions, to look again within each new context what an 'umbrella' means. This involves what others have called the engagement in local knowledge over the primacy of specialised knowledge.

The phenomenological dictum to allow things to show themselves in the ways they show themselves is asking the therapist to have faith in dwelling with the richness and vitality of expressions as they appear.

In the case I refer to, this principle translated ontically into a sense of being compelled, swept along, and fascinated; and when respected, allowed apparently authentic client issues to be revealed in a way that neither client nor therapist anticipated. In this sense I would say that this faith of not knowing was conducive to the free emergence of the client's ways of being beyond planning, willing and conscious control.

The occurrence of client insight is an indirect rather than a direct consequence of phenomenological process

A psychotherapist who values the aesthetic quality of phenomenological process does not vigorously and directly pursue the facilitation of self-insight. Rather, she directly pursues a process that progressively heightens the client's contact with his world. Such a therapist thus understands that an insight that does not emerge from a phase of 'closeness' or submersion in an experience, is an insight that may be true, but lacks experiential credibility. The facilitation of such 'closeness' to experience is thus valued as primary, and indirectly facilitates insight.

There are potentially many higher order, integrating insights that can occur in the process of psychotherapy. For example, in this case, the client may say that he realised that taking care of others would be more authentic for him when done from a position where he was allowed to withdraw if he wished. As psychotherapists we may want to facilitate such an insight and become excessively guided by such content. However, such an agenda may obscure an experiential process that could empower the insight in a personally relevant way. In Len's case, he needed to experience the nourishment of withdrawal in image and memory, and then see whether the experiencing of this possibility could actually enhance interpersonal life. This would constitute real confidence regarding the insight. Without this experience we would probably call the insight 'ungrounded' and needing to be propped up by excessive 'self talk'. A true insight that is experientially grounded thus tends to reduce the necessity for conscious remembrance or continual affirmation.

In following a client's therapeutic movement in a phenomenological way, we begin by suspending our notion of what is important in content and thereby attend to the present experiencing of what is of concern to the client. In this perspective, psychotherapy proceeds most meaningfully from a centre of concern (cf. Mahrer, 1983) that is 'asking for attention'. Sensitivity by both therapist and client to this phenomenon involves a mutual interest in 'what is there', be it boredom, anxiety, apathy, loss, a pressure to get something off one's chest, or a fear that they would not be able to proceed. 'What is there' is thus best guided by a description of, or sensitivity to, the 'feeling qualities' that are brought to the session. What these feeling qualities are 'about' (that is, the content) may be considered very trivial from a psychotherapeutically greedy point of view. For example, the client may be truly upset about the lack of cutlery in his/her house. Although the therapist may not know what this has to do with anything, he/she begins with the felt meaningfulness of this experience in the moment. Care for such experiencing by client and therapist may result in the unfolding of related *or* unrelated experiences in *content*. However, the subsequent events of the session are considered to be related in *process*. That is, attention to the sense of 'being upset about the cutlery' initiates a mutual process of 'being there'. The medium is the message. Such a process of 'being there' for 'what is' gives more permission to encounter other or related meaningful areas of concern. Such 'process relatedness' in a client constitutes a manner of being present, characterised by ways of knowing that are not following a logical sequence when one adopts an external point of view. The art of interpretation in psychotherapy too often serves to interrupt this 'process relatedness' by prematurely attempting to make content-sense out of the phenomena that are occurring. This is best done in retrospect in which a kind of content logic does appear. However, experiential sequence is related in a less linear way. As facilitators of experiential sequence, our theoretical understanding may sometimes help us, but more crucially our capacity to be descriptively present to the emerging phenomena serves the process better.

In the case I presented, the client began with a sense of loss of a friend and ended with a sense of hope that he would not drive people away if he was simply himself. It would not be difficult to construct a logical relationship between the content of these experiences. However, the path from the beginning to the end of the session was certainly a surprise to me. I did not know whether or how he would experience the joy of 'being in his own world', nor did I know how important this experience was as a process-related issue to the outcome of the session.

Such a recognition of 'process-relatedness' pays tribute to Husserl's notion of the 'life-world' as the preconceptually specific, vital matrix, or flow of happenings which any conceptual system refers towards.

In this way Husserl wished to ground our reflections. With reference to psychotherapy, we thus become concerned with assisting the client to become more faithful to her experience – to speak from this sense of being-in-a-situation. This involves a degree of 'closeness' to experience in which insights emerge from such a process. I am not excluding the importance of insight here, as it is an essential ingredient of our encounter with our world. However, I wish to contextualise insight as part of a larger rhythm of distance and closeness to our lived situation.

Client insights are thus a class of phenomena that cannot be willed; only facilitative context can be more or less given.

The total phenomenological process in psychotherapy is best conceptualised as taking place in the shared world that is progressively forged between therapist and client

If the therapist embodies a phenomenological presence to phenomena, he is not just a listening or non-participant observer. He allows himself to be affected. Such participation is far more holistic than theoretical understanding. It includes bodily sensation, sharing of images, and emotional receptivity to the phenomena encountered. The therapist appears to be required to 'heal' or 'move' the experience in him/herself if he/she is not merely to be rendered helpless or overwhelmed by the phenomenon. Psychotherapy in the phenomenological tradition is thus ultimately shamanistic in that the therapist draws on healing powers within and without. In the psychotherapy session a reference was made to how 'both Len and I dwelt with the mood of despair' when co-jointly present to 'an absence of a space where both self and other could be'.

In this case, something first moved for me in that I called on the gifts of childhood. Then something moved for Len in that he remembered experiences of enchantment. My access to what I call the 'gifts of child-hood', that is, playfulness and even a magical, non-logical conception of things, helped Len to find more of his own resources which were, in a sense, already there.

So it would seem that a psychotherapist within this perspective is not merely passive as an experiencer and witness of the client's phenomena. One is receptive, even bodily and emotionally, but may become active at times, supported by one's level of empathy. One's activities as a therapist are thus not merely theoretically informed but are grounded in a felt participation in the emerging experience. One's 'healing power' does not just reside in one's ability to reflect under-standing but more truly in one's contribution to the joint encounter with that which appears. Such active collaboration at least reduces isolation and at best facilitates new and supportive experiential processes.

It would thus seem that the use of the self (cf. Satir, 1987) is not merely a source of interpersonal learning for the client where the boundaries of an I–thou relationship may be progressively negotiated. Rather, a psychotherapist who values phenomenological process is not primarily centred on the vicissitudes of transference and encounter, but often transcends issues of the self and other. In this mode of collaborative presence, the client's experience becomes shared and thus moves from the 'smaller space' of isolation into the more 'confirmed space' of the 'between'.

The psychotherapy situation, in this conception is considered to be a joint venture in which neither the power of the therapist nor the power of the client is primary. In such a joint venture, neither therapist nor client is exclusively the source of the emerging reality. Both the therapist and client change in this process, and the work is done together. In some way, not only is the client called upon to account for the phenomena of depression, pain, finitude, confusion, and so on, but the therapist in each new situation is called upon to account for these phenomena as well. Although the contexts of these phenomena may be unique to the client, these phenomena involve structures of human existence that are not merely subjective. We participate uniquely in the modifications of human existence, and such general themes are both larger than us as well as uniquely and intimately experienced by us.

A psychotherapy that is fundamentally informed by the value of phenomenological process is less likely to result in finding simple 'answers', insights or solutions, and more likely to result in an experience of growing complexity that enhances personal identity

Van Den Berg (1974) has lucidly elaborated on the psychological implications of living in contemporary complex society. Since Freud's time, authoritative and traditional structures have broken down further. Thus psychotherapy in the modern idiom has to deal with multiple problems of self, society, and desire. In this context, the Freudian problems of psychological repression are often overshadowed by the more dizzy problems of meaning and lack of given foundations.

In modern times, mental health indeed seems to require more flexibility than previously. Psychotherapy would thus require something more than the appropriate expression of feelings or the attainment of rational thinking.

Phenomenological process facilitates openness to multiple profiles of existence. It speaks of Heidegger's notion of 'letting-be-ness' where we are called to be open for the ambiguities of life without too much reductionism according to our ego-oriented concerns.

In his book, *The New Gnosis*, Avens (1984) notes how both Heidegger and the archetypal psychologist, James Hillman demonstrate a phenomenological perspective to the multiple qualities of Being. Hillman explicates a polytheistic vision in which 'many gods' live in us and in the world. Each one is to be honoured in its realm and allowed to speak without being reduced to another. In a less imaginary language, Heidegger pays tribute to the pre-Socratic Greek world-view where Man/Woman is called upon to become open for the multiple profiles of existence beyond category.

Their implicit criticism about the way we often attempt to solve our problems is that we prematurely accept our narrow range of resources. In Hillman's terms, we could say that we do not have access to a fuller range of 'gods' or powers. He indicates, for example, that the power of Hercules proved impotent in the 'underworld' where the power of Hermes was more appropriate. Their suggestion is that we should rather focus on increasing our capacity for openness to a greater 'pantheon' of resources and support before feeling compelled to attack the 'dragon' with a water pistol.

The implications for psychotherapeutic practice are that we are more likely to value the facilitation of multiple experiences in the client as contributing to the 'widening' of the client's openness to existence, and are less likely to over-value the content of particular insights and conclusions. Such relativising of the content of insights acknowledges that something, which is true in one context, may not be true in another. This vision involves a 'process-conception' of mental health where harmonious co-existence of multiple ways of being crucially informs the content of the client's overall experience. Psychotherapy then essentially increases the repertoire and flexibility of the client's ways of being and, such multiplicity acts as more of a resource than more linear attempts to solve life's existential problems.

As an example of the facilitation of multiple experiences in the client and the widening of the client's openness to existence, I refer to the atmosphere of thickness in the consulting room with Len. In this process, Len experienced the ambiguities of a number of different moments of experience. At one moment, he felt independent, the next, dependent; at one moment he felt stoical, the next magically imaginative. Psychotherapy that respects such multiplicity does not seek to make the client prematurely commit himself to one of these ways of being as a solution to his existence. Rather it seeks to help the client to differentiate the complexity of psychological life in such a way as to find a valid place for all of them. Such differentiation promotes existential living; in other words, a living that is always more complex than any essential rules and regulations would prescribe.

If I wish to remain faithful to the experience of the session, I have to say that therapeutic movement had more to do with the movement of this thick quality than any specific insights that occurred.

The client's experience of growing complexity may thus provide a larger context within which questions and concerns often change before being directly answered.

The 'thickness' in the session was a feeling-description of the juxtaposition of images trying to find place and form. Thickness occurs with mixing, where 'substance' changes through fraternising. Thickness was the announcement of the 'between' and the intercourse of images. The therapeutic work progressed through even more thickening; of near and far, here and then, sleep and wakefulness.

> Mirrors shift. Valleys echo. The ten thousand things, confused for a moment, pause ...
> towards memory towards dream.

I thank the client concerned for permission to utilise this session. Identifying details have been omitted or disguised.

8
Globalisation and the Complexity of Self: The Relevance of Psychotherapy

I have been wondering about the future of psychotherapy in an increasingly plural and global culture and would like to share some emerging reflections based on my engagement in both theory and research. These thoughts have been informed by a number of related questions and contexts that I will need to touch on. They are:

- How culture and the nature of the self is changing through globalisation.
- How psychotherapy has evolved historically to essentially address problems of the self.
- How an empirical–phenomenological study of clients' experiences of psychotherapy may help to clarify the possible tasks of psychotherapy within an increasingly global culture.

In considering these questions and contexts, I would like to suggest that the essential task of psychotherapy will continue to be relevant in a more global world where the plural challenges of living 'in the borderlines' of multiple contexts pose both great freedoms as well as challenges for human identity.

1. Globalisation and self-identity

Although Ritzer (1993) has referred to the 'MacDonaldisation' of the world, other social theorists of globalisation have extended their analysis beyond the economic dimensions to consider its implications for our cultural experiences and sense of self-identity.

Within this spirit, Featherstone (1995) does not see a form of globalisation that results in a homogenisation of culture where tradition gives way to American consumer culture. Rather, he sees it as much more complex than that. In his book, *Undoing Culture: Globalisation, Postmodernism and Identity*, he provides evidence for multiple forms of mutual cultural exchange. In this view, there is a greater mixing and 'syncretism' of cultures that were formerly held as separate. He asserts:

- More people are crossing cultural boundaries than ever before and have multiple affiliations that question taken-for-granted stereotypes. The way that he expresses this is that more people live between cultures, 'on the borderlines'.
- There has been a shift in the global balance of power away from the West to the extent that it cannot now avoid listening to the 'other' or assume that the latter is in an earlier stage of development. (p. 12)

He concludes this stage of a much more detailed exposition by saying:

The process of globalisation then, does not seem to be producing cultural uniformity; rather it makes us aware of new levels of diversity. (pp. 13–14)

For the purposes of this chapter, we can leave him here and ask about the implications of such a trend for the practice of psychotherapy. In order to approach this question, we first need to take an excursion into the history of psychotherapy.

2. What the history of psychotherapy may tell us about its central task

Philip Cushman (1992), in a helpfully provocative interpretation, looks at how the history of psychotherapy is intertwined with the history of the United States of America, and characterises the psychotherapist as the 'doctor of the interior'. He claims that this can apply across a range of psychotherapeutic theories – psychodynamic, humanistic, self-psychology, and cognitive therapy.

In the context of the present analysis, I would like to agree with certain aspects of Cushman's argument, but put a different emphasis on his analysis of self. This difference in emphasis centres on the extent to which the psychotherapeutic task addresses historical issues and the extent to which it addresses more universal, existential issues.

I agree with Cushman's understanding of the popularity of psychotherapy expressed by him as follows:

> Psychotherapy is so accurately attuned to the twentieth century cultural frame of reference that it has come to provide human services that are crucial, perhaps indispensable, to our current way of life. (Cushman, 1992, p. 24)

As such, he sees psychotherapy as 'emblematic of the postmodern era' and insightfully traces various theoretical and practical developments in psychotherapy since Freud. He shows how these changes of emphasis mirrored nuances of concern in our postmodern culture – concerns that centre on the challenges of forging an individual self in a rapidly changing world.

He sees these challenges as having an essentially historical source, and therefore, psychotherapy as addressing these historical, essentially capitalist nuances. So, for example, with Freud, psychotherapy addresses a morally overbound self, with Winnicot and Kohut, a bounded, lonely self, and with humanistic psychology, an empty self. In these ways, according to Cushman (1992):

> Psychotherapists shape, maintain and heal the realm of the private that the modern era has located within each self-contained individual. (p. 22)

The problems of this self-contained individual with their different historical and cultural nuances can essentially be understood within the context of capitalist culture.

So Cushman sees the problems that psychotherapy addresses as being a fundamental product of a particular era. He builds on the work of Taylor (1989) in this regard, who characterises the self of the current era as bounded, masterful, and hypertrophied – a kind of self that is suffering from a condition of 'cramp' and 'contraction'.

In the development of this argument, Cushman also draws on Foucault (1980) to articulate the historical 'rise of the self-contained individual', and he pursues some of the dangers of such an individualistic agenda for mental health. Cushman sees the individualistic agenda of our culture as having

> resulted in moral illiteracy, confusion, isolation, loneliness and self-pre-occupation leading to the need for the social practice of psychotherapy. (1992, pp. 27–8)

So, in this view, psychotherapy is a practice that attempts to heal the 'illnesses' of this masterful, bounded self.

The difference in emphasis that I would like to put on this is to suggest that the central task or essence of psychotherapy, although addressing our current historical–cultural occasion, essentially addresses a more universal, existential dilemma that still applies in other cultures and other historical eras, though with different nuances.

The more fundamental, existential issue may be about the nature of human identity and the question of 'belonging'. This is a very old story and goes back to the mythological mists of various ancient cultures (for example, the story of Adam and Eve being thrown out of the Garden of Eden).

The existential question is: What am I part of; what is me, and what is not me? This is a question about the self, about how the part relates to the whole, the 'inner' to the 'outer'. And I would like to suggest that religion, the family, and community life has not been adequate to addressing this task in recent times.

Thus one may want to make a distinction between an existential, more universally human level, in which, as human beings, we have the question about the problem of belonging in common, and a cultural, historical level, in which the nuances of this task can emerge in diverse and even urgent ways. This can mean:

- There *is*, as Cushman suggests, a particular postmodern dilemma in the way we experience our sense of personal identity.
- But that, in facing this historical nuance of the overbounded, self-contained individual, we are also facing its deeper existential question of belonging – and that this dimension is transhistorical and transcultural.

So, what the history of psychotherapy may tell us about its central task is that it has been a secular way of addressing an existential task in ways that religions and communities did in other ways, in other times and places.

And it also tells us that the particular problem of self-identity is changing, that self-identity has become overbounded and too rigid, and that this has constituted symptoms of felt emptiness, isolation, and inner conflict.

We now turn to the results of an empirical–phenomenological study of clients' experiences of psychotherapy towards the end of the twentieth century. I do this in order to suggest that the essential experience of psychotherapy may continue to be relevant in a postmodern, increasingly global culture of 'living in the borderlines' where the personal tasks of belonging become even more complex.

3. Clients' experiences of psychotherapy

In this section, I have been extensively informed by the empirical–phenomenological study that I reported on in Chapter 5. However, here I wish to reflect on some of the implications of this study for psychotherapy within an increasingly global culture.

With this in mind, the phenomenological–methodological goal of the study of seeking an invariant structure of psychotherapeutic self-insight may provide some clues for considering what is still relevant about psychotherapy in relation to the increasing global challenge of 'living on the border lines'.

The concern with formulating an invariant structure involves a question about what makes something what it is. And this involves a description of its essential constituents and how these constituents interrelate to form a meaningful whole. The articulation of such 'essences' of the experience of psychotherapy is based on an analysis of particular concrete experiences that were lived through by psychotherapy clients. The value of such a methodology for addressing the concerns of the present chapter is that we are looking for transferable essences that may 'survive' changes in form. By understanding such essences, we could then imagine these essences still being able to occur in different historical and cultural forms. Thus the 'substance' of psychotherapy would not be attached to what it looks like from an external point of view, for example, two people sitting on chairs. The substance such as its intention, experience, and values could be expressed in different forms. This is what Husserl, the founder of philosophical phenomenology meant by 'imaginative variation'. That is, if we were to change this or that element, does it still retain its essence – what makes it what it is? So, for example, one could have many different kinds of tables, with different numbers of legs or no legs, but it could still have a surface of some kind to put things on. Thus, a 'surface' is one of the essences of what makes a table a table. It is the invariant structure that may tell us something about what can survive about psychotherapy in an increasingly plural culture and global world.

The empirical–phenomenological study was not carried out at the time to make a cultural or comparative point. Nevertheless, the psychotherapy clients who made up the informants of the study could be said to have lived 'on the borderlines' as articulated by Featherstone, earlier. They were people who saw in psychotherapy the potential to help them with struggles with the sense of themselves, issues of belonging, and who they were in relation to others and a wider world.

The ten people (six men and four women) who had been in psychotherapy for a minimum of four months were asked to describe a situation in psychotherapy in which they saw or understood something which carried a greater sense of freedom. All could recognise such an experience, and an analysis of their diverse experiences *did* reveal some invariant themes that tell us about the basic 'substance' or 'essence' of such an experience. As I described these findings in greater detail earlier in the book, I will here merely summarise them as a platform for a further discussion about the relevance of psychotherapy:

- Firstly, there is a personal narrative work that makes sense of personal identity – where one has been and where one is going, in the context of wider relationships with others, the world, culture, and sometimes God or a higher purpose.
- Such personal sense-making occurs through clients moving back into the concrete and specific details of their lives. Such details are credibly woven to form a patterned, meaningful story that makes sense of many things for them. The nature of the therapeutic relationship is such that it gives enough safety, permission, and freedom to honestly explore such personally credible sense-making. There is an emotional healing to such sense-making in that a greater sense of personal agency becomes clearer in the weaving of details and patterns – like seeing more about where to walk because one is on higher ground.
- Even deeper than this increased sense of personal agency, is the achievement of a more complex experience of their own personal identity, and this complexity constitutes the 'sense of freedom' that they were referring to when responding to the research question. The sense of freedom is essentially an experience of 'being more than ...'.
- Being more than what I had previously thought and felt.
- Being more than what I had said up till now.
- Being more than any premature judgement of myself – good or bad.
- Being more than any 'thing' of self-enclosed entity that reacts to forces and causes.

So the study revealed that, paradoxically, in returning clients to the concrete details of their lives, psychotherapy is a work of *un-specialisation*, of *de-role-ing*, a sense of complexity of personal identity that is 'more than' any definition can capture. Psychotherapy clients thus move beyond previous levels of self-enclosure and objectification. Such experiences of a more complex self credibly transcend premature self-definition – and it is this experience that may continue to be relevant in a postmodern, increasingly global culture.

4. Concluding thoughts

A world of living increasingly 'on the borderlines' as articulated by Featherstone, emphasises an existential dilemma in an unprecedented form. How do we achieve narratives of personal meaning in a historical situation where the givens of narrative, the centre does not easily hold – narratives of religion, community, and even science do not easily hold.

The results of this study would indicate that the psychotherapy clients were not primarily engaged in problems of the 'private interior' as Cushman contends. This is part of the story, but the task is more relational. It is not so much that, in psychotherapy, the private interior is 'protected, understood, cared for, healed, and made to thrive' (Cushman, 1992, p. 58). Rather, it is that psychotherapy engages in a more existential, universally relational task that is an ambiguous project of self and other. It is a work of personal meaning-making that requires more fluidity and more personal artistry than ever before, and which can be addressed by the following essences of psychotherapy, whether that term survives or not:

- A work of personal narrative that is experienced as true to the felt, concrete details of one's life that undoes premature specialisation and objectification of identity, and creates a space of some fluidity and freedom.
- A work of personal meaning-making that is complex enough to move and understand itself within a plurality of contexts.

How different cultures and the future will give different forms to these essences remains to be seen.

9
Freedom-Wound: Towards the Embodiment of Human Openness in Psychotherapy

I take my task here as a kind of weaving. I wish to throw the net wide and show how Martin Heidegger and Medard Boss have offered me an understanding of the human realm, and its grounding in Being that has intimately informed how I am as a psychotherapist. They have communicated this human realm, between sky and earth, not just in philosophically logical ways, but also in evocatively human ways that may be 'held' and embodied. It is in this spirit that I wish to use the term 'freedom-wound' in order to indicate and evoke what I will call the 'soulful space' of being human – how we are grounded in both great freedom and great vulnerability. Such ambiguity may describe the essence of a human kind of openness, and the lived understanding of such ambiguity may be shown to give direction to psychotherapy in the following ways:

- Such understanding welcomes psychotherapy clients to the human realm as wound and freedom. Such 'wound' and 'freedom' is not merely historical and social but is given, and can be taken up and lived in more welcome ways. There are 'wounds' and vulnerabilities that can be avoided or can be 'healed', but there is a great vulnerability that cannot. There are many freedoms that can be taken away or fought for, but there is a great freedom (with its responsibility) that cannot. An existentially oriented psychotherapy may give deep permission to clients to encounter and experience a kind of 'settling down' into these dimensions as they come through in the unique vicissitudes of their own life, and to take them up and live them forward.
- Such understanding sees so-called psychopathology as flights and distortions of the human freedom to which one is called and also as

the forms of refusal to the human vulnerabilities and limits that are existentially given. In this respect, one of the ways that Heidegger has served us is to indicate the relevance of grounding the understanding of human beings in a larger ontological context from which he/she is not separate. Such non-separation is the ground of a 'calling' beyond us yet intimate to us, and as such, cannot be fully understood by humanism, cognitivism, or psychologism. So-called psychopathology thus goes beyond psychology to the so-called spiritual and moral realms of our response to 'callings' that are not just 'within' our 'minds', but are 'there' in the mutual arising of being and beings.

Essentially I wish to articulate an existential stance of 'belonging to freedom-wound', also metaphorised as 'soulful space', between sky and earth embracing ambiguity. But first I will speak of 'belonging to freedom' and then of 'belonging to wound'. So, although the ideas are intricately interconnected, I would like to proceed by highlighting these emphases as a way of holding them apart in holding them together. I will adopt this artificial device in the following way:

- A focus on freedom. This section considers the kind of nothing that we are and how we objectify and turn self and others into 'things'.
- A focus on vulnerability. This section considers what has been called 'narcissism' and how we can refuse the call to embrace human vulnerability and inter-human vulnerability.
- Embracing ambiguity: between sky and earth. This section attempts to set out a holistic vision of the interconnection between freedom and vulnerability. The shape of such 'occurring together' of freedom and vulnerability is metaphorised as 'freedom-wound', and alternatively as 'soulful space'.
- Towards the embodiment of a human kind of openness. In this final section, I would like to honour the Daseinsanalytic understandings of Heidegger and Boss as giving direction to therapy, and encouraging a particular kind of invitational presence for the therapist to embody. I would also like to indicate, however, how an increasing focus on the 'lived body' and 'attunement' (which has its seeds in Heidegger and Boss) has nevertheless set me off in a direction with a somewhat different emphasis in terms of psychotherapeutic practice. This has to do with my increasing concern with the notion of a client's access to his/her 'experiencing-before-formulations' and the possibilities of client direction 'from there'.

1. Belonging to freedom

I would like to begin by quoting Heidegger (2002) from the Zollikon Seminars, the publication that documents his encounters with Medard Boss and psychiatry students. In these quotations I see the seeds of an ontological freedom that can be taken up ontically as a responsibility and task:

> Freedom is to be free and open for being claimed by something. (p. 217)

> Beings are and are not nothing ... [human being's] distinction and peril consists of ... being open in manifold ways to beings as beings. (pp. 74–5)

In the Zollikon Seminars, Heidegger claims that it is not that he wants to make philosophers out of the psychiatry students whom he is addressing, but that he would like them to become 'attentive to what concerns the human being unavoidably' (p. 115), even though this may not be easy to articulate.

In his encounters with psychiatry students in the seminar series over its 10-year history between 1959 and 1969, Heidegger summarises the essential insights of Being and Time, as well as the sense and spirit of his later work. Within this very broad context, which includes a consideration of spatiality, temporality, intersubjectivity, embodiment, and language, he speaks in a way that we never lose sight of a 'clearing' that makes all things possible. Indeed, as he says explicitly: 'Spatiality and temporality both belong to the clearing' (p. 225). In other words, space and time are not 'independent variables' into which all beings (including human beings) are slotted, but space and time are themselves shaped from the events of the clearing in which human existence intimately participates. He articulates these fundamental existential structures in more challenging ways: spatiality as the possible 'free and open' into which things can come; temporality as the possible then, now, and not yet which carries both continuity and discontinuity; embodiment as a 'bodying forth' of ways of being; discourse as the medium by which all things disclose themselves as something and interact in some. But even more fundamental than that is a 'clearing' which grounds these possibilities, making these possibilities possible. This 'clearing' is the 'something-eventing' rather than nothing', the 'is' that includes both the revealed and the concealed, and opens the possibilities of intimate participation.

This 'clearing' is not human consciousness as in an idealist fantasy of it: such a position would enthrone human existence and human consciousness as the source of all this. Nevertheless, human being, as dwelling ecstatically 'out there' together with beings and participating in the 'clearing' carries the essence of the clearing forward in intimate ways. To quote Heidegger:

> He is not the clearing himself, not the entire clearing, nor is he identical to the whole of the clearing as such. (p. 171)

Yet human being in his/her essence does carry an opening power that is enacted by his/her embodied perceptions and actions. This is the essential source of human freedom; not fundamentally in the freedom to choose or to act (which is nevertheless part of this freedom), but to be a domain of standing perceptually/receptively open to what is encountered, to be the 'there' of being (dasein). Why this can be called a kind of freedom is that it gives room to perceptions and meanings. It is a kind of freedom that both reveals and conceals, and which co-participates in the event of being. Living on the edge of time I occur as a gathering and am the 'there' for the coming together of possibilities and relationships that can be carried forward into the aliveness of something new. It should be emphasised that we are speaking here ontologically: this kind of freedom is something we *are* rather than something we *decide* to do or not – it is part of the essence of being human. To quote Askay (2001):

> Dasein can only be free in the sense of 'freedom of choice' because it is primordially exposed to the free and open dimension (that is, the clearing) of being in the first place. (p. 312)

Yet this is not an absolute freedom as if everything was inside an individual being's own personal consciousness, and as if there was no 'otherness'. Falling far short of totality, human openness means that it is an openness for ... and this involves an acknowledgement of being claimed by the concerns that come with such 'otherness' as well as the claims of one's own situated and embodied existence, its relationality, and the 'room' that both otherness and situated existence needs. So 'being there' is also a 'being there for' – it is essentially an opening that has 'care' as its nature.

Michael Zimmerman (1992) in a paper on ethics and responsibility articulated how freedom is not a human possession. At the ontological level, we 'belong' to freedom and can ontically take this up and authentically be of service to the task of freedom, which is to 'let beings be'.

Such given ontological freedom and responsibility to be the 'there' can be lived out ontically in different ways. There are multiple ways of being the 'there' and perceptually attuning to otherness such as in boredom, in anger, in sadness, in desire. In appropriating Meister Eckart's notion of *'Gelassenheit'* or 'letting-be-ness', Heidegger indicated something of the care-full possibility of freely standing in a serene welcome that allows beings their 'otherness' and their own freedom to be. This is the 'sky of welcome', the hospitality of home-rooming things and beings that can become themselves more and further. We will return to this ontic possibility of granting freedom based on its ontological foundation when we consider one of the dimensions of psychotherapeutic welcome a little later.

In considering this relationship between the givenness of ontological freedom and its ontic possibility of being taken up, I would like to move closer to a particular implication of the ontic experience of freedom: a freer and more 'spacious' sense of personal identity. This implication may give insight into one of the central liberating powers of psychotherapy.

In Chapter 10, with reference to spirituality, I will discuss in more detail the problem of self-objectification and its releasement, how we are always more than our contexts (also see Frie, 2003 and Zimmerman, 1981). In not being enclosed upon ourselves, human identity cannot be essentially defined in a 'thing-like' way. Human identity can never be finally objectified, it is essentially nothing. I will emphasise this dimension just for the moment even though it is far from the whole story. But as a counterpoint to a growing technological world-view which has found it useful to isolate objects and things, a meditation on our nothingness may help us remember how we may get lost in specialised, objectified views of ourselves. Such specialised, objectified views of one's own identity, if clung to too tightly, may forget the 'room to move' that the openness of being has granted us in our essence. In the forgetfulness of our primordial belonging, the need to belong does not go away, even if it means belonging to some 'thing', some general category, some specialised turning ourselves and others into grasped objects. This strategy of objectifying self and other has become particularly difficult to sustain in these postmodern times where the traditional narratives do not easily hold their centre, and where the task of belonging has become an extremely complex challenge.

In Chapter 5's phenomenological study of clients' experiences of psychotherapy, a picture emerged in which the complex story that unfolded between therapist and client constituted forms of self and world that were 'more than' previous self-definitions. This kind of self-insight was characterised as a direction which freed self-understanding from the objectification of self and other. One generic power of conversational psychotherapy may thus be to help clients recover their sense of human identity in ways that always transcend any form of objectification. Here, I would just like to highlight one component of this experience, that is, the nature of the 'sense of freedom' that occurs. As may be recalled, an invariant structure that was intuited was the experience of 'being more than ...' and, as such, of moving beyond previous experiences of self-enclosure.

But also, as may be recalled, such experiences of freedom were also experienced in relation to particular limits and restrictions, the 'from where' of freedom. 'Belonging to freedom' is thus inclusive of a complex historical experience; it is a situated freedom, and although grounded in nothingness, 'works' in relation to the immanence of 'this' embodied, historical situation. The metaphor 'between sky and earth' may then indicate something of the nature of a human, embodied freedom and not an imagined one that is merely 'beyond it all'. And here we come to vulnerability.

2. Belonging to wound

In talking of the claim of ontological freedom and the ontic experience of situated freedom we have begun to touch on the nature of a 'wounded' kind of freedom that forms 'soulful space', the human realm between sky and earth. But we have not yet come explicitly enough to articulating the existential nature of human vulnerability with its task of suffering and sojourning the human realm and meeting others there. Again I would like to start this section with Heidegger (2001):

> Dasein is that being whose being itself is at issue. (p. 124)

> Being human, as such, is distinguished by the fact that to be, in its own *unique* [my italics] way, is to be this openness. (p. 121)

There is a question and a certain quality of aloneness in this.

Just as a great freedom and responsibility is given with human beings' intimate participation in the clearing, there is a profound vulnerability that is given with human existence. The source of vulnerability paradoxically 'comes from' human beings' openness to the world to receive–perceive. And Heidegger has characterised this as 'care'. Zimmerman (1992) elaborates as follows:

> By defining the being of Dasein as care (Sorge), Heidegger emphasised that human existence is essentially concerned about itself, other people, and things in the world. (p. 60)

It is as if each of us is formed as a passionate question, an incompleteness that lives with us and to which we respond. This 'care' is incarnate in our flesh and shapes the ways that things come to us.

This is the 'wound of earth', of walking *this* path rather than *that* path, of loss and the possibility of not-being, of physical pain and the pain of not being at home, of being thrown into this circumstance, culture and time, of being situated and defined by self, body, others, language, and culture.

In living a human life we come with the seasons, with dryness and wetness, with the rhythms of darkness and light, of going away and coming back, of continuities and great discontinuities, with its janus-face of both potential anguish and renewal. Framing and permeating all this is finitude; there, in the possibility of not being, and there, in the fragility of flowers, in the beauty of a sunset, and in the passing of a smile.

I want to say that the essence of all this speaks of an existential vulnerability that is the foundation of its specific circumstances. And this is the 'wound' of human openness that grounds the experience of vulnerability. The very nature of the human sojourn carries an inevitable question: how to live with the implications of this wound that speaks of an unfinished self that cannot be irrevocably grasped, that speaks of temporal uncertainty, and that speaks of falling from the oneness of belonging. Far better to try and deny such vulnerability and to embark on a voyage of great refusal. And here we come to narcissism.

As will be elaborated on in Chapter 12, 'narcissism' as a psychological term has been characterised as a whole style of being-in-the-world that tries to defend against the great vulnerability of feeling needy and incomplete. Something of the understanding of such a possibility for living can be indicated with reference to the myth of Narcissus. Essentially, a beautiful young man becomes fixated and fascinated by an illusion: that his image in a pool of water can be grasped and possessed. He becomes enamoured with this surface image of himself to the exclusion of all other possible relationships. The core quest is to become at one with the beautiful picture. This story can be taken as a metaphorical indication of trying to avoid the vulnerability that comes with openness and relationality by pursuing a quest that tries to live as if it were possible to be in control of the source of 'otherness'. Like all of us, he finds himself in the human realm, feeling a sense of disconnection from an absolute guarantee of 'nourishment' and continuity. This is a state of vulnerable longing, of being in need, of feeling the ways we are not complete. So Narcissus embarks on the journey of great refusal. By binding himself to himself, he attempts to 'puff up' and maintain forms of self-sufficiency that strain against the spoiling of such self-sufficiency. The psychoanalytic tradition has been helpful in considering a number of strategies of living that are implicated in the narcissistic journey. These include trying to turn the 'self' into something 'objective' that can be held onto, into a beautiful 'thing' that is stable and admired, or into an ideal fantasy that is 'above it all'; of seeking others as 'mirrors' of one's wholeness and completeness, or of 'merging' or identifying with another or group who seem fixed, strong, ideal, or special. With different emphases and nuances, these psychoanalytic writers have indicated the different strategies of self-sufficiency: how to deny the acknowledgement of aging and death, how to pretend to be in the stance of 'I don't need'. In these ways the flight from openness, relationality, and vulnerability are pursued. The futility of this quest as an absolute possibility is finally indicated in Narcissus's mood of despair in which, in one version of the story, he kills himself.

The story also implies a different possibility, the existential task of embodying openness and vulnerability, the possibility of bearing this wound and even finding it as a gate and passage to that which is humanly possible and which I will metaphorise as 'soulful space', the intertwining of freedom and vulnerability. But before that I would like to indicate the gift of 'belonging to wound'.

This gift involves what Eugene Gendlin (1997a) calls the 'life forward direction' which may require an openness to what may come in vulnerability. In this vulnerable openness there is a leaning towards the life that is not yet, and the 'newness' of being touched by an aliveness that always includes the possibility of pain. This 'hunger' for what may come is not just towards the past, as if to be at one with a mother at the beginning, but rather a leaning into the matrix-not-yet, the freshness of what presents itself. In the flow of relational life there may be a nourishment of the play of home and adventure, the gift of belonging to wound. So there is an existential wound that one can bear that remains open and does not contract into self-enclosure.

The one from home is transformed by this adventure and such a 'self' is never self-enclosed but is always in the openness of relationships.

So we come back to freedom and towards the intertwining of freedom and wound in soulful space; the freedom of being incomplete; the nourishing brightness that can come in such unknowing, carrying with it the possible tenderness of the human space of welcome.

3. Belonging to freedom-wound: Embracing ambiguity in 'soulful space'

Belonging to freedom-wound, we are intimate with 'being-in' and 'being-with'. In these terms, the openness of being is not forgotten and the nature of such openness is *in* its 'withness' and *in* its 'in-the-worldness'. This may be taken together with Heidegger's (2001) earlier quote that 'beings are and are not nothing ...' (p. 74). Heidegger is indicating a 'being-open' that is never separate from 'being open for ...', the claims of one's unique situatedness. A further and more explicit quote from Heidegger (2002) takes this further:

> Now how is it with consciousness? To stand in the clearing, yet not standing like a pole, but rather sojourn in the clearing and be occupied with things. (p. 225)

Belonging to freedom-wound can translate into the ontic capacity to welcome historical incompleteness and human vulnerability. Ongoing participation rather than the survival of a 'fixed' self can become welcome. In such free participation one is changed *in* the participation, and thus one 'wears' the freedom to be vulnerable in an existential way. The mood of this is not just a serene 'letting-be-ness', but rather the moods of being moved and touched in many different ways at different times, the gift of wound. Through these moods and multiplicities there may also be the poignant taste of being willing to be the 'there', to be hospitable, and to be a unique place of gathering for a new 'showing' of historical eventing (Richardson, 2002). We could also put it this way: the recovery of our nothingness paradoxically empowers the freedom to be someone-in-particular and incomplete.

To bear and take up the marks of finitude in our own carrying forward, and the marks of another in our sojourn, brings us most fully to the characterisation of 'soulful space'.

In being 'more than' any way we objectify ourselves and in being 'more than' any way our contexts objectify us, there may be a sense of great space and freedom. However, freedom-wound is more complex than this. It is not just 'space' but a 'soulful space' in that the 'wound' of human unfinishedness is also embodied.

'Soulful space' takes its essence in human participation and historical relationality. Intimately within this sojourn, there is a mixing of 'what one goes through' alone and with others, the stretching of the seasons, and the specific vulnerabilities that is more complex than a 'serenity' of vastness. Rather, this is the taste of belonging between sky and earth, the 'we-feeling' of mutual vulnerability.

In living forward we carry the given freedom of 'more than' any objectification of ourselves and others, and in living forward we carry the given vulnerabilities of situatedness and finitude. We are able to say 'givenness' because we do not start with beings, but with the grounding of beings in being. Such belonging to freedom-wound provides the possibility of an intersubjectivity that grants both freedom and empathy; a 'soulful space' where we meet as fellow carriers of freedom-wound.

This human realm is thus an ambiguous space (Sallis, 1973) that includes freedom and vulnerability and other tensions of intimacy and aloneness, self-assertion and love, productivity and play, home and adventure. Within this context, so-called psychopathology can be understood as a flight from the openness of freedom and the refusal of human vulnerability. And here we come to the implications of such an embodied understanding of freedom-wound for psychotherapy.

4. Towards an embodiment of human openness

A question that now arises: how may an existentially oriented psychotherapy be informed by a lived understanding of 'belonging to freedom-wound'?

Heidegger traces the Greek roots of the word 'analysis' to also mean 'to loosen'. And this implies bindings. In this regard he has referred to metaphors of 'unravelling a woven fabric'. One could say that conversational psychotherapy in general addresses the repetitions and premature ways that we have defined others and ourselves. But more distinctively, the analysis of human being as a 'belonging to freedom-wound', places existentially oriented psychotherapy within an ethical context and conscience that is 'there', beyond the relation between drives and society. This 'calling' is something Medard Boss was very attentive to. He used it as a basis from which to understand psychopathology and as a basis from which to characterise the existential therapist's essential activity. I would like to briefly acknowledge these two contributions before moving on to my own increasing emphasis on the 'callings' of the lived body.

Psychopathology as truncated existential possibilities

Condrau (1986) has characterised the essential question in relation to illness as:

> *How* is a person's freedom to carry out his potentialities impaired *at any given time*; *what* are these potentialities; and with respect to *which* entities does this impairment occur? (p. 69)

By means of italics Condrau emphasises the words 'how', 'what', 'at any given time', and 'which' potentials. Thus, contained within this understanding of illness is how it is in relation to living forward, its context and meaning. One may say 'so far, so psychoanalytic ...'. But note that he is not as interested in the 'why' question – for him, a focus on 'why' is speculative, philosophically unsustainable, and may obscure the phenomenological presence to, and description of, the specific potentialities that cannot be carried out. It is in this spirit that Medard Boss, his colleagues, and students have studied and articulated the particular existential potentials that are truncated in different pathological forms. I cannot do justice here to these descriptions that have been pursued among other places in Boss's books: *The Content and Meaning of Sexual Perversions* (1949), *Psychoanalysis and Daseinsanalysis* (1963), and *Existential Foundations of Medicine and Psychology* (1979). Suffice to say that such a 'seeing' of specific existential potentials gives the 'illness' a direction and 'calling'. For example, Merdard Boss could recognise in the case of a sadistic pervert, the extremely frustrated desire to be at one with a lover, where the patient could only express the wish to devour and own (Boss, 1963, pp. 186–208). And here we come to the second important contribution, a contribution to practice:

Anticipatory care and the invitational presence to 'let be'

Boss saw in Freud's 'free association' the seeds of a practice that could be reframed within a deeper existential context. Initially, he was not as interested as Buber or the object-relations theorists in the phenomenon of interpersonal encounter in itself as the major focus for therapeutic activity. Building on Heidgger's notions of 'anticipatory care' and 'letting-be-ness', he wished to invite patients to become more 'open to' what addressed them as they dwelt with, and attended to, their experiencing. He understood how such 'experiencing' was not 'inside' and separate from the world, but always in the relational presence of the potential callings and claims of being-there, between sky and earth. In anticipatory care he thus had great faith that if he turned patients back towards 'themselves' rather than towards him, the relation between being and beings could begin to do its work of restoring existential possibility and the remembering of belonging to freedom-wound. The direction 'comes from there' and he deeply welcomes and gives permission to this possibility, even encouraging this direction by means of his 'why not' question. The therapist's attention in this mode is thus a listening for the healthy potential that is implicit. Such an attention is embodied in a certain kind of invitational presence and raises the question: How is it possible, accompanied by a lived understanding of freedom-wound, to represent such callings in a way that a client can authentically integrate and take up as his own? And here we come to a direction for practice that I have personally increasingly pursued with greater emphases, that of the 'lived body' as a primordial form of participative knowing in all this.

Therapist as experiential guide and existential companion

I am increasingly interested in what I would call experiential–existential psychotherapy. In my view, this focuses essentially on two things: firstly, the therapist's own existential presence to 'freedom-wound' that allows her or him to be a place of welcome and permission. And secondly, the therapist's ability to honour and facilitate the client's experiential process, moment by moment, as it is engaged in attending to the growing edges of her/his experiencing. It is with this latter concern that I have considered the notion of attunement, the lived body, and how experiencing becomes open to a vast range of implicit meanings and callings that move within our bodily relation to self-world-happening; and how language can serve such opening and appropriation.

This is a large subject and I would just like to indicate the central import of Eugene Gendlin's philosophy of implicit entry for psychotherapy.

Here, as in other important moments in this book, I am again indebted to Gendlin's exposition of how we are bodily in situations, and how we bodily know in ways that exceed any precise formulation or patterning of it. This place of excess is where meanings can be felt before they are thought. Such a 'felt sense' indicates a prereflective understanding of one's specific experience that functions intelligibly. Gendlin's elaboration of the practice he calls 'focusing' then involves attending to a 'felt-sense' that is bodily grounded and builds on Heidegger's understanding of how emotional attunement opens the world in different ways. But Gendlin notes that the 'felt sense' can include but is 'more than' than emotional attunement. Rather the bodily felt-sense functions as the background knowing of a situation-for-one-as-a-whole before lifting out or formulating its distinctions. Heidegger is indicating something similar when he writes of *befindlichkeit* as 'locating' or 'finding-oneself-in-relation'. Such self-finding in felt ways involves both an attention to the body as well as an attention to the *meanings* implicit in such a 'felt sense'. And making implicit meanings explicit needs language. So the lived body allows interactions and meanings to be felt from 'before' clear distinctions are made, from the 'more' of what is there. Such 'before distinctions are made' is the way the body 'carries' meanings. Such 'carried meanings' felt in the body are important for psychotherapy to engage with for two reasons: firstly, because it is the place where fixed meanings are carried, the potential repetitions of the past; and secondly, because it is also paradoxically the place where 'finding-oneself-in-relation' is potentially larger than these fixed meanings, thus providing a larger relational context and direction. In the 'more' of one's bodily 'felt sense', one finds both wound and freedom, embodied history and being 'more than'. So focusing on and languaging, both the fixed meanings as well as the possible directions within 'the more' of the felt-sense can provide the two central gifts of freedom-wound:

- The sense of personal agency that is given with the freedom of 'being more than'.
- The greater degree of self-acceptance that is given with the common vulnerabilities of an embodied human life.

So 'focusing' is both an embodied and languaged process that moves in the existential direction of freedom-wound. It provides a bodily sense of what we 'carry' but also provides a bodily sense of continuity with contextual potentials that 'come from' the relational vastness of being-in-the-world. Who knows how far this goes. Yet such gatherings are very specific. To quote Gendlin:

> Whenever we enter the experiencing of anything that is being talked about, we immediately find an intricacy with vast resources that goes beyond the existing public language. (Gendlin, 1997b, p. 37)

So this kind of 'locational dwelling' and 'self finding' presents both our 'carried' relatively fixed meanings, as well as the implicit 'moreness' from where fresh living-as-possibility and living-as-letting-be-ness can be constituted: 'freedom-wound'. The essence of deep psychotherapeutic change is then in the client's growing trust that is two-fold: firstly, through experience that he/she can be productively informed and nourished by her/his matrix that which is given with the lived body's capacity for a recollection of being: home; and secondly, through the experiencing of his/her capacity to take up and 'live forward' new meanings, fresh perceptions, and engagements: adventure. It is then no wonder that depth psychology has concentrated so much on 'mother' and 'father'. The increasing trust of an unmediated belonging to home and adventure empowers a sojourn that enters the complexity of 'soulful space' between sky and earth. Experiential–existential psychotherapy then holds fast onto the understanding that although one cannot walk for another, accompaniment is both possible and helpful.

While Medard Boss took Heidegger's existential of 'bodying forth' into the specific arena of psychosomatic medicine, how meanings may be lived or truncated, he may not have focused sufficiently on the implications of the lived body's attunement for psychotherapeutic practice.

In my view Gendlin provides a practice that emphasises an experiential knowing, a knowing by virtue of being, an intimate inhabiting, an 'embodying of the presence of things that is pregnant with meaning' (Ferrer, 2002, p. 122). Such bodily mediated intricacy is greater than conceptualisation. So, how as psychotherapists do we protect and facilitate this 'fertility' and 'generativity'? How do we honour and give phenomenological respect to the lived process by which languaging and embodying interact?

We are only on the way towards understanding the nature of the invitation to clients to bodily dwell with preseparated multiplicity, to be the practitioners themselves of 'how' they find words that carry forward presence, and of how therapists embody and language such service. For the therapist to be both a guide and a companion, this may be the challenge.

Part III Spirituality: Embodying Freedom and Vulnerability

This section on spirituality attempts to show how phenomenologically oriented thought approaches the tension between psychological and spiritual levels of discourse, finally locating human embodiment as the integrating 'place' where both human vulnerability and spiritual freedom can happen. Martin Heidegger, particularly in his mature writing, has been important in providing a poetic understanding of human existence that cannot be separated from its broader spiritual context.

Chapter 10 pursues a particular nuance of this integrating vision, the distinction between psychological and spiritual freedoms. The discipline of psychology has generally articulated a view of personal identity formation that is intimately grounded in interpersonal interaction. We thus become 'something', and this can easily lead to a feeling of being like an object, with all its securities, insecurities, and constraints. But is there a source of freedom from the objectification of such self-definition? In this chapter, I consider how Heidegger offers a counterpoint to self-objectification through a view of self that is an 'unspecialised openness'. The relationship between a specialised self-concept and this greater openness of identity is elaborated. This provides a framework for understanding psychological freedom as the achievement of more flexible definitions of self-identity (as that which often occurs in psychotherapy). But it also provides a framework for the more provocative task of understanding spiritual freedom as a fundamental insight in the 'nothingness' of self per se (as sometimes occurs within the context of spiritual practices or mystical experience).

Chapter 11 further develops this broad understanding of psychological and spiritual freedoms. It uses accounts of lives and interactions from the Zen spiritual tradition, as well as case studies from psychotherapy, to illustrate the kinds of self-insight that occur within these two contexts. With reference to the Zen tradition, the nature of the kind of insight that accomplishes experiences of spiritual freedom is illustrated. With reference to clients' experiences of psychotherapy, the nature of the kind of self-insight that accomplishes a greater degree of psychological insight is illustrated. The central concern of this chapter however, is how these levels of insight and experiences of freedom become integrated into one's everyday life. The phenomenon of 'tacit understanding' thus comes into focus as the way that both psychological and spiritual insights become embodied and lived. Such embodiment is a form of integration that has then become prereflectively tacit to functioning, and as such, lives more naturally without too much reminder or thought of it.

If Chapters 10 and 11 concentrate on the nature and possibility of the psychological and spiritual freedoms that may be given to human existence, Chapter 12 concentrates on an articulation of existential vulnerability as a crucial component of human spirituality. It does this by developing a phenomenological and existential perspective on what has been called 'narcissism'. The myth of Narcissus is used as a touchstone in order to understand the great flight from human vulnerability and thus achieve the omnipotence of self-sufficiency and exclusive self-love. This great refusal of the limits, 'unfinishedness' and relationality of human existence, is juxtaposed with an alternative path, one that welcomes and embodies existential vulnerability. The metaphor of 'soulful space' is used to name an existential achievement and an alternative response to the call of Narcissus. As such, the development of 'soulful space' provides human spirituality with a creative 'wound', and this provides a foundation for interpersonal empathy and care.

Chapter 13 comes back to the theme of spiritual and psychological integration in relation to current discourses within the field of Transpersonal Psychology. It provides a phenomenological perspective on transpersonal development as a dialectical movement between effortful discipline and realised 'grace'. Some implications of this paradox are taken forward to indicate a basic open and non-deterministic dimension of our depths that enters 'nature' and 'time' in unknown ways. In this view, we cannot compartmentalise the 'transpersonal' as something that comes later, or as a stage to be achieved. There do indeed appear to be 'stages' of integration but the transpersonal dimension is not a stage. Rather, the tension between the 'personal' and the 'transpersonal' is revealed from the beginning as constituting a fundamental existential ambiguity which is always calling. The chapter thus proposes an 'ambiguous focus model' of transpersonal development in which there is a dynamic tension in our sense of self between the possibility of 'non-separative being here' and more specialised forms of self experience and engagement. So there appears to be a tension between the 'personal' and the 'transpersonal' that functions in any moment and forms a deep motivation and creative tension in the human heart. The chapter concludes by indicating the lived possibility of sustaining the integration of focus on whole and part, unity and difference. In living such a focus the inner peace of such a wide embrace may come to visit.

Chapter 14, the concluding chapter of the book, attempts to offer four defining characteristics of embodied enquiry that may be seen to thread themselves through the book. Such a thematic integration, while acknowledging the company of seminal phenomenological thinkers such as Husserl, Heidegger, and Merleau-Ponty arrives at a position that is most informed by the philosophy of Eugene Gendlin. The chapter concludes by considering the central implications of an embodied perspective for the three topic areas of the book: emphasising the achievement of empathic understanding in qualitative research methodology, emphasising the facilitation of a more bodily grounded yet flexible sense of personal identity in psychotherapy, and emphasising the possibility of meeting mystery in palpable ways in spirituality.

10
Psychological and Spiritual Freedoms: Reflections Inspired by Heidegger

The theme of freedom is perhaps an important dimension of spirituality. But can we find a view of freedom that gives the person both a sense of transcendence as well as a sense of intimacy with the embodied vicissitudes of being-someone-in-particular?

This chapter exercises a particular interpretation of the work of Martin Heidegger as it throws light on the problem of self-objectification and its 'releasement'. This interpretation, which is based on what Michael Zimmerman (1981) calls Heidegger's 'practical–dramatic' theme, is developed in the direction of a more psychological language in order to clarify the notion of experiential wholeness and its appropriation in individuated existence. Thus, although I make reference to Heidegger's thought on a number of occasions, the central thrust of the chapter involves a personal reflection on the depth of human identity by a psychologically oriented person who has been inspired by Heideggerian thought. This reflection on the depth of human identity exposes a paradox in which the psychological notion of 'ego-strength' is enhanced by the experience of 'egolessness'. The nature of this paradox is pursued as an alternative to a conflict model which views 'ego-strength' and 'egolessness' as separate movements of development. As part of this task, the chapter also considers the relationship between two levels of freedom: psychological and spiritual. Examples from the practice of psychotherapy are utilised to distinguish a conception of psychological freedom from that which is considered to be the essence of spiritual freedom.

1. Vision

Martin Heidegger finally felt most at home with poetry. If one follows his philosophical development one can see how his concern always to speak of the mutual belonging of beings, things, and world led in this direction. In his appreciation of the poetry of Rilke and Holderlin, Heidegger (1971) heard a way of speaking in which depths of meaning were invoked by the remembrance of the interface and rhythm of things, where nothing occurs in isolation. He spent his life attempting to articulate some of the implications of this vision as a counterpoint to a growing technological world-view that found it useful to isolate objects and things and find 'independent survivors'.

It is in this remembrance of how things stand out, of how the 'thing' always speaks of things beyond itself (the peasant's shoe, of the earth), that his vision of human identity may be interpreted.

2. The rhythm of human identity

The emphasis of much useful psychology has demonstrated the centrality of the interpersonal matrix out of which a sense of personal identity emerges. We know ourselves through others. This dialogue of self and other encourages specialised self-perceptions. Here is the changing mirror of self-definition. This mirror displays a paradoxical challenge: to re-establish self-definition in changing circumstances. The call of the 'other' carries promise of new adventures; the excitement or fear of someone different, of new perceptions to be found. The 'other' is a demand or an invitation and calls for a 'yes' or a 'no'. The call of self-sameness, with all that supports it, carries promise of security, of being-at-home. This desire for a degree of continuity, of finding the 'familiar', is in creative tension with the call of the 'other'. Both calls never seem to cease and both calls support the search for a specialised perception of self or a sense of identity that would make personal choices and committed acts intelligible. Ongoing self-definition is thus a 'conversation' in which a Greek chorus is never too far away.

In living a human life we 'become someone' and live the rhythm of self-sameness and otherness. Within this rhythm there is always the dimension of a present self to uphold or a future self to attain. This rhythm may be viewed as one way of describing the destiny and formation of our specialised self-perceptions – a destiny which, without further recourse, can easily fall prey to a powerful self-misunderstanding and alienating motive; that is, the futile quest to objectify the self.

Heidegger would like to remind us of another potential rhythm which may be viewed as a rhythm of ontological depth. It refers to the possibility of remembering our unspecialised nothingness as a counterpoint to our specialised self-perceptions.[1]

In remembering the vanishing depth out of which self-definition is dialectically woven, Heidegger speaks of our fundamental and non-specialised perceptual openness to the world. In this view, human existence intimately participates in a 'spaciousness' or 'clearing' which gives beings and things a 'place' to be revealed and concealed. In characterising human existence as the 'shepherd of Being', he wishes to indicate that human identity is most essentially and radically defined by not being enclosed upon itself. It is thus most basically characterised by metaphors such as 'openness', 'lighting', and the 'there'. In this vision, human existence has its essence in its transcendence; it is being itself most when it is 'lost' from itself, 'there' for the things and beings that are. In its fundamental nature, human identity can thus never be finally objectified; it is essentially nothing.

Such nothingness does not refer to an experience of nothingness. In fact, Heidegger, in his concept of *Gelassenheit* or 'letting-be-ness' indicated that our essential nothingness, when uncomplicated by objectifying concerns, allows an experience that is more akin to fullness than emptiness. This is because the myriad meanings of the world can reveal themselves more fully to a perceptiveness that is not overly concerned with self-definition and the procrustean selectiveness of finding a world that is relevant to such specialised interest. In this context Heidegger thus speaks of the possibility of being simple in our presence to things, where the motive for self-finding disappears. It is here that he is most lucidly the philosopher of wonder and naivety.

In being discontinuous with the motive for self-finding, we are continuous with, or available to, a world which can show faces of interconnections that are new and not merely the specialised-world-for-a-specialised-self. In allowing our nothingness to be, we provide the space in which the world can show its open-endedness, its freedom. In granting things their free possibilities, we find a freedom at the foundation of our own identity; a freedom that is not merely the freedom to choose or decide, but the ontological freedom that provides space around our premature self-definition.

The claim to be made is that there is a nourishment to a rhythm of self-finding and self-losing in which both movements can be mutually supportive. Within this perspective, it will be shown that, paradoxically, 'self-losing' provides access to an experience of wholeness that is primordially 'given' to us and that excessive self-objectification ironically attempts to find a 'self' that can never be whole: ironic, because the very desire for self-objectification is grounded in a hope for wholeness. The notion of experiential wholeness is thus an elusive concept to grasp and it is to the development of this theme that we now turn our attention.

3. The source of the experience of wholeness

In its fundamental openness, the foundation of human identity is nothing-in-particular and this is not something that can be lost or gained as if it had an objective nature. It is whole in the sense that it cannot be divided as if we were put together as elements or bits and pieces. This level of wholeness is of a different order to the dilemmas of lack and fullness experienced through the limitations of situated life. It is a wholeness in regard to one's fundamental identity, that is, a 'centre' of subjectivity which is complete as an irreducible foundation to 'being there'. Wholeness, in this sense, is never something we can 'become' as we become a particular self or other. The issue of wholeness cannot be fundamentally solved in either of these directions. As regards this issue, we are deeply confused by our historical experiences of pain, separation, and threat in which an incomplete situation is felt to be an incomplete self. Thus the search for an objectified self begins.

The wholeness at the source of human identity is, however, always already there, obscured by the relentlessness of the quest to become something-in-particular. Tragically, we seek wholeness somewhere else, in the particularity of objectifying self and other. We can only become transparent to the wholeness we already are to the extent that we are relieved from the felt necessity to attain an objectified self from which to experience and act.

The problem is thus fundamentally not our wholeness; the problem is the relationship between our wholeness and our committed self-assertion and expression.

Specialised and committed self-expression is essential to human existence. We soon learn that we avoid making choices at our peril. Resistance to a fully human incarnated life in which we are historically and interpersonally situated results in a fundamental dishonesty, which constitutes the source of much psychopathology. Such a 'pattern of non-commitment' (Angyal, 1965) leads to neurotic cognitive and behavioural pseudo-attempts to avoid being someone unique and specific. One example of this pattern is where a person engages in obsessive and ritualistic activity which obscures his attention from the 'voices' of his more direct situation, where he may have to commit himself to a need or course of action for which he would prefer not to be responsible. It would thus constitute a tragic destiny if one felt that the recovery of our nothingness and sense of ontological freedom required the avoidance or eradication of being-someone-in-particular.

On the other hand, specialised self-binding without access to the nourishment of unspecialised self-possibilities also constitutes forms of psychopathology; psychopathologies of boredom, alienation, and ennui which are increasingly becoming the signs of the times. Psychotherapy patients are presenting less often with traditional symptoms and more often with a global sense of meaninglessness and deadness. Such a syndrome constitutes the lack of vitality that is inherent in the excessive objectifying of self and other.

We are thus looking for a mutually inclusive relationship in which self-finding and self-losing are not necessarily contradictory tendencies. Indeed, an attempt will be made to show that these capacities may mutually support each other in a way that may enhance mental health and human functioning.

In pursuing this problem, namely the experience of wholeness in the midst of self-definition, the question may be more fruitfully posed in terms of temporal metaphors of movement, access, and rhythm rather than spatial metaphors of structure and state.

4. The ontological and the historical

The Psychoanalytic Movement, culminating in the theoretical sophistication of Jacques Lacan (1977), acknowledges a profound sense of loss of the experience of wholeness at the centre of individuated life. This tradition would see the loss of wholeness as an event of personal history in which oneness with the mother constitutes the original wholeness. As soon as we use the mother as the prime metaphor for wholeness, we are tempted to also see the futility of such wholeness, as the inevitable separation is visualised. We then focus our psychodynamic understanding on the dilemmas of further historical and interpersonal bindings and separations.

It is easy to see how we, in our psychoanalytic thinking, confuse the source of wholeness with 'mother' rather than the ontological and undivided nature of our nothingness at the centre of identity. We may understand the depth of our 'countertransference': because we in our personal history may unconsciously confuse the loss of our wholeness with the loss of unity with 'mother', we will also confuse the source of our wholeness in our psychoanalytic theory. It is a confusion of different orders: the ontological with the historical. Further exploration of the difference of these categories may prove fruitful.

Within a materialistic world-view, it is tempting to envision the source of the experience of wholeness or completeness in the light of a physical occasion or circumstance – that is, historical fusion with mother. There is thus a wholeness or completeness that is based on circumstance. But is the experience of wholeness fully described by this circumstance? In other words, is the answer to the question, 'what is it about the nature of humankind that makes the experience of wholeness possible?' the fact that we 'come from' our mothers? The source of the experience of wholeness may more centrally be envisioned to 'come from' our essential unobjectifiable nature. Although psychoanalytic writers have speculated on different qualities of undifferentiated experience in infancy, it is asserted here that the wholeness of our unobjectifiable nature is best described in an ontological context rather than in a historical context.

The experience of completeness or wholeness in such a context is thus of a different order to the completeness envisioned in the occasion of infancy.

The sense of completeness that is felt when 'we' are transparent to our non-objectifiable nature is not a completeness in the sense of being infinitely nourished by a mother – endlessly protected from changing states and suffering. The completeness that 'comes from' one's nothingness is not the finding of a *situation* of completeness – it is not a completeness in which suffering is avoided – but the completeness in which the seeking for self-as-object is recognised (at different levels of implication) to be unnecessary. Such completeness is markedly different from a completeness that is sought in objectified forms.

It is suggested that access to such a sense of completeness can live side by side with the essential ongoingness and incompleteness of historical life. The non-confusion of these two levels, the ontological with the historical, constitutes the basis for a relationship that is paradoxically supportive. That is, access to a sense of ontological completeness supports the fuller acceptance of historical incompleteness and human vulnerability. Because one is not essentially seeking completeness in the impossible vicissitudes of the past, present, or future occasion, one is more fully here – incarnate in all the things that confront one.

In order to elaborate this point in traditional terms, one could say that 'ego-strength' partially involves the capacity to accept historical incompleteness and human vulnerability, and that 'egolessness' involves the sense of completeness inherent to the unspecialised openness of being there. In terms of this exposition 'egolessness' is then a powerful source of 'ego-strength'.

One or two other implications of this relationship may be noted with reference to perception and the content of experience.

When we are transparent to our nothingness, we do not find a 'self' as an object of experience; we find the 'world' in the sense of being turned 'without' rather than 'within'. Such a world 'without' is not just the 'objective' world as defined in a Cartesian sense. Rather it is a world, which constitutes depths of relationships beyond purely objectified concerns; it has a depth beyond the narcissistic reduction to the 'known'. It is thus not a nothingness, which turns away from the interpersonal realm. Indeed, in such a remembrance, one will objectify others less. This constitutes the possibility for a more human form of relatedness, a form that provides 'shape' to the experience of intimacy and aloneness. Such an access also constitutes forms of perception that are more naive[2] than the specialised perceptions constituted by objectifying motives. This does not mean that the world 'as it really is' is found to be 'one thing' as in the objectifying fantasy of it. But such naive perception does involve an openness to new configurations of meaning in which ongoing participation, rather than the survival of the self-concept, is emphasised. As an identity one is in actuality more of a question than an answer, supported by what we bring and what has been brought.

5. Self-objectification and its release

The question still in mind: how can the ground of our identity, which is our essential nothingness (that is intrinsic to us right now rather than lost in an exclusively historical sense), become transparent to us in the midst of individuated life? How can such nourishment be regained?

In order to approach this question, some more distinctions about the nature of specialised self-formation need to be made. It involves the distinction between a specialised self-concept and specialised self-capacities.

Our specialised self-concept, that is, the specialised view that we have of ourselves is always more restricted and prematurely fixed than all the potential memories, capacities, and historical experiences that make up our specialised self-capacities. Formation of such specialised self-capacities in themselves is not the power that obscures the nourishment of our nothingness. It is not such capacities that essentially exclude the freshness of perception that our simple presence brings. Rather it is the relentless activity of our self-concept that binds naive perception. Naive perception, as the child of our nothingness, becomes obscured by a confusion of status. Rather than naive perception being more fundamental than specialised perception, the self-concept, fuelled by its greedy motive of appropriating all to itself, assumes itself as the legitimate foundation of perception. In this act, it denies its ground and embarks on the pseudo-search for a nourishment it is always negating. The sense of loss at the centre of the specialised self-concept motivates a search for wholeness. But the search for wholeness is sought by specialised perception; a futile and reductionistic quest.

Excessive reference to premature self-definition as a foundation for perception becomes implicit to psychological life. In encountering the world, we thus 'begin' from these implicit references rather than 'begin' from the indeterminate openness of the situation with the benefit of secondary access to our historical references. The confusion of status refers to the ordering of two phases of psychological movement: our simple presence to things and the specialised relevance of things. The specialised relevance of things becomes the foundation of perception, motivated by the need for security where the self-object is supported. Understandably so; almost inevitably so, as the pains and the threats of our historical separations have overwhelming power to determine the felt necessity for self-objectification.

If the picture is beginning to look rather bleak, fortunately there is another side to the story. If the objectifying tendency of self-definition is relentless, ceaseless in its efforts to pull itself up by its bootstraps, the object-transcending tendency of our fundamental nothingness is also relentless, constantly threatening the self-sufficiency of specialised self-perception. Such a non-linear rhythm most commonly constitutes a tension and lives in the following way:

Intrinsic to the structure of a specialised self-concept and its limits on perception is a 'voice' that undermines its self-sufficiency. Such a voice is the 'conscience' of our nothingness; it reminds us of our exile. When the experience of such fundamental loss is listened to but misunderstood, its form becomes symbolised and grasped in terms of personal and mythological events and themes; and an intelligible story emerges which attempts to name or capture the experience. Thus, for example, we may symbolise such loss in the events of our childhood, which, no matter how much they provide further occasion for loss, do not fully speak to the loss of which we are talking. So too, we may symbolise our loss in the form of the 'archetypal' patterns of partial ways of being such as the 'persona and the shadow'. Although such metaphors may remind us of the direction of our 'home', such collective themes, if classically used, may themselves become objectified and serve anew, albeit more flexible, self-object to be grasped. In this regard, the voice of our nothingness is relentless and would sacrifice all the 'gods' as they turn one into another, finally acknowledging the lack of substantiality at the centre of their existence.

However, listening to any symbolisation of our fundamental loss constitutes a re-evaluation of the primary status of the self-concept as foundation of perception, and to this extent, the symptoms of our alienation become less severe.

Such a course is better than the other response to the conscience of our nothingness. This other response involves the severe self-misunderstanding which has already been described as the futile attempt to seek wholeness by intensifying the objectifying of the self, as if wholeness can be successfully reduced to take on specialised form. One example of this futile quest would be the vicarious attempt to achieve a more 'complete' or better self by denying aspects of one's unique situation and attempting to become like someone else through self-control and vigilance.

The destiny of intensifying the objectification of self as response to our sense of incompleteness tragically increases self-fragmentation with its symptoms of confusion and lability. Within such a destiny, many selves-as-objects that are 'within' one clamour for validation and survival. In various stages of response, such a person may feel the uncanny discontinuity of these different self-objects and experience annihilatory anxiety or emotional impotence.

The most direct response to the whole problem involves the clear recognition of the perceptual limitations of specialised self-presumptions and a commitment to *Gelassenheit* or 'letting-be-ness' where naive perception born out of our nothingness may begin to be recovered.

This 'returning', where an implicit commitment is made to the primordial status of our non-objectifiable nature, initiates a new rhythm in which self-expression is in greater dialogue with non-specialised perception. The rhythm of nothingness and self-expression can thus live as either an ambivalent tension or a mutually supportive rhythm in which the self-concept is willing to 'bow down' to naive perception. Specialised self-expression uses all its historical capacities, but is informed and nourished by its open ground. This gives the person a degree of flexibility and spontaneity of thought, feeling, and action she otherwise would not have. In this rhythm, the self-concept may or may not find itself as self-sameness. But the person does not feel threatened as a greater nourishment is trusted.

It is important to note that such fixed-identity transcendence does not, therefore, mean the obsessive or fearful avoidance of self-expression with all its historical continuity. In fact, one feels freer about representing such identities because of their ontological non-centrality. Becoming someone-in-particular is less tentative because there is not as much at stake compared to a position where the 'ego' as a fixed identity is to be irrevocably achieved. Indeed in the latter case, becoming someone-in-particular may be avoided because of its non-playful and anxiety-laden implications.

If the remembrance of our non-objectifiable wholeness were sought through the process of psychotherapy, the unique elaborations of self-objectification would be increasingly recognised in personal and perhaps mythological contexts. Thus, the recognition of repetitive personality structures can point to their transcendence. Such greater freedom in turn contextualises existing personality structures within a more playful context. For example, one person may realise that he is still living as if identified by parents as an 'over-demanding child'. This identity may still be lived out in the form of guilt in which his emotional needs are repressed in adult relationships. Realising this, he feels less guilty when asking for support and he is not necessarily a 'demanding child' when doing this. Such freedom in turn opens up other ways he can sometimes be a child – such as in being spontaneous or astonished. An example of a mythological elaboration of self-objectification is where a person realises that he has been living like Athena, always preparing for battles and government, far away from home where Hera contemplates the hearth. What is important here is how these patterns still live in us rather than the full recovery of their earlier occasions. Such psychological themes with their myriad responses are many and constitute a complicated series of modifications of the fixating potential of human identity. Without access to 'self-losing' such fixation and self-objectification becomes self-reinforcing. Psychotherapy which focuses on our uniquely situated and historical formation reminds us in vivid and compelling ways about the depth of our objectifying activities, with its many levels of coherent organisation in different areas of life – how we did (do) it and how it was (is) done to us – and we begin to discover a context or series of stories which make our unique forms of objectifying unworkable and unnecessary.[3] In such a process of discovery we have, in a sense, lost ourselves in the release of a particular form of self-objectification. The ever-widening story that unfolds between therapist and client thus co-constitute forms of self and world that are less fixed than previously.

The process of psychotherapy does not, however, facilitate such a direction in an amorphous manner without reference to the historical and thematic details of the client's unique situation. Such uniqueness is paradoxically given increasing strength and flexibility by the kind of self-finding that is based on self-losing; a 'finding' whose validity is revealed by naive looking rather than asserted and defended by specialised concerns.

In such a rhythm there emerges an increasing willingness to be somebody and to not be somebody, and this gesture is implicitly learnt in psychotherapy. However, this is not necessarily the central goal of most psychotherapies, nor should it be. Such an issue involves the difference between psychological and spiritual freedoms. But it may help to remind psychotherapists of the way their specialised concerns limit the depth of such an experience in their clients, and to be more sensitive to the call of nothingness 'within' the client.

6. Psychological and spiritual freedoms

In the process of psychotherapy, one can have an insight into the restricting power of one's particular organisation of self and world; perhaps how it came into being and something about the power which maintains it. One can also have an insight into the possibilities for living, which this structure has obscured and perhaps feel a more unambivalent invitation to embody some of these possibilities. Such specific forms of self-insight pave the way for actualising a more flexible self-perception, perhaps one more in accord with the freedoms and limits of human existence.

Although such an insight is made possible by our intrinsic nothingness, it is not necessarily an insight about our nothingness; that is, the structure of our identity as a whole. There is a profound difference between the kind of insight that allows us to grasp a more flexible self-as-object and the kind of insight that relieves the quest for object-seeking per se.

Although in the specific insights of psychotherapy there may progressively be hints and echoes of the structure of human identity itself, such an insight is not necessary for the occurrence of specific self-insights into one's particular situation. In fact, it is suggested that most psychotherapeutic orientations successfully manage to operate on the basis of a self-misunderstanding; a self-misunderstanding about the ground of identity based on a Cartesian world-view. Such orientations are successful because they usually have flexible visions of human identity, at least more flexible than the ones by which their clients are living, and this allows significant healing to take place. However, it may be conceived that the co-constitution between therapist and client could structure a more flexible 'self' that is nevertheless articulated in such a way as to obscure the further call of one's nothingness. For example, in a situation of psychotherapy a client may become preoccupied with the fear of death. The therapist may focus excessively on the historical losses in the person's life as an important component of the fear. In this process the client may become freer concerning the unambivalent mourning of loved ones. This is undoubtedly helpful but would be limiting if it were felt that the meanings of the 'call' to attend to the themes of death were exhausted by these historical meanings.

Such degrees of psychological freedom do not thus necessarily lead to what will be called 'spiritual' freedom, that is, the freedom from the necessity for objectification of self, other, and world. This kind of self-insight, however, does appear to have a relationship to the growth of psychological self-insight. Even in the Zen tradition where spiritual self-insight is directly and radically pursued, there appears to be a relationship between one's degree of specific and situated self-insight and the readiness for mature spiritual self-insight. Breakthroughs of one's 'original nature' although occurring at different developmental states, appear to be most stably remembered and 'lived from' when they occur in a particular context; a context where a person has achieved a degree of non-preoccupation with uniquely personal and historical issues which would otherwise only be relentless (implicitly or explicitly) in their need for attention. If this were so, then the 'spiritual' quest would be insidiously misunderstood by the limits of a particular preoccupation. Thus a person who is phobically avoidant of personal commitment could use the 'language' of spiritual freedom to support his neurosis. Clear differentiation of these kinds of freedoms is thus important, and more work needs to be done specifically to articulate their relationship and relative modes of action (Engler, 1984).

In conclusion, suffice it to say that a non-linear rhythm of human identity, of self-finding and self-losing, may provide a vision that contextualises the possibility for both psychological and spiritual freedoms. In such a context, the psychotherapeutic and spiritual traditions could sit down with Heidegger and remember the forgetfulness of Being.

11
How Does Liberating Self-Insight Become Tacit Understanding?

One of the concerns of a more embodied spirituality involves the ways in which experiences of freedom come to be integrated and lived within one's everyday life.

This chapter attempts to clarify the question of how liberating self-insight becomes tacit understanding. I hope to show how the terms used in this question are useful and that they are able to clarify experiences that are central to both psychotherapy and spiritual awakening. The approach taken can broadly be called phenomenological in that the seamless flow of everyday experiences is used to give substance to concepts such as liberating self-insight, tacit understanding, and integration. Descriptions from two sources are used – from the reported lives of well-known Zen masters and from experiences of clients in psychotherapy. Regarding the former I draw heavily on the biographical accounts of Zen masters that are summarised in the book *Crazy Clouds* by Perle Besserman and Manfred Steger (1991). The vignettes from psychotherapy are taken from my PhD thesis on self-insight in psychotherapy (Todres, 1990) and have been modified to exclude possible identifying details.

The broad question is concerned with how insights that occur in psychotherapy or spiritual awakening may become integrated into one's everyday life. The pursuit of this question is assisted by an enquiry into a number of related questions:

- What is liberating self-insight?
- Is there a difference between the kinds of liberating self-insights that occur in psychotherapy and those that occur in Zen enlightenment experiences?
- What is tacit understanding?

The chapter concludes with some thoughts on how Jung's notion of the transcendent function is useful in furthering our understanding of the awakening of consciousness.

1. What is liberating self-insight?

A number of philosophical traditions such as Buddhism, postmodern thought, eco-systemic theory, and existential phenomenology (see Wilber, 1995) have pointed out in different ways how the 'self' is different from a thing. In the previous chapter I reflected on how Martin Heidegger unfolded an ontological perspective in which the rhythm of human identity is not just defined interpersonally, but participates in a vanishing depth that is fundamentally open, that it is most radically and essentially defined by not being enclosed upon itself, and that, as such participates in an ontological dimension of freedom.

This kind of consideration sets the scene for defining liberating self-insight as a *direction* that frees self-understanding from the objectification of self and other. How deep can this go? Well, very deep, if we take the life and thoughts of the Buddha seriously: deep enough to look at each other without conclusion, open to what is arising as if for the first time.

However, there appears to be a difference between experiences of such a direction that commonly occur in psychotherapy and those that occur in Zen enlightenment. In psychotherapy, a person may have an experience in which the way one has become defined becomes more flexible so that new possibilities of living and feeling can be accommodated. For example, in psychotherapy, Michael realised that he always responded to criticism as if he deserved a reprimand. He had not realised before how much he was living according to a definition of himself in which he was stuck in time, as if still responding to a critical mother. He became aware that he had developed a 'self' in which he attempted in many ways always to be beyond criticism. For example, he was often preoccupied with the length of his beard and the cut of his suit. This insight helped him realise that he need not live and act as if he was still standing there trying to be perfect. The direction of this self-insight was a shift in personal identity in which he became less objectified as the 'potentially reprimanded one'. So his identity became less fixed, and he embraced a greater ambiguity in situations and began to learn a balance that was neither self-demeaning nor overly self-assertive.

However, although such an insight was made possible by his intrinsic nothingness, it was not an insight about his nothingness, that is, the structure of the depth of his identity as a whole. There is a profound difference between the kind of insight that allows us to grasp a more flexible self-as-object and the kind of insight that relieves the quest for self-definition per se. And here we turn to the Zen tradition.

After serious Zen study and practice, Layman Pang encountered Baso with the question:

> 'What kind of man is it that has no companion among the thousand things?'
> Baso said, 'Swallow up all the water in the West River in one gulp and I'll tell you.'

Layman Pang experienced an opening of identity. Into what? Nothing in particular. Implicit here are some of the principles of the Buddhist tradition – interdependence, emptiness, no boundary. Yet even these words did not define him or his experience.

This kind of self-insight indicates a shift in personal identity not just to where a person is less defined than previously, but to where self-definition is not possible, to where it does not exist. In this phase of experience the emptiness of self is emphasised.

In a period of great social inequality, Rinzai talked of the 'true man of no rank'. Likewise, after much searching and committed meditation, Bankei was suddenly struck with the insight that 'all things are resolved in the unborn'. These experiences indicate a vanishing depth of personal identity in which one finds oneself with the birds and the trees, and even then: what is this? No clinging to self high or low. We may thus be ready to define liberating self-insight as an understanding which allows personal identity to shift in a direction that is less restricted by one's previous enacted definitions. In the case of psychotherapy, this can lead to a more flexible self-concept: one more in accord with the limits and freedoms of human existence. In the case of spiritual practice, this can lead to a fundamental re-evaluation of personal identity as a whole, where the boundaries of the self are experienced as 'convenient fictions' and understood as empty of independent existence. Liberating self-insight in this view is thus a wonderful solution. But in our lives it is also a problem and it is to this problem that we reluctantly turn.

2. When things are either/or: The problem of dissociativeness

This problem refers to how someone can have a self-insight that does not appear to make a difference to the way he or she subsequently feels or lives. The term 'dissociation' is used here, not in the narrow psychiatric sense, but in the broader way in which Wilber (1995) used it, to indicate a failure to adequately integrate emergent differences.

During psychotherapy, Sharon was exhilarated to realise that she had been living as if her older sister were a parent and that this need not be so. Her personal identity had been bound up excessively with either trying to please her sister or rebelling against her. This insight liberated her to acknowledge strengths within her that were independent of her sister's judgement. This more flexible identity functioned to allow her to live a more independent life. However, this emerging independent identity functioned best when she was not in her sister's company. When with her sister they would fall into old mutual roles where her sense of strength was obscured by a sense of helplessness and frustration. It took time for her to apply her more flexible sense of herself to a number of specific situations. Her insight, even though she lost the full impact of it, became rooted enough to serve as a reference point by which new skills could be learned in specific situations. So she had to learn the nuances of things like 'Where is my strength when my sister flatters me?' or 'When do I sometimes allow dependence on her?' The moral of the story? Liberating self-insights can occur generally, but do not always function locally. Or as the Zen idiom says: 'Where is your Zen when you tie your shoelace?'

Ikkyu, a Zen master of the fifteenth century, was uncompromising in his demonstration of freedom, metaphorical homelessness, and no place to stand. He vociferously rebelled against the Zen institutions of his day, calling his brethren 'phoney monks in cow skirts'. When Ikkyu's Zen teacher was asked who his successor would be, he referred to Ikkyu by saying, 'it will be the mad one'. It could be said that he did not fit in. There are numerous indications in his utterances and deeds that he represented the essential emptiness of self and world. However, it was only when he was 77 and settled down with his blind lover who was in her late 30s that there are indications that he significantly integrated his freedom with the specific complexities of leading an interpersonally confirmed life. Towards the end of his life, Ikkyu commissioned a portrait of himself that indicates something of this integration. He is painted in a grey, empty circle denoting the essential emptiness of things, while his lover, Lady Shin, is dressed in professional finery and playing her musical instrument. This vignette should not be taken to value either absolute or relative values over each other, but rather raises the possibility that experiences of emptiness of self can remain dissociated from the world of form and mutual definition.

After a deep enlightenment experience Hakuin attempted to have his experience confirmed by a well-known Zen master, Dokyo Etan. In answer to a well-known koan from Dokyo, Hakuin responded: 'In Joshu's *mu* there is no place to put hands or feet.' Fair enough: swallowed the river. Dokyo immediately grabbed Hakuin's nose, gave it a good twist, and laughed saying: 'I found some place to put hands and feet.' Dokyo then continued to give him a hard time to prod him out of his 'emptiness addiction'. The general point is that in human development and spiritual awakening, dissociation happens. It happens after achieving more flexible self-definitions in psychotherapy and it happens after experiences of no-self. So if such experiences are only part of the story of awakening what else do we need to consider?

3. What is tacit understanding?

The notion of 'tacit understanding' is explored in order to indicate a form of functioning by which an insight or learning has been integrated into a person's everyday thoughts, feelings, and actions. Philosophers such as Michael Polanyi (1996) and Hubert Dreyfus (1972) have penetrated deeply into how we learn very specific things like riding a bicycle or playing chess. Although different terms are used such as tacit knowledge, intuition, and implicit understanding, such authors are concerned with the application or functioning of knowledge in our everyday lives. In this vision we are not disengaged cognitive beings who have learned the rules of operating and then apply this to concrete situations in a pre-given world. We are seldom that separate or knowing-in-advance. Also, the world is seldom something objectively there, independent of how we reveal it.

In this regard Merleau-Ponty (1962) has indicated how we belong to the things we learn and how knowing is only one productive phase in which we distance ourselves from something in order to find a new relationship to it. For example, in learning how to relate to an elephant, what is it enough to know? The most fundamental things are taken for granted – that we share space, move with gravity, and have outsides and insides. In a certain sense, we belong together. As we learn about elephants, we learn helpful details such as when they need to eat and sleep. We develop discrete bits of information about them. But ultimately no amount of learning these discrete bits of information is sufficient for learning how to relate to an elephant. This is because, as Merleau-Ponty noted, perception and understanding are not based on our capacity for picking up rules but rather, on ongoing participation in which constant living adjustments are made, often before they are understood. We learn as participants, and the known (as approximate style rather than definitive bits of information) is in constant dialogue with the surprise and unknowingness of perception and participation. So what are the implications of this for liberating self-insight? Just this: that an experience of liberating self-insight does not necessarily function in specific situations, and that although a liberating focus has occurred, it may not yet belong or be tacit to a person's complex functioning in everyday living.

In noting five stages of skill acquisition, Dreyfus and Dreyfus (1986) write about the level of expertise in which we are intimately familiar with a situation where the specifics of the situation is tacitly informed by a background context of understanding that operates spontaneously without us having to remember or be conscious of the principle on which it is based. As they so succinctly put it, 'we seldom "choose our words" or "place our feet" we simply talk and walk' (Dreyfus & Dreyfus, 1986, p. 32).

In psychotherapy, Shirley experienced a number of self-insights in which she understood that a deep sense of mistrust of others had been necessary when she was growing up, but was not necessary in her present life. This was a relief for her, and her sense of personal identity was experienced in a more complex way than previously. This more complex personal identity allowed her to become much more inviting of interpersonal relationships. However, it took time for her new understanding to become tacit and to function in a more open way without effort and conscious choice. She knew that such tacit understanding had begun to occur when, for the first time, she allowed someone else to see the level of her distress by weeping. This had not occurred for many years and when it happened with her boyfriend, she later realised that her body was beginning to respond organically and naturally to situations of trust without requiring much conscious processing. This level of tacit response reflects a level of understanding that Eugene Gendlin (1981) calls a 'felt sense'. He uses this term to indicate a preconceptual understanding of one's specific experience that functions intelligibly. Such tacit understanding is felt, is there as a whole, and provides an intelligible referent for thinking about, feeling about, and acting from.

When Zen masters demonstrate tacit understanding of no-self, it can look really crazy since it happens spontaneously, preconceptually. In retrospect, however, one can reflectively lift out the nature of the insight that was demonstrated.

Fuke, a Zen fool who was a contemporary of Rinzai, used to

> roam the streets ringing a bell and crying out: 'When it comes in brightness, I hit the brightness. When it comes in darkness, I hit the darkness. When it comes from all directions, I hit like a whirlwind, and when it comes out of the blue, I flail it'.

Hearing this, Rinzai instructed one of his monks to grab Fuke and demand, 'if it does not come in any of these ways, what then?' The monk did as he was bid. But Fuke only wriggled out of his grasp and said, 'tomorrow there's a nice free lunch at the Monastery of Great Compassion'. When the monk returned and told Rinzai what had happened, Rinzai said, 'I was always intrigued by that guy' (Besserman & Steger, 1991, p. 35).

In responding to the monk's challenge, Fuke does not hesitate by trying to formulate or remember the insight in general. Rather, out of tacit understanding an answer comes which is transparent to a number of the implications of no-self such as present-centredness, flexibility, great creativity, and inclusive love. Fuke responds from his 'felt sense' of all of this without necessarily taking time to 'know it' in an explicit way. In Fuke's case, the liberating self-insight of no-self appears to have become tacit and is trusted as a source of action.

4. Integration: The transcendent function

Let me return to the title of this paper: How Does Liberating Self-Insight Become Tacit Understanding?

In liberating self-insight, the context for one's personal identity broadens, and in the case of Zen enlightenment experiences, no-self is hit. Such shifts in personal identity may be sudden and contain a new holistic reference point for living. However, working out the implications for living in specific situations is more gradual, and requires time and refinement.

The sudden and the gradual need to converse: a creative tension is set up in which the general nature of the new position meets the specific nature of complex situations. Carl Jung referred to this process as the workings of the transcendent function. Although this term has been shown to be problematic (Dehing, 1993), the phenomenon of which Jung was writing is instructive. In Jung's view, there is a creative tension that can occur between divided parts of our functioning, and there appears to be a pull towards harmonising or integrating these divisions. So in the process of psychotherapy, a person eventually finds a way to 'walk their talk'. When this has happened sufficiently and becomes tacit understanding, the 'walk needs little talk'.

To illustrate, John had a series of dreams in psychotherapy in which he saw himself in a divided way – as a 'good guy' that represented his public face and as a 'bad guy', of whom he was ashamed and who lurked in the shadows. The 'good guy' was only able to function at the cost of great self-vigilance and lack of spontaneity. The dream of his divided selves initiated a creative tension in which the divisions 'stuck in his throat', demanding some kind of reconciliation. He could no longer simply pursue one side of himself, even though it seemed socially safer to do so.

A resolution began to occur, first as a liberating self-insight and then, more gradually, as tacit understanding. The liberating self-insight occurred suddenly in a further dream in which he saw his 'bad' self as merely 'instinctual' rather than 'bad'. This helped him to separate the phenomenon from the judgement. Tacit understanding grew gradually, as he found ways to enact a more complex self-image that was both social and instinctual. In the beginning he noticed that he would err on one side or the other. But by 'bumping' his insight against specific life situations in actual encounters, he became less and less preoccupied with the implications of his insight. His new identity was an 'and' rather than an 'either/or'.

In the case of spiritual awakening, the creative tension can initially be very strong – like a leaden ball which can be neither swallowed nor spat out. The tension is between the ahistorical and the historical, the personal and the impersonal, the absolute and relative, all time and just-this-moment. And can such integration ever be complete? In the Zen tradition, there are many stories that illustrate the drama of comfortably harmonising emptiness with form. In this area, the term 'harmony' is better than 'integration' as one is not trying to achieve a simple synthesis but rather a plurality that is co-dependently supportive.

What does comfortably exchanging this moment with emptiness look like? Again, it can look pretty crazy:

> One day when Tanka came to visit Pang in his cave, the Layman (Pang) didn't get up from his seat. Tanka raised his fly whisk, symbol of the Zen master's authority. Pang raised his wooden hammer.
> 'Just this or is there something else?' Tanka asked.
> 'Seeing you this time is not the same as seeing you before,' said Pang.
> 'Go and belittle my reputation as you please,' said Tanka.
> 'A little while ago, you were bested by my daughter,' replied the Layman.
> 'If that's so, then you've shut me up,' Tanka said.
> 'You're dumb because of your intrinsic nature and now you inflict me with dumbness.'
> Tanka threw down his fly whisk and left.
> 'Master Tanka! Master Tanka!' Pang called after him. Tanka did not look back.

'Now he's come down not only with dumbness, but with deafness too!' said the Layman.

(Besserman & Steger, 1991, p. 19)

So how does liberating self-insight become tacit understanding? In the case of psychotherapeutic development, new, less-fixed possibilities for self are seen and serve as a helpful reference. The reference may be held as a symbol, metaphor, or self-image and is enacted in different complex situations. Over time it comes to function skilfully and naturally without much thought. In the case of spiritual awakening, no-self is experienced and also serves as a helpful reference. However, the reference can never be held absolutely and one learns in specific complex situations to sustain the implications of enacting the unity of emptiness and love – groundless context and this careful moment. This enactment never ends, and tacit understanding and liberating self-insight become an ongoing dance of closeness and distance.

12
The Wound that Connects: A Consideration of 'Narcissism' and the Creation of Soulful Space

The last two chapters have emphasised the notion of freedom as a central dimension of spirituality. But a more embodied spirituality would ask for an inclusive perspective that could embrace both freedom and vulnerability. This chapter, therefore, tries to remedy the emphasis on freedom by reflecting on the nature of existential vulnerability. It revisits the theme of narcissism that was introduced in Chapter 9 in greater detail and articulates a more embodied understanding of the relationship between freedom and vulnerability. Two quotations may indicate this direction:

> There is a crack, a crack in everything, it's how the light gets in. (Cohen, 1992)

> We know separation so well because we've tasted the union. The reed flute makes music because it has already experienced changing mud and rain and light into sugarcane. Longing becomes more poignant if in the distance you can't tell whether your friend is going away or coming back. The pushing away pulls you in. (From a commentary on Rumi's poetry, Rumi, 1997, p. 47)

These quotations provide some indication of the concerns and direction of this chapter: the phenomenon of human vulnerability as an existential given. This phenomenon can be metaphorised as 'wound' and announces both a great dilemma and potential gift. The dilemma refers to that of Narcissus and his great flight from human vulnerability. The 'gift of wound' refers to what will be called 'soulful space', a freedom *for* vulnerability, in which the humanising potential of 'wound' connects us empathically with others. The meaning and sense of 'soulful space'

150

can be clarified and evoked through encountering and dwelling with the issues raised by what has been called 'narcissism', and this chapter wishes to explore some of the implications of this encounter.

A compassion for vulnerability may be an important existential task in a world that still easily lurches towards fantasies, systems, and technologies of hoped-for invulnerability and purity, with its vision of a great transcendent winner; a vision of power rather than inclusive empathy.

Much theorising and jargon surround 'narcissism' as a technical term within psychoanalysis and the field of psychopathology. Yet, in spite of this, the discourse refers to patterns of experience and behaviour that are instructive when considering some of the central existential dilemmas of being human. It may be an unfortunate term as it has been used like much of psychiatric terminology to diagnose and judge the behaviour and experiences of others in a way that negatively values a certain kind of self-absorption. It has been elaborated to characterise a whole style of being-in-the-world that tries to defend against the great vulnerability of feeling needy and incomplete. As such, there has been much theorising about the defensive styles that are adopted, (see, for example, Mollon, 1993) and in its extreme forms, a diagnostic category called 'Narcissistic Personality Disorder' has been constructed. Yet the discourse surrounding this phenomenon points to a complexity of experiencing that is best spoken of in terms of metaphor and poetic narrative, and here is where the dry logic of psychoanalytic theory becomes more alive, and where one may resonate with some of the existential dilemmas revealed beyond this specialist discourse. The existential themes centre on a 'wound of longing', how we bear this wound, and even find it as a gate and passage to some of our deepest existential possibilities. This dimension touches our human concerns to a degree that has been called 'spiritual' or 'ontological', and this discourse may speak further about how a certain kind of opening to the 'wound of longing' can invite us towards homecomings of great participation and belonging.

The aims of this chapter are two-fold: firstly, to indicate how the myth of Narcissus and the way it has been taken up by the psychoanalytic tradition can be expressed in more phenomenological and 'experience-near' ways. In this pursuit, guidance has been taken from Gendlin's experiential phenomenology (1973) and his distinction between the logical and responsive orders (1997b). This chapter thus adopts a style that attempts to be both evocative and logical in the way that it proceeds in order to present the potential 'aliveness' of the emerging phenomenon.

Secondly, the aim is to evoke and articulate the phenomenon of 'soulful space' as an authentic response to narcissism. The word 'soulful' is not used in a primarily religious sense, but rather as an adjective that has gained currency in Western culture as reflected in dictionaries such as the Concise Oxford Dictionary and Collins Shorter Dictionary and Thesaurus indicating 'full of sentiment or emotion', 'evoking deep feeling', and 'not mechanical or heartless' (Allen, 1990; Makins, 1995). If, as will be shown, narcissism centrally involves a flight from vulnerability in order to attain a kind of 'freedom *from* wound', 'soulful space' refers to a different kind of freedom or 'spaciousness' that can tolerate or embody the vulnerability of 'soulfulness', a 'freedom *for* wound'. The chapter concludes with a description of 'soulful space' that combines both freedom and vulnerability as an existential possibility. Rather than being summative, this final stage of the chapter will prioritise an evocative style that invites an embodied 'holding' of the ambiguous 'felt sense' of 'soulful space' as 'freedom-wound'.

1. The drama and myth of Narcissus

Essentially, the Greek myth of Narcissus unfolds a drama in which Narcissus, a beautiful young man, becomes fixated and fascinated by an illusion; that his image in a pool of water can be grasped and possessed. He becomes enamoured with this surface image of himself to the exclusion of all other possible relationships. The core quest is to be at one with the beautiful picture. This fascination binds his energy and attention, and the drama unfolds through a number of stages, as the futility and desperation of his quest to possess his image becomes apparent. In one version of the myth, Narcissus finally kills himself in the mood of despair and isolation.

This tragic story has been interpreted in a number of ways. One way that psychologically minded people have interpreted it is as a metaphor for how we can become alienated from the nourishment of our lived experience by turning ourselves into an image or object. This surface image of ourselves is always elusive and precarious, yet Narcissus is desperately enthralled by the hope of grasping and attaining this 'great love'. There is the sad image of him leaning over the pool and extending his grasping hand towards his image under the water, only to find that the image ripples away and evades him, leaving his desperate longing insatiate. He lives with this insatiability and, as the story unfolds, tries to find compensations and various strategies that will either soothe his pain or keep his hope alive.

The tragedy of this drama is about how such fire of longing pro-gressively drowns in the mood of isolation. Ovid, the Roman writer who chronicled this drama, evokes the scene and mood of isolation as follows:

> There was a clear pool with shining silvery waters, where shepherds had never made their way; no goats that pasture on the mountains, no cattle had ever come there. Its peace was undisturbed by bird or beast or falling branches. (Ovid [43 BC–AD 17/18], 1955, p. 85)

So what we have in the myth of Narcissus is someone who possesses great beauty and potential, and who is not being carried forward into the richness and possibilities of relational life. There is a shocking dep-rivation in which his longing is mocked. And it is the mocking of his longing that has been contemplated by the psychoanalytic tradition in interesting ways.

Self and other

Freud and others have written about the naturalness of what they call 'primary narcissism' (see, for example, Morrison, 1986). According to this view, babies are naturally inclined to respond to confirmation that their desires and longings can be fulfilled. They are passively or actively demanding of such responsiveness in what Freud saw was a self-preoccupied way. When they are nourished in this way, both physi-cally and emotionally, they receive confirmation that their feelings and desires are welcome. The field of 'me' becomes a productive source of information and direction, and forms the basis of a degree of inner freedom and vitality. This has been called 'healthy narcissism'.

But both 'primary narcissism' and 'healthy narcissism' may be unfor-tunate terms in that the actual experience may not be one of exclu-sive self-absorption as indicated in the myth, but rather unproblematic relationality and responsiveness at that level. Both Freud and Klein (Livingstone Smith, 1995) have been noted as having a conflict model of relational life. This view assumes that to be so-called self-involved in pleasure is different from the action of being in relation with another. Both Kohut and Winnicot appeared to understand this and articulated a view of early self-other relationships in which self-reference is not the opposite of relating to others. For Kohut (1971), self-feeling is not antithetical to relationality. Winnicot (1965) makes this kind of com-plementarity even more explicit. He speaks of how babies come to enjoy the space of their own play. Such 'own-ness' is not narcissistic self-exclusiveness but an interpenetrating field of self and other – never only self and never only other. So, for Winnicot, and some intersubjective theorists (Stolorow et al., 1987), narcissistic isolation, as in the myth of Narcissus, is never primary and exclusive but rather only occurs as a contraction of the more original interpenetrating play of going-on-being, in which self and other play hide and seek.

When there has been sufficient welcome and interaction of this kind, a person develops a certain strength, which the psychoanalysts have problematically called 'ego-strength'.

> He knows not only what he does not want but also what he wants and is able to express this irrespective of whether he will be loved or hated for it. (Miller, 1987, p. 50)

But if psychoanalytic thinkers have written extensively on the 'ways the longing is mocked' by self and others, how may we describe this 'longing', its feeling and landscape?

The wound of longing

Before it turns into a sense of shame and deficiency, there is simply a vulnerability given with the human condition. Let us approach this slowly before we describe it more fully. In opening towards it, it may come like the song indicates: 'Sometimes I feel like a motherless child, sometimes I feel like a motherless child, sometimes I feel like a motherless child, far, far from my home.' So one aspect of opening towards all this is a sense of disconnection from a source of nourishment and continuity: a tear in the sense of simple going-on-being. There is a felt vulnerability of need and incompleteness, of wanting; a sense of something missing, and a stretching towards what may come. The energy of Eros is always leaning towards the life that is not yet, and in the experiencing of the multiple circumstances of living we are accompanied by this vulnerability that knows the softness of flesh and the relief of welcoming the one who returns. One may also move towards what this is in the salt of tears, of loss. One existential writer expresses an aspect of this vulnerability as follows: 'To be human means to be torn' (Kastrinidis, 1988, p. 179). There are different paths towards this opening: the throb of sex, the pain of an aching back, hunger that would swallow the world.

So, in opening to the sense of vulnerability in these ways, what is revealed is this human realm of what we go through. Leonard Cohen expresses this well in his song *Here it is*: 'Here is your sickness, your bed and your pan; and here is your love for the woman, the man' (Cohen, 2001). What may come with this sense of vulnerability is a longing, as if our body knew its heart's desire. And how can we interpret the heart's desire? The psychoanalytic tradition has literalised this to an actual event: oneness with mother. To quote one psychoanalytic thinker: 'They are trying to re-experience the missing connectedness of their primary attachment' (Livingstone Smith, 1995, p. 124). However, the feeling of connectedness for which we long may not be essentially back there in time as an event or person (even though this may be one occasion for longing). Rather, the feeling of connectedness that the body seems to know may be implicitly right here and now in the flow of relational life. So, in opening to the wound of longing and vulnerability, one may stand open and trusting to what may come and what may be longed for. But equally one may not. One may come to hate a state of vulnerable longing and embark on a journey of great refusal. Some implications of this refusal to admit vulnerability and longing are now explored.

Some forms of refusal to the wound of longing and the realm of vulnerability

When admitting vulnerability and longing, 'self' may be open, flowing and dynamic: vulnerable to a range of relational, embodied, full-feeling; not freezing self into an object or falling into partial grasping of a self-image. There is less a sense of repetition, more novelty, and less preoccupation with the boundary that says: 'I am this only'.

But we can be shocked, and are shocked, into refusing vulnerability and the flow of longing and what comes, by an action of self-contraction. We are shocked into a self-contraction in different ways and may not easily get back into the flow of intimate relational life – here we may remember the drama of Narcissus. Psychoanalytic writers have articulated these reactions in different ways but, in their meditations on the narcissistic ways of flight from vulnerability, emphasise the doomed attempts to 'puff up' and maintain forms of self-sufficiency that strain against admitting otherness. It may be helpful to briefly indicate some of these ways and their implications in relation to the question: how does one refuse vulnerability and longing?

Hating the self that is vulnerable or longing

Before one defends strongly against vulnerability and longing, one may simply hate these feelings or the self that has them, and experience great shame.

> In shame the pain concerns the image of the self ... the self as weak, defective, pathetic, exposed and violated. (Mollon, 1993, p. 74)

There is a shock of painful self-consciousness in which one looks at oneself as a problem to be solved, an object to be changed. One may become very attuned to what others expect and may experience an embarrassed self-consciousness when one violates this expectation. In shame, one has been captured by the other and experiences great self-doubt in the other's gaze. In its extreme forms, it is as if the other is saying: 'You are nothing without my approval or admiration' and in the extreme forms of self-doubt, it is as if one is saying to oneself: 'I am nothing without what I should be.' In this shock of self-objectification, of viewing oneself from an outside perspective, one may become pre-occupied with one's body as sick, as breaking up, of its shape needing to be altered; there is a painful standing out.

The strategy of self-sufficiency: 'I don't need'

Then there may be the path of refusing vulnerability by trying to pre-tend that one does not need others or otherness; addiction to the feeling of self-sufficiency. For, Narcissus, in a sense, there is no other and he tries to feed himself *with* himself. In this trajectory we can try to 'puff ourselves up' with images of our own specialness or strength. The jar-gon for this dimension has been referred to as 'grandiosity'. The con-struction of a more perfect, ideal self is attempted; one that one is in control of, and that can armour oneself against personal vulnerability. When this feels relatively successful one may feel somewhat elated, but in a rather precarious way. Exposure to the limits that come with the acknowledgement of personal vulnerability are rejected in different ways: aging, death, the uncontrollable contingencies that come with this human realm. Others may detect a note of aloofness, arrogance, or scorn in one's voice at these times as if the tone says 'I don't need you and am more or better than others'. A victorious mood of the self-sufficiency of being in love with one's own mirror image may leave the other feeling redundant. There may be a lot of energy expended on these images of specialness, strength, or goodness in different ways.

However, to be less than this specialness or strength is to become 'only ordinary', and to fail. The self-esteem that was based on the ideal image crashes, and a feeling of great depression may ensue in what feels like the 'dreaded truth' of one's deficiency in the face of one's failed ideal self-image. One variation of the precariousness of keeping an ideal self-image going is that it may flicker like an unstable movie projector, and the unstable sense of self-esteem may fluctuate between feelings of expansive ideal identity achievement and feelings of deficiency and ideal identity failure.

The strategy of seeking others as mirrors of an ideal self

Another aspect of Narcissus's strategy was to use others as a mirror of the ideal self he was trying to attain and forever possess.

> Narcissistic individuals demand that the world provide them with unqualified, unremitting reassurance of their being-a-whole. (Kastrinidis, 1988, p. 169)

One may go into a rage when this is not forthcoming. Or one may feel deeply insulted when others do not help to feed oneself with one's own desired image. Ironically, one's need for others is very great in this quest, as the possibility of success in self-sufficiency needs a great deal of support. One becomes exceedingly sensitive to others' views of oneself as so much is at stake. Words can bring one down and it can feel like one is fighting for one's soul. One may be afraid at the power that others have in this mirroring need. This can constitute a deep ambivalence about others' power: great desire for being defined by others yet great fear about being possessed in such a way. In such forms of interpersonal sensitivity and extremity, a lot of energy is expended on finding a mirror that admires the hoped-for ideal self-image. The need to see oneself in such a mirror can carry the level of panic and desperation that is associated with a life or death issue. When others do not provide this for us, we may experience the kind of insult that 'cuts us to the quick, that assails us where we live, that threatens our identity or our self-image, or our ego-ideal or our self-esteem' (Levin, 1993, p. xiv). We take offence as the image of our ideal self is injured. Or we may become addicted to admiration and do what it takes to keep another mesmerised, whether through masochistic seductions or sadistic control. We may attempt to achieve a painless oneness with a sense of nourishment or power that we control through drugs, alcohol, magic, or fame. (Kastrinidis notes how an authentic fusion with oneness with another is different from this as it 'always leaves open the possibility of pain ...' [1988, p. 178].)

At certain phases on this path, there is a sense of deficient emptiness, as no true nourishment seems to happen; one is trying to live with the kind of nourishment that is 'ghostly' and not very substantial. If one becomes addicted to admiration and puts oneself 'on show', one does not at the core feel loved for the person one is; there is always a suspicion at the centre of this kind of feeling admired. This is the life of compensation. We would 'exchange a walk on part in the war for a lead role in a cage' (Gilmour & Waters, 1975). Something is felt missing and can result in a strategy of self-sabotage that mocks one's own success in this regard as if to taunt: 'Admiration is a pale substitute for true welcome and love'. Here, one may even cynically resign oneself to the absence of feeling respected or understood. One may be left in a chronic state of envy that, somehow, a place in the sun is only possible for others: an endless world of comparing 'haves' and 'have-nots'. One may feel scornful of others' feelings because one cannot take one's own feelings seriously. At its extreme, such pain of envy may fuel a desire to destroy what others have got or to destroy what one cannot possess, rather than have the desired object or person belonging to someone else. This is a sad, predatory state of affairs, of stalking empty corridors, pale in the shadows.

The strategy of merging with a great or special 'other'

A further interpersonal variation of seeking a fixed, strong, ideal, and special self is by identifying or merging with another who seems fixed, strong, ideal, and special: 'You are great and I am part of you.' One enters into the relief of an 'I' that is 'we' and who always wins the cup. We would defend to the death this 'we', this great hope for oneness without vulnerability. To be someone's twin, give me similar clothes; to be a fan, to find a hero, to join a cult, we would pay the price gladly. And at the end of the war we were just following orders.

In all these ways, psychoanalytic writers have indicated a flight from vulnerability and longing. They have done this in theoretically dense ways but there are rich insights when read metaphorically and with a light touch. Their insights, particularly with regard to psychotherapeutic and spiritual directions, can be fruitfully enhanced, and I would like to move on to a vision of possibilities inspired by A.H. Almaas and Eugene Gendlin. Both of these writers are helpful in moving towards an understanding of 'soulful space': Almaas, by considering the kind of 'spacious freedom' that characterises the essential openness of human identity; and Gendlin by inspiring a vision of 'soulfulness' that is embodied, deeply felt, and open.

2. An essentialist approach: A.H. Almaas

In his writings on narcissism, Almaas draws extensively on the psychoanalytic tradition but reframes these insights to characterise 'everyday' narcissism as a universal dilemma, and just as relevant to his primary concern that of spiritual practice. In his view, what has been referred to as Narcissistic Personality Disorder is 'basically a severe form of the narcissism of everyday life' (Almaas, 1996, p. 27).

Almaas sees the central problem of narcissism as the act of self-objectification, the attempt to flee from the rich and textured seamlessness of immediate experience by using the filter of thought and self-definition. He thus sees such self-objectification as almost inevitable. In such acts of self-objectification, we identify and define ourselves partially. What this means for Almaas is that we fail to live our multidimensional capacities and true patterns. He has a definite view about what these true patterns essentially are, such as value, strength, intelligence, will, nourishment, peace, and a number of other positive essential qualities that come with what he calls the 'essential self'. He has a tantric view of all the narcissistic strategies in which our radiant potentials are hiding. Thus, poor self-esteem hides an essence of intrinsic worth and value; arrogance can transform into an essence of the humble openness of 'not knowing'; a sense of grandiosity can transform into an essence of a sense of personal uniqueness and destiny; the need for mirroring can transform into an essence of the capacity to perceptually 'drink in' the world free from the need of self-affirmation; a feeling of betrayal and rage can transform into a determination not to betray one's own process; the intolerance of insult to self-esteem can transform into a capacity to forgive life its changes and a differentiated ability to look after oneself; shame and the dilemma of oneself-as-object can transform into the essence of peacefulness about the flow of how one appears; the search for invulnerability can transform into the deeper essence of one's indestructible true nature; the painfulness of the wound of longing can transform into the essence of compassion, one that connects rather than separates.

For Almaas, all this is possible if one clears the way for 'essential self'. It should be noted that he is not speaking here about the extremes of Narcissistic Personality Disorder, but of a path of spiritual development beyond 'everyday' narcissism. His deepest solution to the act of self-objectification is to move towards dis-identifying with all the ways we define ourselves and are defined by others. To not identify means to not objectify, and he recommends forms of self-enquiry that gradually face all forms of self-objectification until the multiple 'diamond' facets of 'essential self' can be restored and shine through in their myriad radiant forms.

> This means we are not looking self-reflexively at ourselves or con-ceptualising ourselves ... If we are not experiencing ourselves self-reflexively and conceptually (whether with old or new concepts), then we are experiencing ourselves immediately, directly, and non-conceptually. (Almaas, 1996, p. 130)

At certain stages in the radical deconstruction of structured identity, there is a sense of free presence that sees through the substantiality of these forms of self-identity. There may be a sense of great space and freedom. This wonderful mysticism can touch a sense of timelessness and completeness: Boddhidharma's 'vast space, nothing holy'. However, this is not the same as the more complex phenomenon that I wish to call soulful space. It is possible to become too enamoured with 'free presence' and the resolution of human vulnerability into vastness. Such spaciousness can become dissociative if it is not integrated with the historical specificities of 'me meeting you' in all life's specific occasions. It is to this that I wish to return a little later.

For now, I would just like to express a degree of caution about Almaas's essentialism. One's 'true pattern' may not be essentially 'there' as essential contents existing in themselves such as 'love, peace, strength, value'. Rather, these contents may be better understood as derivatives of a process that occurs in life; a life of interaction in which phenomena are co-created as one meets the specifics of history and situations. Emphasising and honouring such specifics grant forms of experience that exceed any ways of categorising them and give much more nuanced qualities, emotionally rich with aspects, which, who knows, exceed any conceivable essence no matter how skilfully articulated. Such novelty is 'wet through' with the events of time and meetings that have never before quite happened like this. And here we come to Gendlin.

3. An existential approach: Eugene Gendlin

In a paper explicitly on narcissism, Gendlin has criticised the way that the cultural discourse on narcissism has developed.

> What is *called* 'narcissism' (anything other than the imposed order) is much more and different than the term implies. (Gendlin, 1987, p. 12)

He notes a number of distinctions that need to be made and that have not been made and how this has led to a conflation of two different kinds of self-activity: one, the process of self-focused attention in which complexity and richness emerge and two, the structure-bound process of defining self, other and world, in which there is a freezing of such process (see also Gendlin, 1964).

In what Gendlin calls the 'life forward' direction, there is an acknowledgement of the 'unfinishedness' of human identity and desire, and how the body knows a sense of what is needed and what the next step could be. This is an existential approach in that there are no final, unconscious contents to be realised; the content of experiencing is always more than, and richer than, any way of summarising a particular unconscious potential or content. The body knows a sense of wholeness that is open rather than frozen. It is not a totalised or final wholeness unable to admit the novelty and specificity of new happenings. We are always potentially invited into a greater whole that is open and fertile. Such a coming to wholeness enjoys the sigh of recognition, but the openness of this wholeness welcomes the longing of what still may come. Such 'being-in-process' is expressed in a similar spirit by a psychotherapist in the Heideggerian tradition: there is '... a readiness to receive whatever it is that wants to show itself, to serve as an opening for the gathering of Being through a calm, self-composed waiting upon or attentiveness to Being' (Kastrinidis, 1988, p. 180). So the body knows intimately the taste of unfinishedness, and even more, of separation, being-torn, and longing. And the body recognises the taste of wholeness, of being at one, of being continuous with something much greater; a moving whole that is already adventuring. The body knows that it can be let into a sense of relatedness and process, invited into the flow of carried forward wholes.

To grasp wholeness as content, a summary, a finished meaning is to freeze the openness and rhythm of going-on-being, and is to fall into objectification. In our '... preoccupation with any single possibility (ideal or even wholeness), [we] lose [our] freedom to take up [our] full inheritance as a diverse, ever evolving presence in the world' (Kastrinidis, 1988, p. 174). In such preoccupation and grasping for a fixed ideal self, we would lack the freedom of being-incomplete, the nourishing brightness of what can come in such unknowing. The body affirms the value of hungry longing and quivering vulnerability as the human space of welcome.

The dilemma of Narcissus is not that being-in-process has become unavailable to him but that he does not like such a process and tries to solidify it as a hoped for achievement of invulnerability and self-sufficiency. Here we may remember some of the strategies that I have indicated.

So we have been coming to what I wish to call 'soulful space' in hints and turns, and I would like to take this a bit further.

4. The creation of 'soulful space': Mountains and valleys holding one another

At core, the human heart of Narcissus is simply the vulnerability that is given with the human realm, between earth and sky. But then, there is a panicked flight from this into a hoped-for freedom: the 'freedom from otherness', in which one is self-sufficient and complete.

The notion of 'soulful space' wishes to indicate a different kind of freedom – a 'spaciousness' in which vulnerability is not avoided, but rather, embraced. Soulful space is the mixing of vulnerability and the kind of freedom that embodies a willingness to 'wear' and 'move' within the vulnerabilities of this human realm. Both Almaas and Gendlin indicate the kind of 'flow' of 'being-with' that can embrace human vulnerability, need, and 'unfinishedness'.

Soulful space may also be metaphorised as freedom-wound, the kind of human openness in which we feel 'touched': a different kind of freedom from the freedom that is 'above it all'.

Soulfulness embodies the 'valleys' of many heart-felt historical moments. It includes the many things that we are touched by in opening to 'otherness' and the seasons of time. Soulfulness is history and the marks of being historical beings.

As one goes through this 'manyness', there may be a growing sense of the taste of this inclusiveness, this mixing, this holding space, this stretching of the seasons of time. There may be a growing taste of the fertility of flow, and the taste of the freedom of a space that can hold and move with the 'manynesses', its specific vulnerabilities. And this mixing always carries more than just the feeling of spaciousness that just 'lets go'. Rather, it is a spaciousness that also 'lets in'. For within the intimate touching of what one has gone through, there is a treasure coming from such 'salt' that is more complex than the peace of space and the freedom of flow.

> If we can only let go but cannot take hold, if our only concern is with space or spirit, then we may never be able to fully commit ourselves to work with our own circumstances or with other sentient beings. (Welwood, 2000, p. 19)

In this taste there is also the acknowledgement that living forward means separations and bindings, so there is also pain – a beautiful pain in living forward, and in giving up what we have embodied. This beautiful wound is the human realm. It is the realm that Narcissus would reject. It is not the kind of pain that withdraws into isolation. Rather, it is the mellower wound of longing that is worn gladly as we look deeply at one another and care for one another as fellow carriers. The wound sings the song of separation and longing, and the body (whatever that is altogether) remembers both connection and separation; a soulful space where we can deeply meet. And does this mellow wound disappear? If it did, great love would disappear. Could it be an important source of human compassion?

Carl Jung is standing on this road when, towards the end of his life, he wrote:

> I am astonished, disappointed, pleased with myself. I am distressed, depressed, rapturous. I am all these things at once and cannot hold up the sum ... and it seems to me that I have been carried along. I exist on the foundation of something I do not know. In spite of all uncertainties I feel a solidity underlying existence and a continuity in my mode of being. (Jung, 1961/1995, p. 392)

The treasure of the wound of longing is the taste of the beauty and poignancy of human participation; the essence of relationship, the 'we-feeling' in mutual vulnerability. Soulful space: to be a place where this can happen: not just 'soulful', merged in the cry; not just 'space', the presence of flow and impartiality. This 'we feeling' in mutual vulnerability may finally be the place that grounds more humanised forms of institutions and cultures, an existential achievement that would remember and take heed of Narcissus in his different forms.

13
Embracing Ambiguity: Transpersonal Development and the Phenomenological Tradition

This chapter addresses the growing field of Transpersonal Psychology and wishes to argue that this area of psychology requires more philosophical clarification at a foundational level if it is not to succumb to some of the limitations of a world-view that seeks predictable lawfulness and progression in matters transpersonal. It would be ironic if the field of Transpersonal Psychology were to begin by privileging developmental models which are mainly progressive, systematic, and essentialist in conception, and where the steps of psychological/spiritual growth are framed as a historical system that is closely allied to the 'known' and the 'predictable': little place for 'grace'. This chapter attempts to clarify this concern by situating human identity within a broadly phenomenological–philosophical tradition. As such it wishes to articulate a vision of the development of human identity that 'always already' has a transpersonal dimension which functions in dynamic ways in our everyday lives. In this view, we cannot compartmentalise the 'transpersonal' as something that comes later, or as a stage to be achieved. Rather, the tension between the 'personal' and the 'transpersonal' is revealed from the beginning as constituting a fundamental existential ambiguity which is always calling. In this way, a more embodied understanding of transcendence that 'lives' may be articulated.

Vision I

The arguments of evolutionary development are compelling and elegant. With the eyes of evolution I am able to look at myself from an 'outsider' perspective as an organism like other organisms, subject to laws of time and space. Evolution connects me to time and my ancestors. It gives me a future, a great adventure. It makes my work meaningful, contributing to the march of things. When I look at my sons I feel like a man.

But I appear to participate in another dimension as well, in which the march of time as progression disappears. If we switch focus, we may notice in the midst of everyday experience, a coming up *with* time rather than *from* time. With this focus, we are present to an open dimension, a discontinuity, in which we are not defined by chronological time, but participate in a freedom that is 'always already' beyond self-enclosure and is an essential part of the story of who we are.

So evolution can be seen as one story. And while I will willingly participate in stories, so that stories story me, there appears to be an awakening from these stories while in the midst of them – and if not an awakening, an intuition, that we participate in this 'other dimension': not evolving, never evolving, but always already expressing something that does not need to be completed, and is as full and complete as it will ever be.

So how should we view development? There is development and there is no development, and Transpersonal Psychology may work further to articulate this relationship between development and no development.

I believe that the phenomenological tradition provides one place to begin.

1. Some touchstones from phenomenology

This section will attempt to show that, beginning with Husserl's articulation of the concept of 'intentionality' and moving on to Heidegger's notion of 'being-in-the-world' and Merleau-Ponty's conception of the 'intertwining', the existential–phenomenological tradition is concerned with a non-dualistic vision of existence that can serve as a foundation for philosophy and psychology. While these thinkers often moved into the traditional questions and problems of philosophy, a phenomenologically informed Transpersonal Psychology could stay a bit longer with the experiential qualities of such a non-dualistic vision.

Husserl was initially concerned with a potential self-deception in human thought; of how the boundaries and structures of thought could lead to a replacement of what the thought was referring to. His motto became 'back to the things themselves' and he established the beginning of a phenomenological approach, which wished to remain faithful to the holistic quality in the way things are connected. He

wondered about the extent to which we could suspend our precon-
ceptions when we are in front of any phenomenon, whether it is a
perception, thought, or image, so that its essence is not prematurely
lost. His understanding of 'intentionality' loosened the Cartesian
boundaries between mind and matter. Intentionality describes a connectedness between consciousness and the objects of consciousness
before self and other are separated out. His concept of the lifeworld
describes a stream of experiencing which cannot at its root be objectified in terms of fundamental boundaries. These boundaries are made
rather than given.

Heidegger took this thrust further. He criticised Husserl's concept of
intentionality (cf. Zimmerman, 1981) for not moving radically enough
beyond a dualistic position. Although in Husserl's view the boundaries
between consciousness and world, subject and object were artificial,
Heidegger felt that Husserl was equating consciousness with individual
consciousness. For Heidegger, presence as such is a more fundamental
category than any subjectivity or ego. Consciousness is not centred in a
self, as if the self was a container or thing. Subjectivity is rather a secondary modification of what he came to call being-in-the-world. This
move heralded the existential–phenomenological tradition in which
essence does not precede existence. Both Heidegger and Merleau-Ponty
were then able to talk of an order or unity of Being which is fundamentally 'one song' with Becoming or Time. In emphasising the lived
body, Merleau-Ponty (1968) used the term intertwining to indicate a
fundamental intimacy in which perception is only possible because of
our bodily participation in the order and unity of existence. In this
view, the depth of the lived body carried both closeness and distance –
intimacy and separation.

There are many debates and controversies within this broad tradition. However, the central issue that I wish to draw from it is this: that
the self is continuous with, and disappears into, a ground or order of
life (of interpenetrating contexts), and that this order of life gives the
self its qualities, which are the qualities of being-in-the-world. Some
of these interpenetrating contexts include language, culture, developmental structures, and physiological constraints and freedoms.
However, the ground of being-in-the-world is not merely limited to
these existential contexts but involve a 'clearing' or 'openness', which
is the 'space' for these distinctive contexts to occur. The self thus participates in an ambiguous realm in which there are two things occurring together, depending on whether one focuses on the figure or
ground: (i) the openness, intimacy, and continuity of the unity of Being

and, (ii) the changing boundaries of the many ways that Being occurs and the many ways we define ourselves. These two things are never fundamentally separate but Heidegger was concerned with how we can lose perspective and forget this unity of being-in-becoming. It is within this spirit that Adams (1999), in reviewing the implications of phenomenological theorists for transpersonal studies, characterises this unity as 'the interpermeability of self and world' (p. 39).

In applying the notion of development to the deepest experiences of human identity, the perspective of 'Becoming' can be overemphasised in such a way that it loses its transparency to the more unifying themes of 'Being', which are immanent in its movement. The phenomenological tradition remedies this danger by offering a coherent vision of the depths of human identity that is no-thing. This perspective will now be applied as a cautionary standard to our attempts to construct developmental models for Transpersonal Psychology.

2. Turning the question on its head

Aron Antonovsky (1979; 1996), a well-known health sociologist developed an approach, which he called salutogenesis. Instead of asking the traditional question, 'What are the causes of disease?', he asked, 'What are the causes of health?' He was amazed that things did not fall apart earlier and posited that open systems (within which he included human beings), as well as closed systems, were characterised by immanent forces of entropy. In a similar vein, existential–phenomenology, instead of asking how consciousness moves beyond self-enclosed levels of development, is inclined to ask how self-definition manages to occur and be sustained through its various developmental stages. In this view, there is in any moment an ontological openness at the centre of identity, which is always functioning, whether one is explicitly conscious of it or not. In whatever developmental stage one is specifically engaged, the basic openness can shine through and be experienced in different ways depending on the way one interprets it. This basic ontological openness should not be identified with historical stages of development where awareness of such openness may be posited. As Wilber is quick to point out, this dimension should not be confused with pre-personal experience. Nor is it the same as Washburn's (1994) notion of the non-egoic core. Both of these concepts speak of the content of early experience. Basic openness is not a particular form of experience but rather the quality of consciousness when it is not specialised to focus on boundary making. It is what is already the case before thinking.

The implication of this perspective for models of human development is that there is an unpredictable and non-determined possibility in which the timeless can meet time, and this intersection may produce developments that we do not yet understand and have not incorporated into our developmental theories.

Although transpersonal issues such as the relationship between part and whole (Frager, 1989) are worked out in a historical–developmental context, the terms of these transpersonal issues are not themselves historical or developmental, but are ontological; that is, to do with the structural possibilities of being. Wittine (1989) is writing within this spirit when he notes that when working with clients in psychotherapy, their life concerns cannot easily be hierarchically arranged in a developmental sequence, but are interpenetrative.

The nature of such interpenetration of life issues would call us to re-vision development in such a way that the logic of hierarchy is understood to be in tension with a more plural dimension in which complexity and even chaos functions. In this conception, the plurality of qualities is an equal partner to the logic of hierarchy when describing any pattern-in-specificity: this concrete occurrence. Neither the pattern that connects nor the uniqueness of 'just this configuration', this unique flower, can be reduced to one another. Hierarchy organises plurality, but plurality surprises hierarchy with the shock of the new, intimate with emptiness.

I would like to briefly indicate something of the complexity of the plural, qualitative dimension by referring to four relevant perspectives: constructivist social psychology, chaos theory, the archetypal perspective of James Hillman, and spiritually oriented feminism.

Constructivist social psychology

This perspective (cf. Burman, 1994) focuses on the cultural relativity that would partially constitute developmental sequences. It would assert that psychological/spiritual development does not follow a unilinear line of development like the development from crawling to standing to walking. Different developmental issues may thus involve a plurality of styles and sequences, just like there may be a plurality of kinds of intelligence that cannot be simply valued in a hierarchical way. In such an existential vision, 'context' is much more powerful than in theories that emphasise essentialist views.

Chaos theory

Allan Combs (1995), in a far-ranging book entitled *The Radiance of Being*, borrows from the field of mathematics in order to apply an image of 'stillness in chaotic motion' to the field of Transpersonal Psychology. He develops some of the ideas in chaos theory to put forward a view of conscious experience in which its conditions appear to exist on the edge of chaos. What this means is that although human experience may develop a 'gravitational pull' towards certain defined structures at different times, such a process shifts back and forth between pre-dictable patterns and chaotic, non-determined activity. Such chaotic activity introduces a freedom and complexity into the system that cannot be known.

The archetypal perspective of James Hillman

James Hillman (1975/1978; 1988) has been fascinated by how our psychological theorising is limited by the way we are caught up within particular archetypal perspectives. He sees developmental psychology as a myth that is informed by the monotheistic vision that human life moves in one direction starting at infancy. Within this 'clock-time' vision of practical reason, what the child brings is superseded by the more 'realistic' world of adulthood. However, what if we change per-spective and see a 'polytheism' of psychological styles always potentially present, appearing, or hiding in different combinations. Can we become more inclusive in honouring the spiritual qualities of animals, children, and rocks that mix with one another and produce subtle qualities?

Spiritually oriented feminism

There is a growing body of literature, for example, Zweig (1990), which would encourage us to think about how our models of psychological development can reflect traditional patriarchal emphases. A traditional patriarchal view emphasises achievement and linear time. It would thus draw a linear and deterministic relationship between 'development' and spiritual realisation. But what if the relationship was more dialectical, where 'heaven' is immanently here from the beginning, holding, or prodding, and asking for attention without preconditions? We could then re-vision spiritual realisation, not so much as a destination at the end of things, but as a companion walking with us, while playing hide-and-seek. This emphasis of 'spirit as ground' provides Wilber (1995) with one side of his integral approach to the paradox: spirit as destiny, spirit as ground.

The four perspectives in slightly different ways are metaphorically consistent with a phenomenologically informed approach, and the rest of the chapter begins to trace out terms of reference that can accom-modate both Being and Becoming.

3. The 'ambiguous focus' model

In his book *Transpersonal Psychology in Psychoanalytic Perspective*, Michael Washburn (1994) provides fascinating and rigorous details of a developmental approach that accommodates regressive and progressive forces. In this and earlier works (1988; 1990), he speaks of regression as a 'return to origins' before there is an ascent to higher, transegoic levels. His 'spiral to integration' model reflects a dynamic movement in which the Jungian idea of a dialectical tension of polarities underpins individuation. It is beyond the scope of this chapter to do justice to the detailed ways in which he draws on aspects of both psychoanalytic and Jungian theories to form a well-differentiated approach of his own.

Here I wish to support the broad tradition of a dialectical tension, also wish to reframe the terms of this dynamic tension.

The phenomenologically informed twist would argue that a 'return to origins' is not necessarily best seen within a developmental perspective. Rather, it is seen within an ontological perspective (cf. Welwood, 1997) in which a person attempts to integrate their focus on whole and parts: 'whole' involves a perspective of *non-separative being here* and is immanent in the depth of ourselves; 'parts' refer to a more selective mode of consciousness which involves our *specialised engagements* with self and other.

Some differences between this 'ambiguous focus' model and Washburn's may help to clarify the nature of the polarities that call for integration.

For Washburn, there is a non-egoic core that has specific content whether archetypal or infantile, to which one regresses, and then regenerates to progressive stages of development. He calls this 'regression in the service of transcendence'.

On this point I wish to agree with Wilber (1990), who asserts that regression is not mandatory as a mechanism of growth.

In this context, Washburn's use of anthropological examples does not necessarily indicate a backward regression. For example, in their development, the African shaman talks of psychically 'going under the river'. This is not necessarily a return, but a journey of depth into the present moment. The heroic quest of going into the underworld may be more immediately understood as facing the present blocks to openness. This can partially contain unresolved issues from the past, but more centrally contains existential issues that have not yet been confronted. In a sense it could be said that these are from the future or from the depth of the present that includes both past and potential. Or put another way, the 'return' is to the other side, the neglected shadow, in which the nascent potentials have not yet been integrated. This often involves a kind of 'falling apart' that can be experienced in both pleasant and unpleasant ways.

I would prefer to call these so-called regressions, 'openings'. In this view 'regression' is one possible subset of an opening. Essentially, however, the opening is not essentially described by its content as if it were a positive archetypal field of energy, but rather as a quality of presence (which is nothing). The 'non-egoic core' is thus a space or a context that is open and not separate from phenomena – it is the non-specialised dimension of consciousness which speaks of Being, connectedness, and wholeness.

So, if we rename the non-egoic core *'non-separative being here'* and we name the ego *'specialised engagement'*, we can begin to consider a phenomenologically informed model of transpersonal experience.

Human existence is a field of ambiguity (cf. Sallis, 1973). A phenomenological description of ambiguity begins with the possibility that human experience participates in structures and no structures, time and no time, personal, pre-personal and transpersonal, and that even these terms are relative to one another. Choice and circumstance, style and development, culture and gender, all combine to describe the apparent gravity and coherence of identity. Yet even so, holes open up, mirrors shift, and the shout of the unknown is always ready to break through.

In the depth of our bodies there is this ambiguity of non-separative being here and specialised engagement (cf. Merleau-Ponty, 1968). Spiritual maturity could then be formulated as the lived ability to sustain the integration of focus of whole and part, unity and difference. Within this spirit, John Wren-Lewis (1997) characterises us as 'infinitude as multiplicity'.

At various stages of development, we can fall or err in emphasising one side of the polarity or the other – simply being connected *or* making specialised boundaries. It requires a great degree of complexity to sustain both non-separative being here and specialised engagement. For most of us it is either/or – we are unable to live both the woods and the trees.

So it becomes an ambivalent tension: play or work, friend or foe.

And this tension is dynamic in that it asks to be resolved without collapsing one side or the other. It is a truly existential and non-deterministic task. Many choices are made and the experience of self-identity wobbles between openness and closure.

However, 'wobbliness' is often not what we like, and we try to fore-close the ambiguity of unity and differentiation. For example, a person can attempt to lock out non-separative being here as a possibility. This appears to be possible to varying degrees by means of what has been called schizoid, obsessive, driven, or focused strategies. In these different ways, the separative task is raised up and appears to survive for a while as an independent great hope – fame, control, wealth, self-improvement, or some other holy war.

On the other hand, a person can attempt to affirm the other side of the tension, 'unity only', and deny specialised engagement by means of strategies which defocus difference. The boundaries of death, interper-sonal separation, and pain are avoided by a completeness that refuses complexity.

The basic transpersonal question thus becomes: how can a vision be sustained in which both unity and difference are one song, where ambi-guity is not merely repressed, but included and embraced? At a more psychological level, this question has different forms at different times: how do I integrate intimacy and aloneness, self-assertion and love, pro-ductivity and play, excitement and security?

The work of Winnicot has encouraged us to think about how infants are coping with a very complex and fundamental task: how to find a way of being that honours both our difference and our unity with others, things and contexts. Neither separation nor unity is simply and irrevocably given to the infant. From the beginning we are in this ambiguous dimension that is both scary and exciting: scary, because it is so changeable and unknown and intimate with the meanings of death; exciting, because it is so changeable and unknown and intimate with the meanings of freedom. Or vice versa: the ambiguity of fear and excitement. This task is there when we have baby ways of dealing with it and it is there when we have old person ways of dealing with it. Different developmental lines may speak of the ambiguity in different languages. For example, in the sexual dimension, the erogenous zones focus pleasure and connection while announcing distinction and separation: the ambiguity of difference and unity. In the more symbolic interpersonal dimension, the existence of the 'other' calls for a complex relationship: related in some way but separate.

At different developmental stages the task is dealt with by using dif-ferent forms of psychological 'magic'. These capacities such as symboli-sation (or defences such as splitting or repression) have the power to reduce anxiety and increase a sense of mastery over ambiguity. More sophisticated cultural strategies such as ideological attachments and national identities are woven together to master the insecurity of ambiguity. But 'wobbliness' in some area of life or development usually comes to question one's achievements in this regard: the mastery is unfinished. Some extreme forms of 'magic' are even able to close the door on ambiguity for a very long time, even though its consequences are usually more severe than very tight lips.

This reflection on ambiguity thus asks the transpersonally relevant question: In what sense do our developmental achievements meet the mark of harmonising unity and difference? What meets the mark regarding ambiguity? Mastery? Love?

The young child who learns to see that her/his mother is both the source of 'good' and 'bad' achieves a perception of ambiguity in the interpersonal stream. She/he may not become ambivalent about this. She/he may forgive life its changes and may be initiated into a more flexible 'magic' in which the ability to change interpersonal perspective (empathy) is possible. This allows more mastery, more love. But such mastery and love does not meet the mark regarding the deepest revelations of ambiguity.

So what meets the mark? What 'magic' is big enough to lead to a great peace *with* ambiguity rather than a peace conditional on the eradication of ambiguity?

There appear to be different ways of answering this question, but the one I would like to offer is that a focus becomes available in which unity holds diversity, and diversity holds unity. At its most fundamental level this is not just about food, sex, and work, but about presence: a wide world in which non-separative being here and specialised engagement are interpenetrative. In such a focus, ambiguity reconciles with its source, spacious stillness, and the emergent 'stillness in chaotic motion' (cf. Combs, 1995) forms a peace that embraces ambiguity. Yin/Yang. This is a great victory and a great grace.

4. Summary and conclusion

Ambiguity is given to the human realm: between earth and sky. The terms of such ambiguity can be expressed in different ways: unity and difference, openness and developmental focus, non-separative being here and specialised engagement.

Ontological ambiguity describes an existential task that works itself out historically in human development. However, such development, although generally progressive, does not move just by means of the logic of dynamics within the historical system. Because ambiguity participates in a non-deterministic openness and freedom, the pattern only looks coherent by the law of averages. For you and me, much more can happen.

The phenomenological–philosophical tradition is concerned with the unity of being-in-becoming. It is able to provide a non-dualistic vision that does not wish to privilege the categories of 'being-in-itself' (non-separative being here) or 'becoming-in-itself' (specialised engagement). Rather, one song.

Functioning in any moment is an ambiguity that forms a deep motivation and creative tension in the human heart. This creative tension can be avoided or embraced at different stages in different streams of development: the heroic quest. However, at the same time and always, basic openness is there, waiting. No development. Fallen out of dualism. The ontologically prior reality overwhelms all boundaries. This suddenness can enter the stream of time and change it in unknown ways. But this is not yet the complexity of 'one song', ambiguity already embraced. So we come back until unity holds diversity, diversity holds unity.

Vision II

Different existential crises *do* ask one to focus on different boundaries at different times. There is an adventure of development. But this may not be as essentialist in flavour as a progressive theory of development may make out.

So, what about the seasons of time and the maturing process? What is the relationship between this and transpersonal identity?

Maturing happens. The old man of the mountain undoubtedly has something. However, transpersonal identity, like an eternal child, is always trying to interrupt such steady walking.

Being and Becoming. Where do we stand if we do not reduce one to the other?

Is there a language for this 'place', which is not usurped by the serious tones of a system, yet acknowledges the tasks of time?

An abstract summary of such a 'position' may kill its essence and I can understand why Heidegger finally felt most at home with poetry.

14
Concluding Thoughts and Touchstones: A Wide Embrace

The various chapters of this book have focused on different things at different times in order to advance the perspective and practice of embodied enquiry. At times it has reflected on the nature of embodied enquiry directly in relation to qualitative research methodology, psychotherapy, or spirituality. When doing this, it has always acknowledged its historical roots in the phenomenological tradition, and its central indebtedness to the thought of Eugene Gendlin. At other times it has concentrated on demonstrating the practice of embodied enquiry in more implicit ways by practicing embodied enquiry to see what themes and insights are opened up in relation to the three topics.

This final chapter wishes to directly articulate and review the central sensibilities that weave through the various parts and chapters. It does this by elaborating on four constituents of embodied enquiry that may be expressed in the following assertions:

* Embodied enquiry is a practice that attends to the relationship between language and the experiencing body.
* Embodied enquiry marries thought and feeling, 'head' and 'heart'.
* Embodied enquiry, by not relying on thought alone, opens itself to what is creative and novel – the pre-patterned 'more' of the lifeworld.
* The kind of embodied understanding that arises from the practice of embodied enquiry is *humanising* and is much needed in a world that too easily objectifies self and other.

The chapter finally concludes by offering some reflections on how embodied enquiry would reframe the purposes of qualitative research methodology, psychotherapy, and spirituality.

1. Embodied enquiry is a practice that attends to the relationship between language and the experiencing body

From a very young age we have generally been learning the craft of putting our experiences into words. We were embedded in a wide world of preverbal happenings – we knew when something did not feel right, that we needed to reach out or to protect ourselves. We found ourselves spontaneously smiling at a welcome face – or if something did not appeal to us we gestured before we had the words as if to say 'no, not that – there is something else I am wanting'. The happenings of the lifeworld were full of texture and our own intimate and nuanced responsiveness to these happenings. And as we learned to say the words about things and situations to others, we learned to also recognise whether the words worked, and the extent to which they were successful in helping us to live in both shared and personal ways. In this process, other people's understandings would be used to build our own, and our own experiences would be carried forward by others to build their own understandings. And when words worked to *say* what we meant, this was a satisfying experience felt in the body. And when we *heard* words that we could relate to in our own lives, this was also a satisfying experience felt in the body. Conversely we can feel 'cast out' by words and feel the isolation and aloneness of this in our bodies. We can feel words as unworkable and we can be called by our own sense of discomfort to make sense of what we do not yet understand.

So words are not just 'tools' or 'skills' that are performed, but are experienced for how they feel. And this 'how they feel', the 'inner dimension' of language, is an aesthetic quality that is central to the process of understanding. Such language that locates ourselves in relation to others is both personal and interpersonal. When the 'feel' of language is operating we are in touch with its 'aesthetic qualities' and sense of fit. This aesthetic quality to language is the thing that makes words human, and much more than just technical. When we are concerned with the 'feel' of language, its aesthetics, and how it locates us in personal and interpersonal ways, then embodied enquiry, whether applied to research methodology, psychotherapy, or spirituality is a *practice* that cares for the bodily felt sense of how words work. Engaging in such practice then relies not just on sense-making logic, but on the sense-making experience of a person whose body holds a history of many experiences and projects. And this leads us to a consideration of how feeling is a form of understanding.

2. Embodied enquiry marries thought and feeling, 'head' and 'heart'

In a helpful article on Heidegger's notion of *befindlichkeit*, Gendlin (1978) goes back to what he considers to be an important concept in Heidegger's work: how feeling is a form of understanding. *Befindlichkeit* may be roughly translated as 'how one finds oneself'. Gendlin believes that this idea provides a new way of thinking about feeling – that it is through a certain kind of feeling that one finds oneself in relation to one's situation and the world. Feeling is not just something that happens 'inside' oneself but is something that tells us how we are in relation to things around us – space, time, people, our bodies. This is a holistic and immediate way of knowing.

By attending to our feelings we find that our feelings are full of information not just about what is inside our skin, but about the world around us as well. Feeling is not just 'inward' – there is an understanding 'in it' about one's situation. What kind of knowledge is this? It seems that it is not merely 'objective' knowledge – nor is it merely subjective knowledge – it is relational in that it tells one something positional about both oneself and another – the connections between self and other. The immediacy of this understanding is not formulated and already packaged as a clear verbal pattern. So this tells us something about self-locating understanding. It is implicit rather than explicit – 'given' in the 'feel' – a kind of knowing that may not start out as being logical but which carries holistic, not yet patterned, aesthetic qualities.

Gendlin expresses this pre-articulate felt quality of our participation in the world as follows: 'We don't come into situations as if they were mere facts' (Gendlin, 1978, p. 3). Rather, we are there in a much more intimate way – as 'going through things' that are not thematically clear but complex. In this complexity, there is a sense of how things are for us, where we have come from in relation to this, where it may want to go – all this is the holistic sense of our living at that moment.

Again to quote Gendlin: 'When you are asked "How are you?" you don't find only recognisables, but always an implicit complexity. Certainly one can reflect and interpret, but that will be another, further step' (Gendlin, 1978, p. 3).

Speech is certainly involved in apprehending the meaning of our lived situation, but meaning is not simply the outcome of words. Rather, meaning is there in rough form but needs refining and work. So, understanding can be helped by speech, but understanding is more than speech. Understanding disappears into its intimate connections with a vast and textured world of experiential living through – and this living through is what the lived body does as a whole movement – experiencing textures, feelings, situations at many different levels and in different ways. It is 'in' and 'with' the lived body where a number of things happen and interpenetrate: feeling, understanding, and speech are all implicated 'there' in the finding of self and world. So feeling does not occur alone without understanding, and understanding does not occur alone without speech. Heidegger's philosophy is always trying to indicate how things happen together and that our way of splitting the categories of mind and body, thought and feeling, head and heart are artificial.

3. Embodied enquiry, by not relying on thought alone, opens itself to what is creative and novel – The pre-patterned 'more' of the lifeworld

The 'happening together' of 'head' and 'heart' in embodied enquiry may be seen as an epistemological approach that calls forth the world in novel ways. Such an approach may be more faithful to the lifeworld in that the nature of the lifeworld is much more than patterns that can be summarised by language or thought. This dimension has been referred to as the 'excess' of the lifeworld. It means that the lifeworld is 'over-flowing' with dimensions far more than we know. Husserl referred to this as the 'plenum' or 'plenitude' of the lifeworld. This 'beyondness' poses a question for how, as human beings we are related to this flow of happenings. Phenomenologists like Husserl, Heidegger, and Merleau-Ponty want to point out that this 'excess' of the lifeworld is not something unrelated to our own participation. It is not a mystical 'out thereness' but this quality of 'excess' is given to our experience. 'In' our experience *is* the excess of the lifeworld. So human experience has an open dimension that is 'more than words can say'. Within this tradition, Gendlin is very interested in this 'more than words can say' of experience and asks the question: What kind of knowing can be more faithful to the 'more' of the lifeworld? He was afraid that, in our Cartesian tradition, we would become prematurely abstract in the ways we categorised and divided up our experience, because this is what words do. Yet, like Heidegger, he is very respectful of the role of words in understanding, if ... if language is given its proper place. So what is a good relationship between words and the 'more' of the lifeworld? For Gendlin, something else needs to be acknowledged as a faculty that is adequate for knowing in experiential ways the pre-patterned 'more' of the lifeworld.

For Gendlin, it is the lived body as it holistically participates in its living, feeling, and moving that provides the experiential ground of what any words are about. The lived body always knows something about how it finds itself in relation to the 'more' of the lifeworld. It is experiential before it is logical or made into a pattern through reflection and language. Yet, even though not articulate in its lively experience, it is in a sense, faithful, or authentic in that it is in touch with something in an aesthetic way. Merleau-Ponty (1962) spoke of how the lived is greater than the known. The 'lived' in this perspective is what the body lives and in a sense is much more encompassing as a faculty of participative knowing than our reflective capacities alone.

So the lived body is not just an 'object' to which the outside world happens. The lived body is rather the place where the 'more' of one's lifeworld gathers and moves in feeling, speech, and understanding. It is the 'place' where the 'said' and the 'unsaid' can intersect – and therefore can carry the 'aliveness' of understanding. Through *befindlichkeit* one feelingly locates oneself even before things and situations are made explicit. The lived body can enter the aliveness of what is implicit and can use language to make something explicit from 'there'.

Gendlin has taken all these understandings and applied them to the practice of psychotherapy. A therapy transcript from Gendlin indicates the way in which words and the alive 'more' of a person's lifeworld move back and forth in understanding:

> I'm afraid of making the wrong choice, I guess.

There is some silence. Then she says:

> It's not about making a wrong choice. I don't know what that is.

More silence. Then:

> There's something there, like 'I want it all!' that's really childish, like kids wanting everything they see. (Gendlin, 1978–1979, p. 7)

There was more silence and the client found 'in the 'more' of that feeling a whole lot of complex understandings about how some experiences from childhood were implicitly living in her. There is much complexity and implicit information in the more of her self-location. She was checking into her bodily felt sense in the silences, finding understandings in holistic bodily feelings like 'wanting' 'anxiety about choices' and a 'feeling of uncertainty'. These bodily feelings gave her access to the 'more' of her lifeworld at that edge and they also served as a felt reference for the words that best fitted 'just there'. So the lived body gives direction to words aesthetically by a sense of 'fit' or knowing of how a particular word or phrase slots into the whole mesh of the felt context. This felt context remains larger than what is explicit but serves as the implicit alive functioning of whether a word or phrase works 'for' that felt context. Meaning is then felt and not just said. To quote Gendlin: 'The feeling knows how to speak and demands just the right words – feeling has the power to guide speech' (Gendlin, 1978–1979, p. 9). The 'said' only provides a part of the credibility of the meaning. The other part is given by the feel of the context that is carried by the lived bodies experiencing of the 'more'.

Gendlin has called his philosophy a philosophy of entry into the implicit. It is a body-based hermeneutics in which qualitative meanings are pursued by a back and forth movement between words and their felt complexity in the lived body. This movement between the whole of the felt complexity at any moment, that is 'in the more', and the part that 'comes to language' is a practice that keeps open the creative tension between words and the aliveness of what the words are about. A felt sense carried in the lived body faces two ways: it faces the 'more' of the lived world and it faces the possibility of language. This way of doing philosophy that interfaces language and the lived body needs an experiential component that is active, rather than just a 'thinking about'. The phrase 'entry into the implicit' means that the words that are formulated, 'come from' an *action* based on attending to the lived body's sense of felt context in any moment. It is this felt context that is the source of the qualitative dimension. So, by not relying on thought alone, but by attending to the relationship between thought and feeling, a wider epistemological embrace is opened up that may invite more novel dimensions of the lifeworld and what previously may have been hidden. I will return to the potentially spiritual import of this epistemological embrace, but for now, would like to consider the social value of embodied enquiry, its potential to *humanise* our understanding.

4. The kind of embodied understanding that arises from the practice of embodied enquiry is *humanising* and is much needed in a world that too easily objectifies self and other

Words that connect the personal to the interpersonal world is humanising in that they find the 'I' in the 'thou' in Buber's sense. As a philosopher, Martin Buber (1970) was concerned among other things with how

knowledge can either be too personal, as in narcissism, or too impersonal as in forms of objective explanation that abandon the sense of
people like us living there. These two extremes, the overly personal and
the overly impersonal is not, in Buber's sense a fully human world
where there is both I and thou. In a more psychological vein, the British
psychologist and paediatrician Donald Winnicott (1953/1971) put forward the notion of 'transitional space'. Within this perspective a child's
development is healthy to the extent that she is provided with an emotionally facilitative environment where she can progressively relate the
world outside to her own intimate concerns and experiences. If one has
to adjust to the outside world by 'leaving' ourselves too much behind,
one learns to function perhaps efficiently, but may come to feel more
and more personally unrelated to 'all that'. At the other extreme, one
can be so shocked by the demands of leaving oneself behind that one
can withdraw and take refuge in a personal world that has little intersubjective adaptation. Whether one is looking philosophically, as in
Buber's sense, or developmentally in Winnicott's way, words that can
connect the personal to the interpersonal facilitate a form of understanding that straddles the space of 'between', where both self and other
can be with a sense of meaningful aliveness. Within this sense of intersubjective aliveness the world can be 'breathed in' through language
and as such, may have some intimate relationship with oneself. This
form of understanding can be called a 'felt' understanding. If one's own
felt and relevant experiences can find a 'place' in the world, this can be
experienced as humanly confirming that a universe where I and thou
matter is possible.

Embodied enquiry, in its incarnation as empathic understanding,
may be particularly relevant when trying to balance historical, national,
religious, and ethnic identities with a sense of common humanity
underlying these identities. Embodied enquiry, in its open stance, lets
go of pre-packaged identities, to look again at what comes, even the
identities 'within' oneself. Such openness does not deny history and
category, but understands such identities within their relative context.
This means that such categories are not reified as absolute or essential.
But the openness of embodied enquiry, which does not totalise or
essentially objectify self and other, is only possible because of a greater
'nourishment' from the lifeworld. Without this nourishment, the letting
go of hard won identities that has been gained through great suffering,
and passed on to us by our ancestors and kin, would be very difficult.
But the 'nourishment' of embodied understanding is a great help: it is the
empathic aliveness that comes when looking at self, other, and world
afresh. Such empathic aliveness is the lifeworld arriving when language

and body, self and other, known and unknown excess, come together in a movement of embodied understanding that is essentially integrative and inclusive in the ways previously outlined.

It may then be that embodied enquiry does not just have an epistemological concern, but also an ethical one, in that it pursues ways of knowing self and other that stay within the value of the irreducibility of persons to objects, things, or summaries. Perhaps in embodied enquiry Merleau-Ponty meets Levinas by providing a perspective and practice in which the radical alterity of the other is already given to experience by the excesses and 'mores' to which the open body is intimate. Embodied enquiry thus guards and enacts such a foundational understanding of persons in different ways and, as such, can inform the purposes and processes of qualitative research methodology, psychotherapy, and spirituality, among other endeavours. Because this book has concentrated on those three areas, I will conclude with a brief consideration of the import of embodied enquiry for the way it would inform the *purpose* of these endeavours. In this concluding section, I will thus not pursue the specific methodologies and practices that embodied enquiry may encourage within these endeavours. These were indicated at various points throughout the book. Rather, this concluding section will highlight the central 'plot' of embodied enquiry for qualitative research methodology, psychotherapy, and spirituality.

Reframing the purpose of qualitative research methodology: Empathic understanding

Within an embodied enquiry perspective, qualitative research in general would try to put experiences into words in such a way as to show a humanised and intersubjective world where people and world are intrinsically connected.

We may take some direction from Heidegger:

> Phenomenological interpretation must give Dasein the possibility of original disclosing, to raise the phenomenal content of this disclosing into concepts. (Heidegger, 1962, pp. 139–140)

This is Heidegger's way of saying that we need to find methods that have the possibility of authentically bringing forth the unsaid to the said. So it opens the way for the need for engaging the pre-patterned aliveness of experience.

In his writings, Heidegger also raises the possibility of inauthentic descriptions or interpretations that have lost their aliveness and grounding. Again to quote Heidegger:

> Every concept and sentence drawn originally in a phenomenological way as a communicated assertion has the possibility of degenerating. It is passed on in an empty understanding, loses its grounding and becomes a free floating thesis. (Heidegger, 1962, p. 36)

A qualitative research endeavour that is centrally informed by embodied enquiry would thus find ways to re-present and evoke the presence of human phenomena. When successful it would lead to an empathic understanding between people of both the details and the sense of the phenomenon as palpable and alive. This 'aliveness' means that the communicated understanding and sense is open enough to allow individuals to relate to it in personal ways that are unique, while also engaging with elements that may be shared. This play of the 'unique' and the 'shared' characterises the humanised essence of embodied understanding.

Reframing the purpose of psychotherapy: A bodily grounded yet flexible personal identity

Within an embodied enquiry perspective, psychotherapy focuses on the relationship between words and the felt sense of meanings carried in the body. Such meanings are generally organised implicitly in terms of their significance for one's own self-project; how things are going for me, the ways in which personally relevant, past, and future meanings meet in the present. Bodily felt meanings occur in an interwoven way to support an ongoing sense of identity that is both a source of possible security and also a source of possible inflexibility. As a source of security, such self-identity provides a feeling of familiarity and being at home in the world; the rhythm of repetition 'hums' us with some degree of trust towards the next moment. However, the downside of a fixed self is that it can defensively close us off to novelty and the energy that new ways of seeing self and other can bring; the excitement of travel. Self-identity can function in ways that are either too rigid or too flexible. Self-identity that is too flexible is relatively ungrounded and does not have much of a home to come back to, even if only as a stepping stone to further horizons.

The purpose of a psychotherapy that is informed by embodied enquiry is to help clients move towards a grounded yet flexible sense of personal identity that can function between the old and the new, between our ongoing world with both its continuities and discontinuities. An embodied enquiry perspective understands such 'groundedness' as a bodily felt experience that comes with the practice of focusing on the felt sense of the meanings of what one is carrying; it is the 'groundedness' of being rooted in a sense of personal connection to one's history as well as one's present interpersonal and lifeworld environment. An embodied enquiry perspective also understands that such a sense of 'groundedness' comes with the power of words to make sense of one's bodily felt meanings. Such 'groundedness' paradoxically supports a flexibility of identity in that the unknownness and openness of the future can naturally be attended to when one's own identity is not too much at stake. An inflexibility of personal identity is hung onto when one is ungrounded, as the 'known' needs to be reified at all cost.

This purpose of psychotherapy as a way of supporting a grounded yet flexible sense of personal identity is well articulated by Gendlin in his book on focusing-oriented psychotherapy:

> Compared to what we can usually think and feel, what comes from the bodily sensed edge of awareness is characteristically more intricate and multifaceted, and yet also more open to new possibilities. We are not bound by the forms of the past, but contrary to what is often said today, we cannot 'construct' just any narrative we like, either. (Gendlin, 1996, p. 2).

A psychotherapeutic endeavour that is centrally informed by embodied enquiry would thus find ways to help people be more bodily here, thus helping them rely less on 'self-talk' as a way of defining who they are. Such bodily 'being-here' may more authentically ground an openness to the novelty of what comes when one is less preoccupied with the insecurities of self-definition.

Reframing the orientation of spirituality: Meeting mystery

Within an embodied enquiry perspective, spirituality is not understood primarily as an integrated framework of direct beliefs about ultimate concerns and one's meaning and purpose in the universe. It is not something that is thought and known without any experiential referents. Rather, spirituality is a dimension that is *felt* as the quality of one's widest and deepest context. This deepest felt context reflects both inner and relational contexts because experiencing is not just 'inside one's skin'. But neither does it exclude the intimate 'ownness' of one's sense of interior. So even though such an openness 'goes far and wide' and responds to callings beyond the 'self' the direction of spirituality is, paradoxically, the direction of the lived body; spirituality is experienced *through* the body, rather than without the body. Where else can qualities be felt? So, a spirituality informed by embodied enquiry is interested in an incarnate spirituality and the ways in which one's broadest contexts can be embodied and embraced in living a human life. Certainly, the ways that such broad experiences are interpreted are crucial for the way spirituality is brought into everyday living. And the nature of such interpretive frameworks are hermeneutically significant for opening or closing further possibilities for psycho-spiritual development. But such interpretations are grounded by the palpable lived experience of meeting a mystery that is always in excess of the known.

Apart from this psychological reason for pointing to the lived body as a gate to spirituality, there are also ontological reasons for wishing to connect the lived body more centrally to the realms of spirituality. The lived body, whatever that is altogether, is not merely a skin-encapsulated object. Rather, it is more fundamentally a subjectivity that is intimately intertwined with what is there beyond the skin. The lived body is both part of the world as well as a view on the world, as Merleau-Ponty so aptly demonstrated. This means that the lived body is an intersection of I and 'that', and is interactive before it is separate. It inhabits both intimacy and distance in its ways of knowing, whereas thought without feeling emphasises distance in the way that it models the world. So one's access to broader contexts is essentially felt as a whole through the lived body before it is separated into thought-patterns by the distancing categories of thought. It is in this spirit that mystics from a diversity of religious traditions have valued the 'cloud of unknowing' (Anonymous, 1981) or the 'beginner's mind' (Suzuki, 1973) in which 'not-knowing is most intimate' (Dogen & Tanahashi, 1995).

A person, who through the lived body feels the quality of contexts beyond the categories of thought, may experience a sense of mystery at the edge of the known. Yet this sense of mystery, because it can be palpable as it comes to the lived body, may carry a feeling of both aliveness and warmth (because something new is always flowering and fluid and is there to be cared for) as well as a great tranquillity (because there is something timeless and still about this mystery that is also experienced as the ground of one's own being). So an embodied spirituality lets the living dimension of mystery live *as* mystery without reducing it to known categories of thought (which would make it smaller than thought). Living mystery twinkles most at the deepest and widest spaces of the 'more than can be represented'. The embrace of the body gives such mystery not its knowability, but a feeling of its palpability.

A spiritual orientation that is centrally informed by embodied enquiry would thus be concerned with practices and ways of bodily embracing the widest contexts present to experience. The meditative traditions may be helpful guides for such pursuits.

Already curious
This bodily here

With
And nearly not

Grateful.

Notes

Foreword

1. Owen Barfield (1981) *Histroy, Guilt and Habit*. Middletown, CT: Wesleyan University Press.

10 Psychological and Spiritual Freedoms: Reflections Inspired by Heidegger

1. This term may be used interchangeably with the more familiar term 'self-concept' if it is understood that both terms also imply a specialised perception of the world; in other words, they are intentional rather than merely intrapsychic structures.
2. In using this term in the chapter, I do not mean to suggest that this form of perception is amorphous, lacking all forms of meaningful structure. Rather, I am using the term to indicate a form of perception which is more multiply determined than less naive forms of perception which begin with a more tightly specialised interest.
3. Psychoanalytic theory provides valuable insights into the degrees and kinds of intensity by which a person clings to a particular organisation of self and world. Such theories offer compelling descriptions about the fears and fantasies, which serve to maintain such structures.

References

Adams, W.W. (1999) The interpermeation of self and world: Empirical research, existential phenomenology and transpersonal psychology. *Journal of Phenomenological Psychology*, 30 (2), 39–67.

Allen, R.E. (ed.) (1990) *The Concise Oxford Dictionary of Current English*, 8th edn. Oxford: Clarendon Press.

Almaas, A.H. (1996) *The Point of Existence: Transformations of Narcissism in Self-Realization*. Berkeley, California: Diamond Books.

Anderson, R. (2001) Embodied writing and reflections on embodiment. *Journal of Transpersonal Psychology*, 33(2), 83–96.

Anderson, R. (2004) Intuitive inquiry: An epistemology of the heart for scientific inquiry. *Humanistic Psychologist*, 32(4), 307–341.

Angyal, A. (1965) *Neurosis and Treatment: A Holistic Theory*. New York: Wiley.

Anonymous (1981) *The Cloud of Unknowing*. London: SPCK.

Anstoos, C.M. (1987) A descriptive phenomenology of the experience of being left out. In: F.J. van Zuuren, F.J. Wertz and B.P. Mook (eds) *Advances in Qualitative Psychology: Themes and Variations*. Berwyn, PA: Swets and Zeitlinger, pp. 137–155.

Antonovsky, A. (1979) *Health, Stress and Coping*. San Francisco: Jossey-Bass.

Antonovsky, A. (1996) The sense of coherence: An historical and future perspective. *Israel Journal of Medical Sciences*, 32, 170–178.

Askay, R. (2001) Heidegger's philosophy and its implications for psychology, Freud and existential psychoanalysis. In: M. Boss (ed.) *Martin Heidegger: Zollikon Seminars*. Trans. F. Mayr & R. Askay. Evanston, Illinois: Northwestern University Press, pp. 301–316.

Avens, R. (1984) *The New Gnosis: Heidegger, Hillman and Angels*. Dallas: Spring Publications.

Barton, A. (1974) *Three Worlds Therapy*. Palo Alto: Mayfield Publishing.

Bergbom-Enberg, I. and Haljamae, H. (1993) The communication process with ventilator patients in the ICU as perceived by staff. *Intensive and Critical Care Nursing*, 9 (1), 40–47.

Bernstein, R.J. (1988) *Beyond Objectivism and Relativism: Science, Hermeneutics and Practice*. Philadelphia: University of Pennsylvania Press.

Booth, W. (1987) *The Rhetoric of Fiction*. Harmondsworth: Peregrine Books.

Boss, M. (1949) *Meaning and Content of Sexual Perversion*. Trans. L.L. Abel. New York: Grune & Stratton.

Boss, M. (1963) *Psychoanalysis and Daseinsanalysis*. Trans. L.B. Lefebre. New York: Basic Books.

Boss, M. (1979) *Existential Foundations of Medicine and Psychology*. Trans. S. Conway and A. Cleaves. New York: Jason Aronson.

Boss, M. (1985) Is psychotherapy rational or rationalistic. In: *Review of Existential Psychology and Psychiatry*, Vol. XIX, pp. 115–127.

Brice, C.W. (1984) Pathological modes of human relating and therapeutic mutuality: A dialogue between Buber's existential relational theory and object relations theory. *Psychiatry*, 47, 109–123.

Bruner, J. (1990) *Acts of Meaning*. London: Harvard University Press.

Buber, M. (1970) *I and Thou*. Trans. W. Kaufmann. Edinburgh: T. & T. Clark.

Burman, E. (ed.) (1994) *Deconstructing Developmental Psychology*. London: Routledge.

Charmaz, K. and Mitchell, R.G. Jr (1997) The myth of silent authorship: Self, substance and style in ethnographic writing. In: R. Hertz (ed.) *Reflexivity and Voice*. London: Sage, pp. 193–215.

Cohen, L. (1992) Anthem. *The Future*. New York: Columbia, Sony Music.

Cohen, L. (2001) Here it is. *Ten New Songs*. New York: Columbia, Sony Music.

Combs, A. (1995) *The Radiance of Being: Complexity, Chaos and the Evolution of Consciousness*. Edinburgh: Floris Books.

Condrau, G. (1986) Daseinsanalytic psychotherapy. In: *Psychiatry and Phenomenology: The Fourth Annual Symposium of the Simon Silverman Phenomenology Center*. Pittsburgh: Duquesne University Press, pp. 63–77.

Cushman, P. (1992) Psychotherapy to 1992: A historically situated interpretation. In: K. Freedheim (ed.) *A History of Psychotherapy: A Century of Change*. Washington DC: American Psychological Association, pp. 21–64.

Day Sclater, S. (1998a) Nina's story: An exploration into the construction and transformation of subjectivities in narrative accounting. *Auto/Biography*, 6 (1/2), 67–77.

Day Sclater, S. (1998b) Creating the self: Stories as transitional phenomena. *Auto/Biography*, 6 (1/2), 85–92.

Dehing, J. (1993). The transcendent function: A critical re-evaluation. *Journal of Analytical Psychology*, 38(3), 225–235.

de Koning, A.J.J. (1979) The qualitative method of research in the phenomenology of suspicion. In: A. Giorgi, R. Knowles and D.L. Smith (eds) *Duquesne Studies in Phenomenological Psychology*, Vol. 3. Pittsburgh: Duquesne University Press, pp. 122–134.

Denzin, N.K. and Lincoln, Y.S. (eds) (1994) *Handbook of Qualitative Research*. London: Sage.

Dilthey, W. (1979) *Selected Writings*. Trans. and ed. H. Rickman. Cambridge: Cambridge University Press.

Dogen, E. and Tanahashi, K. (1995) *Moon in a Dewdrop: Writings of Zen Master Dogen*. San Francisco: North Point Press.

Dreyfus, H. (1972) *What Computers Can't Do: A Critique of Artificial Reason*. New York: Harper & Row.

Dreyfus, H.L. & Dreyfus, S.E. (1986) *Mind Over Machine*. New York: Free Press.

Edwards, D.J.A. (1989) *Cognitive Restructuring through Guided Imagery. International Handbook of Cognitive Therapy*. New York: Plenum.

Ellenberger, H.F. (1958) A clinical introduction to psychiatric phenomenology and existential analysis. In: R. May, E. Angel and H.F. Ellenberger (eds) *Existence: A New Dimension in Psychiatry and Psychology*. New York: Basic Books, pp. 94–124.

Engler, J. (1984) Therapeutic aims in psychotherapy and meditation: Developmental stages in the representation of self. *The Journal of Transpersonal Psychology*, 16 (1), 25–61.

Featherstone, M. (1995) *Undoing Culture: Globalisation, Postmodernism and Identity*. London: Sage.

Ferrer, J.G. (2002) *Revisioning Transpersonal Theory: A Participatory Vision of Human Spirituality*. Albany: State University of New York Press.

Fischer, W.F. (1989) An empirical–phenomenological investigation of being anxious. In: R.S. Valle and S. Halling (eds) *Existential–Phenomenological Perspectives in Psychology*. New York: Plenum Press, pp. 127–136.

Fischer, C.T. and Wertz, F.J. (1979) Empirical phenomenological analyses of being criminally victimized. In: A. Giorgi, R. Knowles and D.L. Smith (eds) *Duquesne Studies in Phenomenological Psychology*, Vol. 3. Pittsburgh: Duquesne University Press, pp. 135–158.

Foucault, M. (1980) *The History of Sexuality, Vol. 1. An Introduction*. New York: Random House.

Frager, R. (1989) Transpersonal psychology: Promise and prospects. In: R.S. Valle and S. Halling (eds) *Existential–Phenomenological Perspectives in Psychology*. London: Plenum Press, pp. 289–310.

Freud, S. (1914) Remembering, repeating and working through. In: *The Standard Edition of the Complete Psychological Works of Sigmund Freud*, Vol. 12. Trans. J. Strachey. London: The Hogarth Press, 1957–1974, pp. 145–156.

Frie, R. (2003) Introduction. In: R. Frie (ed.) *Understanding Experience: Psychotherapy and Postmodernism*. London and New York: Routledge, pp. 1–27.

Friedman, M. (1985) Healing through meeting and the problem of mutuality. *Journal of Humanistic Psychology*, 25 (1), 7–40.

Gadamer, H. (1975) *Truth and Method*. New York: Seabury Press.

Gadamer, H. (1975/1997) *Truth and Method*, 2nd revised edn. New York: Continuum.

Gendlin, E.T. (1964) A theory of personality change. In: P. Worchel and D. Byrne (eds) *Personality Change*. New York: John Wiley & Sons, pp. 100–148.

Gendlin, E.T. (1973) Experiential phenomenology. In: M. Natanson (ed.) *Phenomenology and the Social Sciences*, Vol. 1. Evanston: Northwestern University Press.

Gendlin, E.T. (1978) Befindlichkeit: Heidegger and the philosophy of psychology. *Review of Existential Psychology and Psychiatry*, 16, 43–71.

Gendlin, E.T. (1981) *Focusing*. New York: Bantam.

Gendlin, E.T. (1985) Crossing and dipping: Some terms for approaching the interface between natural understanding and logical formation. *Minds and Machines*, 5 (4), 383–411.

Gendlin, E.T. (1987) A philosophical critique of the concept of Narcissism: The significance of the awareness movement. In D.M. Levin (ed.) *Pathologies of the Modern Self: Postmodern Studies on Narcissism, Schizophrenia and Depression*. New York: New York University Press, pp. 257–304.

Gendlin, E.T. (1991) Thinking beyond patterns: Body, language, and situations. In: B. den Outen and M. Moen (eds) *The Presence of Feeling in Thought*. New York: Peter Lang, pp. 22–151.

Gendlin, E.T. (1996) *Focusing-Oriented Psychotherapy: A Manual of the Experiential Method*. London: The Guilford Press.

Gendlin, E.T. (1997a) *Experiencing and the Creation of Meaning*. Evanston, IL: Northwestern University Press.

Gendlin, E.T. (1997b) How philosophy cannot appeal to reason and how it can. In: D.M. Levin (ed.) *Language Beyond Postmodernism: Saying and Thinking in Gendlin's Philosophy*. Evanston, IL: Northwestern University Press, pp. 3–41.

Gendlin, E.T. (1997c) The responsive order: A new empiricism. *Man and World*, 30, 383–411.

Gilligan, C. (1982) *In a Different Voice: Psychological Theory and Women's Development.* Cambridge, MA: Harvard University Press.

Gilmour, D. and Waters, R. (1975) Wish you were here. *Wish You were Here.* USA: Harvest, EMI.

Giorgi, A. (1970) *Psychology as a Human Science: A Phenomenologically Based Approach.* New York: Harper and Row.

Giorgi, A. (1985a) A sketch of a phenomenological psychological method. In: A. Giorgi (ed.) *Phenomenology and Psychological Research.* Pittsburgh: Duquesne University Press, pp. 8–22.

Giorgi, A. (ed.) (1985b) *Phenomenology and Psychological Research.* Pittsburgh: Duquesne University Press.

Giorgi, A. (1986) Theoretical justification for the use of description in psychological research. In: P. Ashworth, A. Giorgi and A. de Koning (eds) *Qualitative Research in Psychology.* Pittsburgh: Duquesne University Press, pp. 3–22.

Giorgi, A. (1997) The theory, practice and evaluation of the phenomenological method as a qualitative research procedure. *Journal of Phenomenological Psychology*, 28 (2), 235–260.

Giorgi, A., Barton, A. and Maes, C. (eds) (1983) *Duquesne Studies in Phenomenological Psychology*, Vol. 4. Pittsburgh: Duquesne University Press.

Giorgi, A., Fischer, C. and Murray, E. (1975) *Duquesne Studies in Phenomenological Psychology*, Vol. 2. Pittsburgh: Duquesne University Press.

Giorgi, A., Fischer, W.F. and Von Eckartsberg, R. (eds) (1971) *Duquesne Studies in Phenomenological Psychology*, Vol. 1. Pittsburgh: Duquesne University Press.

Giorgi, A., Knowles, R. and Smith, D.L. (eds) (1979) *Duquesne Studies in Phenomenological Psychology*, Vol. 3. Pittsburgh: Duquesne University Press.

Hatab, L.J. (1997) Language and human nature. In D.M. Levin (ed.) *Language beyond Postmodernism: Saying and Thinking in Gendlin's Philosophy.* Evanston, III: Northwestern University Press.

Heidegger, M. (1962) *Being and Time.* Trans. J. Maquarrie and E. Robinson. Oxford, UK: Basil Blackwell.

Heidegger, M. (1971) *Poetry, Language, Thought.* Trans. A. Hofstadter. New York: Harper and Row.

Heidegger, M. (1975) *The End of Philosophy.* London: Souvenir Press.

Heidegger, M. (1977) *The Question Concerning Technology and Other Essays.* New York: Harper and Row.

Heidegger, M. (2001) *Zollikon Seminars.* M. Boss (ed.), Trans. F. Mayr and R. Askay. Evanston, Illinois: Northwestern University Press.

Hertz, R. (ed.) (1997) *Reflexivity and Voice.* London: Sage.

Hillman, J. (1975/1977) *Re-visioning Psychology.* New York: Harper Colophon.

Hillman, J. (1977) *Re-visioning Psychology.* New York: Harper and Row.

Hillman, J. (1981) *The Thought of the Heart. Eranos Lectures Series.* Dallas: Spring Publications.

Hillman, J. (1983) *Healing Fictions.* Woodstock, CT: Spring Publications.

Hillman, J. (1988) Preface. In: J. Allan, *Inscapes of the Child's World.* Dallas: Spring Publications.

Hillman, J. and Ventura, M. (1993) *We've had a Hundred Years of Psychotherapy and the World's Getting Worse.* San Francisco: Harper.

Hobson, R. (1985) *Forms of Feeling.* London: Tavistock.

Hunt, C. (1998a) Writing with the voice of the child: Fictional autobiography and personal development. In: C. Hunt and F. Sampson (eds) *The Self on the Page: Theory and Practice of Creative Writing in Personal Development*. London: Jessica Kingsley Publishers, pp. 21–34.

Hunt, C. (1998b) Autobiography and the psychotherapeutic process. In: C. Hunt and F. Sampson (eds) *The Self on the Page: Theory and Practice of Creative Writing in Personal Development*. London: Jessica Kingsley Publishers, pp. 181–197.

Husserl, E. (1970) *The Crisis of European Sciences and Transcendental Phenomenology: An Introduction to Phenomenological Philosophy*. Evanston: Northwestern University Press.

Jager, B. (2001) The birth of poetry and the creation of a human world. *Journal of Phenomenological Psychology*. 32(2), 131–152.

Jung, C.G. (1961/1995) *Memories, Dreams and Reflections*. A Jaffé (ed.), Trans. R. and C. Winston. London: Fontana Press.

Jung, C.G. (1972) *Two Essays on Analytical Psychology*. Princeton: Princeton University Press.

Kastrinidis, P. (1988) The phenomenology of narcissistic neurosis. *Humanistic Psychologist*, 16 (1), 168–185. Special edition on Daseinsanalysis edited by E. Craig.

Kisiel, T. (1985) The happening of tradition: The hermeneutics of Gadamer and Heidegger. In R. Hollinger *Hermeneutics and Praxis*. Notre Dame: University of Notre Dame Press.

Kohut, H. (1971) *The Analysis of The Self*. New York: International University Press.

Kruger, D. (1988) *The Problem of Interpretation in Psychology*. Pretoria: Human Sciences Research. Council.

Kvale, S. (1996) *InterViews: An introduction to Qualitative Research Interviewing*. London: Sage Publications.

Lacan, J. (1977) *Ecrits: A Selection*. Trans. A. Sheridan. London: Tavistock.

Langs, R. (1982) *Psychotherapy: A Basic Text*. New York: Jason Aronson.

Levin, D.M. (ed.) (1997a) *Language Beyond Postmodernism: Saying and Thinking in Gendlin's Philosophy*. Evanston, IL: Northwestern University Press.

Levin, D.M. (1997b) Gendlin's use of language: Historical connections, contemporary implications. In: D.M. Levin (ed.) *Language Beyond Postmodernism: Saying and Thinking in Gendlin's Philosophy*. Evanston, IL: Northwestern University Press, pp. 62–84.

Levin, J.D. (1993) *Strings and Arrows: Narcissistic Injury and its Treatment*. New York: Jason Aronson.

Livingstone Smith, D. (1995) A brief history of narcissism. In: J. Cooper and N. Maxwell (eds) *Narcissistic Wounds: Clinical Perspectives*. London: Whurr Publisher, pp. 3–15.

Lomas, P. (1981) *The Case for a Personal Psychotherapy*. Oxford: Oxford University Press.

Mahrer, A. (1978) The therapist–patient relationship: Conceptual analysis and a proposal for a paradigm-shift. *Psychotherapy: Theory, Research and Practice*, 155 (3), 201–15.

Mahrer, A. (1983) *Experiential Psychotherapy: Basic Practices*. New York: Brunner/Mazel.

Makins, M. (ed.) (1995) *Collins Shorter Dictionary and Thesaurus*. New York: Harper Collins.

Marcel, G. (1949) *Being and Having*. London: The Dacre Press.

Merleau-Ponty, M. (1962) *Phenomenology of Perception*. Trans. Colin Smith. London: Routledge and Kegan Paul.

Merleau-Ponty, M. (1963) *The Visible and the Invisible*. Trans. A. Lingis, Evanston, Ill: Northwestern University Press.

Merleau-Ponty, M. (1968) *The Visible and the Invisible*. C. Lefort (ed.), Trans. A. Lingis. Evanston: Northwestern University Press.

Miller, A. (1987) *Drama of Being a Child*. Trans. R. Ward. London: Virago Press.

Mindell, A. (1985) *Working with the Dreaming Body*. London: Routledge and Kegan Paul.

Mollon, P. (1993) *The Fragile Self: The Structure of Narcissistic Disturbance*. London: Whurr.

Morrison, A.P. (ed.) (1986) *Essential Papers on Narcissism*. NY: New York University Press.

Moustakas, C. (1994) *Phenomenological Research Methods*. London: Sage.

Murray, E.L. (1974) Language and the integration of the personality. *Journal of Phenomenological Psychology*, 4 (2), 469–489.

Myerhoff, B. and Ruby, J. (1982) Introduction. In: J. Ruby (ed.) *A Crack in the Mirror: Reflective Perspectives in Anthropology*. Philadelphia: University of Pennsylvania Press, pp. 1–35.

Oakley, A. (2000) *Experiments in Knowing: Gender and Method in the Social Sciences*. London: Blackwell Publishing.

Ovid, 43 BC–AD 17/18 (1955) *The Metamorphoses of Ovid*. Harmondsworth: Penguin.

Packer, M.J. and Addison, R.B. (eds) (1989) *Entering the Circle: Hermeneutic Investigation in Psychology*. Albany: State University of New York Press.

Polanyi, M. (1996) *The Tacit Dimension*. Garden City, NY: Doubleday.

Polkingthorne, D. (1998) *Narrative Knowing and the Human Sciences*. Albany: State University of New York Press.

Reed, D.L. (1987) An empirical phenomenological approach to dream research. In F. van Zuuren, F.J. Wertz and B. Mook (eds) *Advances in Qualitative Psychology*. Berwyn, PA: Swets and Zeitlinger, pp. 96–116.

Reinharz, S. (1997) Who Am I? The need for a variety of selves in the field. In: R. Hertz (ed.) *Reflexivity and Voice*. London: Sage, pp. 3–20.

Richardson, L. (1990) *Writing Strategies: Reaching Diverse Audiences*. Newbury Park, CA: Sage.

Richardson, W.J. (2002) *Truth and Freedom in Psychoanalysis. Understanding Experience: Psychotherapy and Postmodernism*, R. Frie (ed.). London and New York: Routledge, pp. 77–99.

Rickman, H.P. (ed.) (1976) *Dilthey: Selected Writings*. Cambridge, UK: Cambridge University Press.

Ritzer, G. (1993) *The McDonaldization of Society*. London: Sage.

Robertson, J. (1999) Writing and re-writing the self: An 'ex-bulimic/woman/ researcher' researching with 'bulimics'. *Auto/Biography*, 7(1/2), 69–76.

Rogers, C. (1951) *Client-Centred Therapy*. Boston: Houghton Millin.

Rosen, E. (ed.) (1982) *My Voice Will Go With You: The Teaching Tales of Milton H. Erickson*. New York: Norton and Co.

Roszak, T. (1992) *The Voice of the Earth: An Exploration of Ecopsychology.* New York: Simon and Schuster.

Rumi, J. (1997) *The Essential Rumi.* Trans. C. Barks with J. Moyne. London: Castle Books.

Sallis, J. (1973) *Phenomenology and the Return to Beginnings.* Pittsburgh: Duquesne University Press.

Sartre, J.P. (1943) *Being and Nothingness.* Trans. H.E. Barnes. London: Methuen.

Satir, V. (1987) *The Use of Self in Therapy.* New York: Haworth Press.

Scott, C. (1978) Psychotherapy: Being one and being many. *Review of Existential Psychology and Psychiatry,* 16, 81–94.

Seale, C. (1999) *The Quality of Qualitative Research.* London: Sage.

Shainberg, D. (1980) Principles, practices, and objectives of non-deterministic psychotherapy. In: G. Epstein (ed.) *Studies in Non-Deterministic Psychology.* New York: Human Sciences Press, pp. 184–211.

Shapiro, K.J. (1985) *Bodily Reflective Modes: A Phenomenological Method for Psychology.* Durham, NC: Duke University Press.

Silverstein, A. (1988) An Aristotelian resolution of the idiographic versus nomothetic tension. *American Psychologist,* 43 (6), 425–430.

Sparkes, A. (1995) Writing people: Reflections on the dual crises of representation and legitimation in qualitative inquiry. *Quest,* 47, 158–195.

Spence, D. (1982) *Narrative Truth and Historical Truth: Meaning and Interpretation in Psychoanalysis.* New York: Norton.

Spiegelberg, H. (1971) *The Phenomenological Movement: A Historical Introduction,* 2nd edn. Vols 1 and 2. The Hague: Martinus Nijhoff.

Stanley, L. and Wise, S. (1983) *Breaking Out Again.* London: Routledge.

Steinbock, A. (1995) *Home and Beyond: Generative Phenomenology after Husserl.* Evanston, III: Northwestern University Press.

Stolorow, R.D., Brandschaft, B. and Atwood, G.E. (eds) (1987) *Psychoanalytic Treatment: An Intersubjective Approach.* Hillside, NJ: Analytic Press.

Suzuki, S. (1973) *Zen Mind, Beginner's Mind.* New York: Weatherhill.

Taylor, C. (1989) *Sources of the Self.* Cambridge, MA: Harvard University Press.

Teyber, E. (1988) *Interpersonal Process in Psychotherapy: A Guide For Clinical Training.* Chicago: Dorsey Press.

Todres, L. (1990) *An Existential Phenomenological Study of the Kind of Therapeutic Self-insight that Carries a Greater Sense of Freedom.* Unpublished PhD dissertation, Rhodes University, Grahamstown, South Africa.

Todres, L. and Wheeler, S. (2001) The complementarity of phenomenology, hermeneutics and existentialism as a philosophical perspective for nursing research. *International Journal of Nursing Studies,* 38, 1–8.

Toombs, K. (1993) *The Meaning of Illness: A Phenomenological Account of the Different Perspectives of Physician and Patient.* Boston: Kluwer Academic Publishers.

Van Den Berg, J.H. (1972) *A Different Existence.* Pittsburgh: Duquesne University Press.

Van Den Berg, J.H. (1974) *Divided Existence and Complex Society: An Historical Approach.* Pittsburgh: Duquesne University Press.

Van Manen, M. (1990) *Researching Lived Experience: Human Science for an Action Sensitive Pedagogy.* London, ON: Althouse.

Van Manen, M. (2000) Professional practice and 'doing phenomenology'. In S. Kay Toombs (ed.) *Handbook of Phenomenology and Medicine*. London: Kluwer Academic Publishers.

Vycinas, V. (1961) *Earth and Gods: An Introduction to the Philosophy of Martin Heidegger*. The Hague: Martinus Nijhoff.

Washburn, M. (1988) *The Ego and the Dynamic Ground: A Transpersonal Theory of Human Development*. Albany, NY: State University of New York Press.

Washburn, M. (1990) Two patterns of transcendence. *Journal of Humanistic Psychology*, 30, 84–112.

Washburn, M. (1994) *Transpersonal Psychology in Psychoanalytic Perspective*. Albany, NY: State University of New York Press.

Washburn, M. (2003) *Embodied Spirituality in a Sacred World*. Albany, NY: SUNY Press.

Welwood, J. (1997) Reflection and presence: The dialectic of self-knowledge. *The Journal of Transpersonal Psychology*, 28 (2), 107–128.

Welwood, J. (2000) *Toward a Psychology of Awakening*. Boston & London: Shambhala.

Wertz, F. (1985) Method and findings in a phenomenological study of a complex life-event: Being criminally victimized. In: A. Giorgi (ed.) *Phenomenology and Psychological Research*. Pittsburgh: Duquesne University Press, pp. 8–22.

White, M. (1983) Anorexia nervosa: A transgenerational system perspective. *Family Process*, 22 (3), 255–273.

Wilber, K. (1990) Two patterns of transcendence: A reply to Washburn. *Journal of Humanistic Psychology*, 30, 113–136.

Wilber, K. (1995) *Sex, Ecology, Spirituality: The Spirit of Evolution*. Boston: Shambhala.

Willis, P. (2002) Don't call it poetry. *Indo-Pacific Journal of Phenomenology*. 2,1, 1–4.

Winnicott, D.W. (1953/1971) *Playing and Reality*. London: Routledge.

Winnicot, D.W. (1965) *The Maturational Process and the Facilitating Environment*. New York: International University Press.

Wittine, B. (1989) Basic postulates for a transpersonal psychology. In: R.S. Valle and S. Halling (eds) *Existential–Phenomenological Perspectives in Psychology*. London: Plenum Press, pp. 269–287.

Wren-Lewis, J. (1997) Beyond the light: The ultimate identity crisis. *Self and Society*, 25 (3), 25–29.

Zahavi, D. (2003) *Husserl's Phenomenology*. Stanford CA: Stanford University Press.

Zimmerman, M.E. (1981) *Eclipse of the Self: The Development of Heidegger's Concept of Authenticity*. London: Ohio University Press.

Zimmerman, M.E. (1992) The search for a Heideggerean ethics. In: *Ethics and Responsibility in the Phenomenological Tradition: The Ninth Annual Symposium of the Simon Silverman Phenomenology*. Pittsburgh: Duquesne University Press, pp. 57–90.

Zweig, C. (1990) *To Be a Woman: The Birth of the Conscious Feminine*. Los Angeles: Jeremy Tarcher.

Index

Lightning Source UK Ltd.
Milton Keynes UK
UKHW02f0633080718
325377UK00022B/929/P